Chag Sameach!

Open this book and let the pages inside
inspire a smile
ignite Jewish pride
teach a lesson or two
enlight and discover
take it all in - from cover to cover.
As you enjoy the Chag from beginning to end
And spend time with family and friends
Remember your Oorah family who cares
And will keep in touch throughout the whole year.

- Rabbi Chaim Mintz

732-730-1000 · OORAH.ORG · THEZONE.ORG · TORAHMATES.ORG · OORAHSPIRIT.ORG

Thinking

Outside

the

Box

Yochanan 'Jeff' Kirshblum

Outside

Thinking

the
Box

Yochanan 'Jeff' Kirshblum

Distributed by:
Israel Book Shop
501 Prospect Street
Lakewood, New Jersey 08701
Tel: (732) 901-3009
Fax: (732) 901-4012
Email: isrbkshp@aol.com

Edited by:
Eliyahu Friedman
(914) 552-3884

Rabbinic advisor:
Rabbi L. Resnick

Cover design, book design & layout:
Levi Chadad
(347) 463-2566

רפוס המעתיק
Hamatik Printing
170 Ross Street, Brooklyn, N. Y. 11211
Tel: 718-782-1391 – Fax: 718-486-5818

ISBN 1-931681-46-5

PRINTED IN THE UNITED STATES OF AMERICA

Endorsements

Congregation Aish Kodesh
of Woodmere
351 Midwood Road
Woodmere, N. Y. 11598
516 - 569-2660

—

RABBI MOSHE WEINBERGER

קהילת אש קודש דוודמיר

הרב משה וויינבערגער
מרא דאתרא

ב״ה

14 Shevat 5763

The story is told of the great *Gaon*, *R' Chaim of Sanz* who had been struggling with a particular line in *Tosafos* for a considerable amount of time. In the back of the *Beis Medrash*, the *Tzaddik*, *R' Yosef Boruch of Neustadt* known as the *"Guter Yid"* was reciting *tehillim*. *R' Chaim* approached the *Guter Yid* and asked him if he can explain the elusive *Pshat* in *Tosafos*. The *Tzaddik* was taken aback and said: *"Rebbe*, I'm a simple Jew, a *"Tehillim Zuger"*, how can I possibly explain the *Tosafos* to the *Gadol Hador?"* *R' Chaim* said, "nonetheless try reading the *Tosafos.*" *R' Yosef Boruch* recited the *Tosafos* with the same sweetness and devotion he infused into his *Tehillim*. In a split second the *Sanzer* called out, "That's it! That's the *Pshat*!!"

When my friend Jeff (Yochanan) Kirshblum asked if I would review the manuscript of his *sefer*, I thought: "Jeff's an *"erlicher Yid"* whose life is devoted to the betterment of his people, an exceptionally bright man who loves *Torah* and loves Jews, but could he possibly have found the time to make a serious contribution to the growing corpus of English *Parsha* literature? I must confess, I was astounded by the *"niggun"* of his *Torah*, the clear, sweet and straightforward way he conveys the timeless truths of *Yiddishkeit*. The *sefer* is filled with the hard earned observations of a hard-working man who has a remarkable grasp of the *Torah's* "heart" and how it continues to beat for each and every one of us. Both Jeff and his wonderful *sefer* are truly an inspiration.

בכבוד רב ובהוקרה הכרת הטוב ונחת רוח,
משה ויינברגר

Yochanan "Jeff" Kirshblum is a Jew with a passion. He passionately cares about Torah, Yiddishkeit, and, most of all, he has a passionate love of his fellow Jew. Jeff was a talmid of mine many years ago and we have managed to keep in close contact.

Over the years, he has spearheaded several programs to enhance the financial security of rabbayim and to help ease the tuition burden of parents. Since Jeff is a very humble and unassuming man, I will not divulge his many activities on behalf of Klall Yisroel and their forgotten Jews but suffice it to say that he was in close personal contact with many of the Gedolim in America who have come to know and love him too.

For the past thirteen years, Jeff has written down his thoughts on the weekly Parsha- thoughts that inspired him to think and feel what it means to be a Jew. He has collected these feelings in these five volumes. Whereas most of the previous commentaries on the Torah appeal to the intellect, Jeff's commentary appeals to the heart of the Jew because it was written from the heart.

There are many novel and original ideas expressed in this work. Though they may not be the "p'shat," the simple meaning, they are certainly within the framework of "shivim panim l'Torah." Jeff Kirshblum, has shown to me everything he has written on the Parshi'os and I personally expressed my delight. They are indeed inspiring and motivating.

May Hashem bless Jeff with the strength to continue his many acts of kindness and compassion. May Hashem grant these volumes of Torah the success they deserve. May the open the heart of every Jew.

Leibel Reznick

Monsey, New York
Menachem Av 5763

This work of Jeff Kirshblum is interesting, fresh and worthy of study. Culled from great traditional sources of Torah commentary, it also addresses the issues and ideas of modern day life. It is easy reading yet thoughtful and inspirational in content. Every Jew has a personal share and portion in Torah. I am delighted that he has chosen to allow us all to benefit from his work and insight.

Rabbi Berel Wein

Jerusalem, Israel

Dedications

Shi-Shi

The world is filled with fathers.
The world is filled with daughters.
Hashem had the perfect plan
when he gifted me with you.
You are wonderful, generous, kind,
and you really know how to make me laugh.
I never expected a parent-child bond
to form as effortlessly as ours has.
Mommy says it is because we are
so much alike and share the same,
kooky, sense of humor.

You know that you are
and always will be my sweetheart.

I am dedicating this *sefer* of Vayikra to you,
in the hope that my devotion to this sefer
will be a *z'chus* for you in the future.

Love always,
Daddy

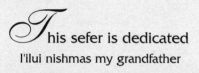

Acknowledgments

*A*cknowledgements are meant to show *hakaras hatov* to all the people who have taken part in an author's experiences while writing a book. While there are many people who fit into this category, I feel the need to express something else.

These *seforim* have been a 17 year project. My dedication to writing them has far surpassed many other commitments in my life. All of my efforts, my time, and my focus would be for naught, if it were not for the incredible generosity and loyalty of two people dear friends who have never shown a deaf ear.

Jay Gelman and Jeff Mansbach – you both recognized and validated my passion. Not only have you made my dream come true, but you are partners in the Torah knowledge that this *sefer* will impart to its many readers. I owe you a tremendous debt of gratitude, one that mere words can never repay.

May you and your families reap the rewards of your chesed in this world and the world to come.

Table of Contents

Introduction...I

⇜ Vayikra

Holiness and humility 1
Animal rights...4
It really should be us on the altar, not the animals....................................7
The merits of our fathers 10
In praise of the dove 11
No man is an island..13
Sacrificial procedures..14
Crop failure 17
Consumed by their own fire 18
The Mitzvos of Parshas Vayikra 20

It's the thought that counts – the Korban Olah 21

Soul food – the Korban Mincha 22

Passing up the sweets...23

Realizing your potential - salting the offering 25

Offering of the erring Sanhedrin 27

To err is human – Korban Chatas...28

If and when 29

Bearing the sin – the Mitzvah to offer testimony 30

A father's pain – the sliding-scale offering 31

The prohibition of separating the head of a bird sin-offering.............33

The prohibition to add oil or frankincense to a meal sin-offering 34

The penalty for the unauthorized use of sacred property 35

Korban Asham Talui 36

The guilt-offering – Korban Asham 36

Restoring stolen property 38

Haftorah Vayikra 40

Tzav

Preparing for Mashiach..43

Enthusiasm is contagious 45

Cleanliness is next to G-dliness..46

"The humble shall inherit the earth" 48

The spark of G-dliness 50

The eternal fire 52

One Kohen, two Kohanim...53

Tree of life 54

The faith of the poor 56

The poor man's bread 57

The inaugural Mincha...57

The meal-offering of a Kohen...60

The sin-offering (Chatas) 61

The burnt sin-offerings 63

The guilt-offering (Asham)...63

From the heart..64

The forty loaves 66

Peace 66

The style of thank you 67

"With a multitude of people is the king's glory" 68

It's the thought that counts 69

Holiness 70

Life and energy 70

Stolen waters 71

The greatest joy 72

Be involved 75

Kashering one's self 76

Haftorah Tzav 77

Shmini

And what would G-d say? 80

Living in the past 81

He who lives in a glass house... 82

Skeletons in the closet 84

A time for humility and a time for pride 85

Down but not out 86

From the heart 88

Assuming personal responsibility 89

The sin(s) of Nadav and Avihu 90

Higher standard 92

"A time for mourning and a time for dancing" 93

Respect for the position 95

The dual personality of wine 96

The answer is the question 98

Laws of Kashrus 100

Why did G-d create ants? 101

The fingernails of our ancestors 103

Socially redeeming values 106

100% glatt Kosher 107

The Mitzvos 108

Haftorah Shmini 111

Tazria

To be or gnat to be 113

One hundred cries 115

Birth & death 117

X & Y 118

Absence makes the heart grow fonder 119

Man's deeds are finer than heaven's 120

"The sins of the fathers are visited upon the children" 121

Compassion, even towards birds..122

The Mitzvos...123

"Life and death in the hand of the tongue" 124

He who has himself as a patient, has a fool for a doctor 127

The soul of his flock 128

The cure for gossip 130

Manufacturer's suggested retail price 133

The Mitzvos...134

It tolls for thee 135

The emporer's new clothes 136

Haftorah Tazria 137

Metzora

But it's true! 140

The Rabbi and the peddler 142

G-d's gift of speech 145

The miracle of Tzara'as 147

Tzara'as is only skin deep 148

Meeting half-way 149

Flying about..150

Second hand smoke..152

French fries for the soul..153

The purification of the Metzora 154

The Mitzvos...160

Haftorah Metzora 164

Acharei Mos

The king is dead..167
Atonement and loss..169
Yom Kippur and the Torah 170
Yom Kippur and the point of creation 172
Two goats 174
The kittle 177
A New York minute 178
Innovations 178
Our mother, the Shechinah..180
Charity begins at home 181
Two kids...182
The great unifier 183
The domesticated man 184
The refined and the hunter 185
Keeping our distance 186
Egypt and Canaan 188
The Mitzvos regarding forbidden relationships 189
The holy land..195
Haftorah Acharei Mos 197

Kedoshim

The ten commandments revisited 200
Unity 205
Be holy 205
In awe of parents 208
Comparative religion courses 210
Idols 'r' us...211
Outstaying one's welcome...212
Sharing your blessings 213
The other theft..217
Theft through words 219
A city called truth 219

The Mitzvos 222

Leading the blind astray 224

Justice must prevail 225

Preserving the life and reputation of others 227

Brotherly love, brotherly hate 228

Love thy neighbor 232

Mixing apples and oranges 233

Forbidden fruit 235

Self-restraint 236

Superstitions 237

Mazel Tov! 238

Whose body is it? 239

No talking during Davening 240

Ghost-busters 241

Respecting the wise 242

Weights and measures 243

The Mitzvos 244

Jewish identity 245

Haftorah Kedoshim 246

∞§ Emor

Say what? 247

Sons of Aharon 250

Hitch your wagon to a star 251

Mais Mitzvah: the Mitzvah to bury an abandoned corpse................253

Mourning..255

The Mitzvos that relate to the sanctity of the Kohanim 260

When the cat is away, the mice will play 267

Make every day count 268

Sanctifying G-d's name 269

The festivals of life..271

Passover 274

Counting the Omer and Shavuos 276

Rosh Hashanah 277

Yom Kippur 278

Succos 279
The four species and the forgotten Jew...............................281
The blasphemer and the showbread 283
Haftorah Emor 285

Behar

Behar 287
7 + 50 = great insights and mysteries 288
Time is the currency of life 291
Faith in the future; faith in today 291
A livelihood 293
The ultimate charity 294
Faith or greed...295
Keeping the lines of communication open...........................296
The Mitzvos of Shmitah 297
The Mitzvos of the jubilee year (Yovel) 297
Laws of wronging another Jew 299
Laws of selling land in Israel 301
Strangers and dwellers...302
Strengthen your brother - the greatest form of charity 304
Your brother shall live with you 305
Empathy..306
Laws regarding Jewish slaves 307
Redemption of Israel...309
Greed and poverty...310
Haftorah Behar 313

Bechukosai

Bechukosai...315
Spiritual rewards vs. material rewards 316
Study in order to do 318
Everything in its season, even blessings 319
Abundance and security 320
United we stand...322

Pride and humility...322

The curses 323

The enemy from within..324

Sevenfold 326

The blessing of the curse 327

Scattering the tradition among the nations 328

The supreme test 329

Everlasting bond: for better or worse 330

The Mitzvos...332

The lesson of Sefer Vayikra 337

Haftorah Bechukosai 338

THINKING OUTSIDE THE BOX

VAYIKRA

INTRODUCTION

✑ APPROACHING TORAH WITH SOUL

What is Torah? Is it a collection of dos and don'ts? Is it a history of the Jewish people? Or is it both—a tapestry interwoven with stories and prohibitions? Actually, Torah is beyond definition. On the surface, it seems to be the story of the founding of our nation and a guide to the principles and laws by which we must live. However, Torah is much more than that; it defies time and space. Its historical truths are as true today in modern society as they were three thousand, five hundred years ago in ancient Mesopotamia, Mitzrayim, and Canaan. Torah's lessons can be studied by the novice and by the scholar. Its appeal is to the young as well as the aged. It delights the mind and gratifies the heart.

Have you ever noticed that a *ba'al teshuvah* embraces Judaism with gusto and enthusiasm, while many of those who were taught about Judaism from their youth go about their religious lives mechanically? You may think that this is because observant Judaism is new to the *ba'al teshuvah*, and all new things are embraced enthusiastically. That, however, is only partially true, as the *ba'al teshuvah* seems to retain his or her passion for Torah even after many years. The reason behind this is that the *ba'al teshuvah* first approached Torah and Judaism on an emotional level. He learned the very same Torah with the very same lessons and morals as others did from childhood, but he learned them with his heart and that stirred the passion of his soul.

This volume will contain lessons and revelations that you may, at some point, already have shelved in your brain. It is my hope that through the words of this volume these revelations and lessons will reach the doorways of your heart.

VAYIKRA

✍ HOLINESS AND HUMILITY

"And He called (vayikra) to Moshe and HaShem spoke to him from the Tent of Assembly saying" (Vayikra 1:1).

Our Sages refer to the book of Vayikra as *Toras Kohanim*, laws of *Kohanim*. Why is it called *Toras Kohanim* and not *Toras HaKohanim*, laws of **the** *Kohanim*?

One who is not a *Kohen* could think that this volume of the Torah does not pertain to him or her. It was written only for the male priests who served in the *Mishkan*. However, the verse says *"Be for Me a kingdom of priests (Kohanim) and a holy nation" (Shmos19:6).* Each and every Jew must strive to be like a priest. We must apply to ourselves the Torah's lessons that were taught to the *Kohanim* in the book of Vayikra. Perhaps that is why this book is referred to as *Toras Kohanim*; it speaks to and instructs each of us, not just **the** priests. In addition, the word *HaKohanim* is found fairly often in the Torah. Surprisingly, the word *Kohanim* is only found one time in the entire

Sefer Torah and that is in the verse *"Be for Me a kingdom of priests (Kohanim) and a holy nation."*

The book of Shmos concluded with the physical aspect of the *Mishkan*. It gave us the list of materials that were to be used, the layout, the holy furnishings, and a description of the priestly garments. *Sefer Vayikra* gives us the heart and soul of the *Mishkan*. It describes the Divine service that was to be performed. The theme of this portion of the Torah is purity and holiness. It describes in detail the holy service in the Tabernacle. It gives us the rules and regulations of purity and impurity. The *sefer* gives us the laws of the holy days in the Jewish calendar; it tells of the sanctity of the Holy Land in the seventh year. It defines sexual morality and immorality. Laws of charity and business ethics are detailed. The *sefer* also contains the blessings for those who uphold the laws of sanctity and purity and, contrarily, the curses that befall those who violate these laws.

The very first word in the *parshah* brings out this theme of holiness and purity. The first word is *vayikra*, "and He called." The word is spelled VYKRa, with a small final letter *aleph*. The Medrash (*Vayikra Rabbah* 1:13) explains that the first two letters are merely prefixes that mean "and He." The root of the word is KRA, "called." KRA is associated with holiness as it is written *"And (the angels) called (KRA) to one another: Holy, Holy, Holy"* (*Yeshayah* 6:3). If we drop the *aleph* from the root we are left with KR which is associated with impurity. *"If there will be a man who is not pure on account of a happening (KR) at night, he shall be sent out of the encampment..."* (*Devarim* 23:11).

Rashi (1:1) points out that when HaShem spoke to Moshe the verse used the word *vayikra*, with the *aleph*. By using the word associated with holiness, HaShem is showing how beloved Moshe was. However, when HaShem spoke to the wicked Bilaam, the word is spelled without the *aleph*, *"And G-d happened (KR) to Bilaam"* (*Bamidba*r 23:16). The Torah uses the term associated with impurity and connotes a feeling of repulsion.

It is interesting to note that in the first verse of Vayikra, Moshe's name came before HaShem's name. In *Sefer Bereishis*, the Medrash asks why did the Torah begin with the letter *bais* and not an *aleph*. We explained that the question was directed at why the Torah started with, *"In the beginning G-d created"* as opposed to, *"G-d created in the beginning."* The latter would have the Torah beginning with HaShem's name and the letter *aleph*. Would it not have been more proper and honorable to begin with the name of G-d?

We answered that HaShem was showing the importance of humility. HaShem was demonstrating humility, by not beginning His Torah with His name. That same lesson is being taught to us here. HaShem gave the honor to Moshe by allowing Moshe's name to appear before G-d's name. Why is the lesson being taught again and why here?

This *parshah* begins the portion of the Torah that deals with sacrifices. An integral objective of the sacrifices was to humble the spirit of man. A prideful sinner will not repent. He will not beg for forgiveness. He feels that he is above supplication and repentance. The *Orchas Tzadikim* (*Shar HaAnavah*) tells us that one who is humble has learned the lesson of all the sacrifices. He also says that the offerings of a prideful person are not deemed acceptable by G-d.

The letter *aleph* stands for *ani* or *anochi*, meaning I or me. The small *aleph* in the word *Vayikra* means that one should humble himself. The lesson of humility, as we shall see, will be the lesson of the sacrifices and that will bring about the spirit of holiness and purity that will endear him to HaShem.

The *Baal HaTurim* (1:1) says that when Moshe was writing this verse, he wanted to spell the word without the *aleph*. He could not bring himself to use the word VYKRA which meant holiness and endearment. Moshe was a humble man. As the Torah itself testifies, *"Moshe was exceedingly humble, more so than any man upon the earth"* (*Bamidbar* 12:3). HaShem insisted that Moshe include the *aleph* in the word VYKRA. Moshe compromised by writing a small *aleph*.

The word *korban* (sacrifice) is derived from the Hebrew *karov* (close) and *kiruv* (to bring close). The purpose of the sacrifices was to achieve a closer relationship with G-d. Pride separates one from his fellow man. Pride separates one from G-d. *"The prideful heart is despised by G-d"* (*Mishlei* 16:5). Humility brings us closer to our fellow man. Humility brings us closer to G-d.

Today, because of our many sins, we have no Temple in which to offer these sacrifices. Our Sages (*Bamidbar Rabbah* 18:21) explain the verse *"We replace the oxen with our lips"* (Hoshayah 14:3) to mean that in our times, when we are no longer able to offer sacrifices in the *Bais HaMikdash*, we replace the offerings with the words of our lips. Our words of prayer and our expressions of *teshuvah* are today's offerings.

ANIMAL RIGHTS

How does the concept of animal sacrifices fit into the contemporary mindset? How does the slaughter of innocent animals bring us closer to G-d? The whole idea of sacrifices seems so barbaric. Were our ancestors savages? Wouldn't it be more humane to serve G-d the way we do today through prayer, fasting, and repenting? Has the behavior and understanding of what is important to humanity really advanced since the dark ages?

Before we address those issues there are two things to consider. The first is that social mindsets do change. Today, western culture regards animal sacrifices as barbaric. We tend to think that moral and ethical views change and evolve over the centuries from a primitive and unsophisticated point of view to a more mature and modern mindset. Today we view slavery as an inhuman form of treatment. Yet, a century and a half ago it was an accepted way of life. This seems to indicate that society is progressing towards a more moral and rational point of view. However, consider the following: A mere decade ago, anti-Semitism was considered the domain of the uneducated. Today, colleges and universities are breeding grounds for anti-Semitism. Anti-Semitism is on the rise in Europe, of all places. A generation ago, an unmarried man and woman who lived together were considered immoral. Today it is accepted without a furrowed brow. A few years ago, same sex marriage would have been considered a bad joke. Today it is a political movement. There was a time when having a child out of wedlock was considered a shameful act. Today, more than half the children born in Washington D.C., the nation's capital, are born out of wedlock. We can readily see that mindsets do change but they do not necessarily change from a primitive point of view to a more moral and ethical point of view. Therefore, all we can safely say is that our view of animal sacrifices has changed in the last 2,000 years; but we cannot say for certain that our present view is more ethically objective and more mature than it was two thousand years ago.

The second point to consider is the whole issue of "animal rights." Aren't they "G-d's creatures" also? The Torah's point of view is very simple. *"Have dominion over the fish of the sea, and the fowl of the heaven, and over every living thing that creeps upon the earth"* (*Bereishis* 1:28). Animal life is for the benefit of man. Animals and the environment are to be used by us in a way that promotes our physical and spiritual wellbeing. Animals have no rights; only humans have rights. However, with our human rights comes human responsibility. We are responsible to see to it that there is no animal cruelty (*Baba Metzia* 32b).

So have our ideas really progressed? In our time, the concept of environmentalism and animal rights have evolved into an extreme and absurd point of view. One group of animal rights activists, People for the Ethical Treatment of Animals (PETA), places animal life on the same level as human life. The president of PETA, is on record stating: "Even if animal research resulted in a cure for AIDS, we'd be against it." PETA believes that using animal in research without the animal's consent is a violation of the animal's rights. In their view animals have rights that are on par with human rights. After all, humans are just another form of animal life. They do not believe that man was created in the image of G-d and animals were not. These extremist groups support the violent destruction of scientific research facilities. PETA has admitted funneling over $70,000 to Rodney Coronado, a convicted arsonist, who burned down a Michigan State University research lab. One "animal rights" group recommended that patients sue doctors who endorse the Atkins high protein (animal) diet. They regard owning pets as a form of animal slavery. An "animal rights" spokesperson was asked "If you were driving down the road and suddenly you saw a baby and a squirrel in the road. Which would you swerve to avoid, knowing that the other one would be killed?" The spokesperson was unable to answer the question.

Now consider this? On Jan 26, 2003, a donkey laden with a bomb blew up outside Jerusalem. Terrorists had detonated the donkey-bomb by means of a cell phone. Fortunately, no one was killed. A few days later, PETA dashed off a plea to Yasser Arafat.

PETA, the group that never before expressed concern about the carnage in Israel, is suddenly outraged: all because a donkey died. Never mind that, according to the Israeli embassy, which keeps track of such grim statistics, 729 Israelis have perished in terrorist attacks since September 2000. It took the death of a donkey for PETA to find its voice.

> February 3, 2003
> Yasser Arafat, President Palestinian National Authority
> Ramallah, West Bank
> Palestinian Authority
> Your Excellency: (I can think of lots of titles for Arafat. Excellency isn't among them.)
> I am writing from an organization dedicated to fighting animal abuse around the world. We have received many calls and letters from people shocked at the bombing in Jerusalem on January 26 in which a donkey, laden with explosives, was intentionally blown up... If you have the opportunity, will you please add to your burdens my request that you appeal to all those who listen to you to leave the animals out of this conflict? We send you sincere wishes of peace.
> Very truly yours,
> Ingrid Newkirk President, PETA

Perhaps Ms. Newkirk would prefer that the Palestinians used suicide bombers instead of burros. Oh, that's right, they usually do.

The Washington Post asked Ms. Newkirk if she has asked Mr. Arafat to stop suicide bombings that kill innocent civilians. "It's not my business to inject myself into human wars," she responded.

On the PETA website there is a shocking slide show presentation.

It compares pictures depicting horrifying cruelty to Jews during the Holocaust with pictures showing cruelty, at least according to them, to animals. The shocking aspect of this comparison is the demented thinking required to make such a comparison.

When the University of Pittsburg Hospital started using arteries from chimpanzees and swine to repair defective aortas in humans, the "animal rights" activists marched outside the hospital in protest. Even though human lives were being saved, the monkeys and pigs did not sign an organ donation form. Better the pigs be spared than humans saved.

The common denominator here is that these so-called animal rights activists are actually individuals who have a warped morality that equates the value of human life with anything else that has living cells. To miss completely the value of human life and its potential precludes one from this discussion of animal sacrifices and their potential to bring us closer to G-d. Issues that are bereft of any spiritual meaning do not pose any idealogical dilemna for true spiritual values.

Thus we see from these two points of consideration that though we may have progressed materialistically from the stone-age to the space-age that does not mean that our spiritual sense of priorities and moral values have likewise progressed. However we still have not answered the original question as to how sacrifices bring us closer to G-d. Let us continue.

✌ IT REALLY SHOULD BE US
ON THE ALTAR, NOT THE ANIMALS

"When a man from you offers a sacrifice to G-dc" (1:2).

ow does sacrificing animals bring us closer to G-d? The Rambam (*Moreh Nevuchim*, Book III chapter 32 & 46) gives two very controversial reasons for the mitzvos of sacrificing. In ancient times, animal sacrifices were considered a universal manner of expressing one's feelings to a deity. HaShem was concerned that should He deny the Children of Israel this mode of expression, they would feel completely at a loss. He therefore permitted the practice, provided that it was clear that the sacrifice was *"an offering to G-d"* and not some other deity. Every sacrifice was accompanied with words of thankfulness or an expression of *teshuvah*, depending on why the sacrifice was being offered. The sacrifice itself just enabled the person to be more fully able to express himself, but the expression of *teshuvah*, the prayer, was the more significant aspect of the entire procedure.

To show that the words of the person were more desirable to HaShem than the animal being offered, G-d greatly restricted where animals could be offered. However, He allowed prayers to be said anywhere.

Another reason offered by the Rambam for sacrifices is that ancient cultures used to worship animals. They believed certain animals had supernatural abilities. The Egyptians worshipped sheep. The Mesopotamians worshipped goats. The Asiatics in the Far East worshipped cattle. These animals were chosen to be used in our sacrifices to show that animals are not to be worshipped. Rather, they are to be used in the worship of G-d.

The Ramban (1:9) strongly contends with these reasons of the Rambam. It is extremely difficult for us to imagine that animal sacrifices were permitted in the sanctuary because it was a standard form of worship in connection with idolatry. The Torah tells us so many times that we should remove ourselves from idolatrous practices. It is inconceivable that the Torah is allowing the most basic form of idolatrous practice in the holy *Mishkan*. Cain's brother, Abel, offered sacrifices before idolatry was introduced into the human experience. Hence, there is no connection between sacrifices and idolatry. In addition, if the sole reason why animals are offered to G-d is to demonstrate that they are not objects to be worshipped, why are there so many detailed laws regarding exactly how to offer the sacrifices?

In order to answer the question of the purpose of animal sacrifices, we must first understand that man has two distinct elements which comprise his totality. Man has an animalistic aspect and a

Divine aspect. Man, like an animal, eats, sleeps, and reproduces. Man like an animal has desires and cravings. Man, unlike animals, has intellect and the ability to control his desires and cravings.

The verse says *"And (G-d) breathed into (Adam) the breath (nishmas) of life"* (*Bereishis* 2:7). The *Zohar* comments that the Hebrew word for breath is *nishmas,* which is derived from the word *neshama,* meaning soul. The verse is describing G-d instilling a soul into man. The imagery is that HaShem was performing mouth to mouth resuscitation. The *Zohar* says that when one breathes into the mouth of another, the breath that was part of him is being instilled into the other person. G-d was instilling into man a soul that contained a bit of G-d himself. Man's soul, emanating from G-d's breath, had Divine characteristics – namely, intellect, the ability to speak, and the ability to control one's desires.

When a person purposely sins (*mazid*), he is rejecting G-d's gift to him that he has the ability to control his desires. When a person sins through ignorance (*shogayg*), he is rejecting G-d's gift of intelligence. When man does not use his Divine aspect, he is placing himself on the same level as an animal (*Kav HaYashar* 21:12).

The verse in Vayikra stated *"When a man **from you offers** a sacrifice to G-d..."* The verse is telling the sinner that, since you placed yourself in the same category as an animal, the offering on the Altar should really be you! You, the animal, should be offered. The Ramban (1:9) says that HaShem, through His great kindness, did not require us to be sacrificed as an atonement. He allowed us to substitute an animal. That is why throughout the portions in the Torah the name YHVH, which refers to HaShem's attribute of kindness, is used and not some other name of G-d (*Sifri Pinchos* 143, *Menochos* 110a).

The lesson of the Binding of Yitzchak was twofold. It demonstrated Avraham's total commitment to HaShem. It also demonstrated HaShem's loving kindness by allowing a ram to be substituted for Yitzchak.

Before a person would offer a sacrifice, he had to place his hands on the animal and confess his sins. We can only imagine that he would look into the eyes of the sad-eyed creature and see himself. He had disregarded G-d's Torah. He abused G-d's gift of "breath of life" and acted like an animal. The sad look on the animal reflects how sadly the person had conducted himself. The sad look on the lamb or calf would seem to say that if only you had not sinned I would live. I must now take your place and be offered to G-d. Bringing a sacrifice was a very emotional experience. In the end, the person would be aroused to do a complete *teshuvah*. Today, we no longer have sacrifices to arouse that same emotional experience. It must come from within ourselves and that is not always very easy to do.

The Ramban (1:9) does mention that the entire concept of sacrifices and its many laws contain many mystical and Kabbalistic concepts. However, we are only speaking in more simple terms to convey some basic idea of what *korbanos* (sacrifices) is all about. If one still feels uneasy about the whole issue of animal sacrifices, he must realize that it is due to his lack of faith and knowledge of Torah and is caused by the polluting influence of the so-called modern mindset.

≈ THE MERITS OF OUR FATHERS

Three types of four-legged animals were used as sacrifices: cattle, sheep, and goats. These animals allude to the merits of our forefathers. Cattle are associated with Avraham. When Avraham was visited by his three angelic visitors, he served them meat of a calf. Sheep are associated with Yitzchak. At the Binding of Yitzchak, a ram was substituted and offered in his stead. Goats are associated with Yaakov. Yaakov covered himself with the skin of goats when he received the blessing from his father, Yitzchak.

When Moshe pleaded with HaShem to forgive the Israelites for the sin of the Golden Calf, he said, "*Remember Avraham, Yitzchak, and Yaakov, Your servants*" (*Shmos* 32:13). Rashi explains that Moshe was saying that if the Israelites are to be condemned with fire, remember Avraham who was willing to be burnt alive for the sake of Your holy name. If the Israelites are to be condemned with slaughter, remember Yitzchak who offered himself to be slaughtered at the *Akeidas Yitzchak*. If they are to be condemned with exile, remember Yaakov who exiled himself from his father's house for the sake of Your name. Immediately after Moshe mentioned the merits of our forefathers, the verse says, *"And G-d regretted the evil that He said that He would do to His people."*

The merits of the forefathers saved the Israelites from extinction. The Medrash (*Shmos Rabbah* 44:3) explains that the forefathers never asked for any reward for their great sacrifices and noble deeds. Instead, they wished that their merits be used to help their descendants. Often, parents work hard their entire lives to accumulate and save money. They do not spend it on themselves but desire nothing more than to leave it for their children to inherit and enjoy. Our forefathers did not leave us any money that we know of. Instead, they left us something far greater: the rewards for their many mitzvos.

The sacrificial animals remind us of Avraham, Yitzchak, and Yaakov and of the many merits they bequeathed to us. Without their foresight and generosity, Israel could not have endured. These animals also serve as a reminder to the person offering the sacrifice that not only has he sinned against G-d, but he has failed to live up to the proud and noble heritage of his forefathers.

◄§ IN PRAISE OF THE DOVE

The only bird that was used in the holy service was the dove. The dove represents all three of our forefathers. The verse says, *"My **dove**, my perfect one – is only **one**; she is the only **one of her mother**, she is the **favorite one** of her that bore her"* (*Shir HaShirim* 6:9).

The dove is described with three phrases and the Medrash (*Bereishis Rabbah* 94:1) says that each phrase refers to one of the fathers. The word "one" refers to Avraham who the prophet Yechezkiel called "one", meaning unique (*Yechezkiel* 33:24). The phrase "one of her mother" refers to Yitzchak who was his mother's only son. The word "favorite" refers to Yaakov who was his mother's favorite son.

Each of those phrases contains the word "one." That is why the verse calls the dove the "perfect one." It represents all three one's – Avraham, Yitzchak, and Yaakov. The nation of Israel is also called "one." The verse says *"Who is like Your nation Israel, one nation in the land"* (*Shmuel* II 7:23 & *Divrei HaYomim* I 17:21). In the *Shemoneh Esrai* of Shabbos *Mincha* we say, *"You are One, Your name is One, who is like Your people Israel, one nation in the land."* Therefore, the dove, the perfect "one," not only represents our forefathers, it represents the nation of Israel.

The Medrash (*Shir HaShirim Rabbah* 1:64) tells of the wonderful attributes of the dove and how they compare to the attributes of the Children of Israel:

> *As the dove is graceful in its step, so too Israel is graceful in its step: when they go up to celebrate the festivals.*
>
> *Just as the dove is distinguished by its coloring, so too Israel is distinguished through circumcision and through tzitzis.*
>
> *As the dove is modest, so too Israel is modest.*
>
> *As the dove stretches forth her neck for slaughter, so too does Israel offer their neck to sanctify G-d's name.*
>
> *As the dove on the altar atones for iniquities, so too Israel atones for the sins of the other nations, since the seventy bullocks which they offer on Succos are only for the sake of the seventy nations.*
>
> *Just as a dove, from the time that she recognizes her mate, never changes him for another, so too Israel once they had learned to know the Holy One, Blessed be He, have never exchanged Him for another.*
>
> *Just as a dove, even if its young are taken from it, never abandons its nest. So too Israel, although the Temple was destroyed, have not ceased to celebrate three festivals every*

year.

> *Just as the dove produces a new brood every month, so too Israel every month produces fresh learning and good deeds.*
>
> *Just as the dove flies far and yet returns to her cote, so too Israel, no matter how far they wander in their galus, they will always return to their home.*

This Medrash reflects wonderfully not only on the Children of Israel, but it also reflects wonderfully on the mindset of the author of this Medrash who is unknown. When we see a dove, what do we think of? Beauty, grace, purity, peace. Yes, but why didn't we think of the Jewish People like the author of the Medrash did? The answer is because we are not preoccupied with our fellow Jews as the author of the Medrash was. His mind was totally consumed with his love and admiration of his brethren. Wherever he looked, he saw his brother and sister Jews. What ever he saw, he saw the Jewish People. That's what it means to be a Jew.

➣ NO MAN IS AN ISLAND

*"When a man **from among you** offers..."* (1:1).

The words "from among you" seem to be superfluous. The verse should have simply said "When a man offers..." We are not a nation of individuals. Each and every Jew is part of a greater entity called Israel. We are each an organ in the body of that entity called Israel. Just as each organ of the human body contributes its efforts to the wellbeing of the person, each of us has his or her part in contributing to the spiritual wellbeing of Israel. When a person sins, it is as though an organ of Israel has become diseased.

Just as a diseased organ affects the entire body, so too do our sins affect our fellow Jews. A sinner cannot simply say "It's my business whether or not I sin. What business is it of yours if I repent?"

That is why the verse says to the sinner *"When a man from among you offers..."* to teach us that every individual man is part of the "among you;" he is part of that greater entity called Israel.

The seventeenth century English poet, John Donne, wrote:

> *All mankind is of one author and is one volume.*
> *When one man dies, one chapter is not torn out of the book,*
> *But translated into a better language.*
> *And every chapter must be so translated...*
> *As therefore the bell that rings to a sermon,*
> *Calls not upon the preacher only,*
> *But upon the congregation to come.*
> *So this bell calls us all*
> *But how much more me...*
> *No man is an island, entire of itself...*
> *Any man's death diminishes me,*
> *Because I am involved in mankind,*
> *And therefore never send to know for whom the bell tolls.*
> *It tolls for thee.*

SACRIFICIAL PROCEDURES

This *parshah* discusses five types of sacrifices:

- The Burnt-Offering, *Olah*
- The Meal-Offering, *Mincha*
- The Peace-Offering, *Shelamim*

- The Guilt-Offering, *Asham*
- The Sin-Offering, *Chatas*

These five are called *kodshai kadashim,* holy of the holiest. They could only be eaten by male *Kohanim* and only within the confines of the *Mishkan* or walls of the *Bais HaMikdash.* The exact procedure for each type of sacrifice differed one from the other; however, here is the general procedure for cattle, sheep, and goats:

1 – The animal was brought near the *Mishkan* or *Bais HaMikdash* and was proclaimed by its owner to be a holy sacrifice. He would mention what type of sacrifice it was to be.

2 – Once inside the sacred grounds, the owner would place his hands on the animal's head and say the *vidui*-confession and atone for his sin.

3 – The animal was slaughtered.

4 – A *Kohen* would catch some of the blood flowing from the neck in a sacred vessel.

5 – The *Kohen* would bring the vessel of blood to the altar.

6 – Some of the blood was tossed against the walls of the altar. The number of times the blood was tossed and exactly where it was tossed depended on the type of sacrifice it was. In addition, sometimes the blood was tossed to the walls of the altar, sometimes it was poured against the walls, and other times the *Kohen* would dip his index finger into the blood and touch the walls. It all depended on the type of sacrifice being offered.

7 – The carcass was skinned and cut up into pieces.

8 – The pieces to be offered on top the altar and the innards were washed and salted.

9 – The parts to be offered were brought to the top of the altar and burned.

10 – The remaining meat was parceled out among the *Kohanim* and eaten. The meat of the Burnt-Offering was not eaten. It too was burned on top the altar along with the innards. The meat of certain Sin-Offerings was also not eaten.

11 – The leftover blood in the vessel was poured down a special opening built onto the bottom of the altar.

The General procedure for a bird sacrifice was as follows:

1 – The bird was brought near the *Mishkan* or *Bais HaMikdash* and was proclaimed by its owner to be a holy sacrifice. He would declare what type of sacrifice it was to be. A bird could only be used for a Burnt-Offering (*olah*) or a Sin-Offering (*chatas*).

2 – The bird was slaughtered but not with a knife. The *Kohen* would use his right thumbnail. The nail was allowed to grow long and was sharpened for this purpose. Also, the slaughtering was done from the back of the neck towards the front, unlike all other acts of slaughtering which were from front to back.

3 – The *Kohen* would press the bird against the walls of the altar and the pressure would leave a blood stain on the walls.

4 – The head was washed, salted, and burned on top of the altar.

5 – The crop, stomach, and intestines were removed and discarded. They were placed in a special waste area near the altar.

6 – The remainder of the fowl was washed, salted and burned on top of the altar. No part was eaten.

A meal offering usually consisted of wheat flour, olive oil, and frankincense (an aromatic gum from the Boswellia tree). The general procedure for a meal-offering was as follows:

1 – Some of the oil was poured into a vessel.

2 – The flour was placed on top of the oil.

3 – Some more of the oil was poured on top of the flour.

4 – The oil and flour were mixed together and kneaded. If the meal-offering was to be baked, then lukewarm water was added to make the dough suitable for baking.

5 – If the dough was to be baked, the dough was put in a griddle or a frying pan or on the floor of a baker's oven, depending on the type of meal-offering, and was baked or fried.

6 – After the baking, the meal-offering had the consistency of a hard pita. It was folded several times so that it would crumble into large pieces.

7 – The offering was placed into a sacred vessel and the remainder of the oil was poured into the vessel.

8 – The frankincense was placed on top.

9 – The vessel was brought to the south western corner of the altar.

10 – The frankincense was moved to the side and a fistful (*kometz*) of the dough (or crumbs) and some oil was removed and placed in a sacred vessel.

11 – The frankincense was placed into that vessel too.

12 – The vessel with the fistful of dough and the frankincense was brought on top of the altar. Some salt was put into the vessel.

13 – The contents of the vessel were poured onto the fire atop the altar.

14 – The remainder of the offering was eaten by male *Kohanim*. If the person offering the meal-offering was a *Kohen*, no fistful was taken from the offering. Instead, the entire offering was burned on top of the altar and none was eaten.

⋙ CROP FAILURE

"When a man from among you offers..." (1:2).

"And he shall remove the (bird's) crop with its innards and cast it eastward near the altar" (1:16).

The Hebrew word for "man" used in the first verse is *"adam."* Why did it not use the more common term for man, namely *"ish"*?

The innards of a four-legged animal constituted an integral part of the offering. Why in the case of birds were the innards discarded?

Rashi (1:2) tells us that the word "adam" was used to hint at Adam, the first man. Just as Adam did not offer anything that was stolen, for everything was his, so too you. You may not offer anything that was stolen. That is the lesson of the word "*adam.*"

Every farmer who had crops growing in his field protected the crops from neighbor's animals and foraging beasts by surrounding the field with a fence. That assures everyone that the animals would only eat food to which they were entitled. The animals could not wander into someone else's field and "steal" the crops. However, birds are not deterred by fences. Birds live off the crops of the farmers. Birds are thieves. Therefore, though the innards were an important part of the sacrifice, the digestive system of the bird, which fed off stolen goods, was not deemed acceptable as part of sacrificial service.

These two verses tell us how important it is to remove oneself from theft, especially when it comes to atonement. As a businessman, I often come across successful businessmen who give substantial sums to charity. Some of these benefactors earn their money in what could be termed illegal, or to put it nicely, questionable means. On occasion, I have had the audacity and temerity to ask them how they could live with themselves since they resort to "questionable" business practices. It was once explained to me that these people rationalize that since a significant part of their money goes to charity, that atones for their devious dealings. Or, at least it relieves their guilty consciences. Perhaps they envision themselves to be Jewish Robin Hoods, robbing from the rich to give to the poor.

However, it is quite obvious from the *parshah* that G-d does not accept and wishes no part of stolen goods. Just as an offering must be accompanied with pure and sincere intentions, so too the offering itself must be acquired through pure and sincere dealings.

✿ CONSUMED BY THEIR OWN FIRE

"And the sons of Aharon the priest shall place a fire upon the altar" (1:7).

*T*he Talmud (*Eruvin* 63a) tells us that although a fire came down from heaven to ignite the wood upon the altar, it is nevertheless a mitzvah to bring a man-made fire and place it on top of the altar. The lesson to be learned here is that we are commanded not to rely upon miracles. We must do things for ourselves.

The High Priest never became unfit for service during the day of *Yom Kippur* and yet the *Sanhedrin* always designated an understudy for the High Priest in case it should happen that he becomes unfit. Even though the understudy was never used, the Sanhedrin did not wish to rely on a miracle (*Tzla"ch Pesachim* 64b).

The twelve Showbread which were placed on the Table in the Sanctuary remained warm and fresh until it was removed from the Table a week later. Still, after it was removed the *Kohanim* would not place the Showbread in a cool place because they did not wish to rely on a miracle to keep it warm (*Yerushalmi Shekalim* 6:3 & similarly *Rashi, Shabbos* 124a).

There are several other instances where the Talmud teaches us the lesson not to rely on miracles (*Pesachim* 64b, *Tosfos Yom Tov. Dimai* 1:1, *Yerushalmi Yoma* 1:4). What all these lesson have in common is that they are all derived from some aspect of the Temple service. Not relying on miracles seems to be a general rule of life. Why is the lesson so often taught in connection to the *Mishkan* and the *Bais HaMikdash*?

Of all the great miracles past, present and future, none can surpass the miracle of forgiveness. Resh Lakish tells us (*Yoma* 86b) that through forgiveness not only is an accidental sin (*shogayg*) forgiven but the sin becomes a mitzvah! Imagine that someone had offended you and your feelings were greatly hurt. The careless offender later comes to beg your forgiveness. You may be able to bring yourself to forgive him but would you now render his offensive act as a praiseworthy deed? Of course not. But, HaShem's forgiveness can do that. It can turn a sin into a mitzvah. That is a miracle!

However, this knowledge is a dangerous thing. Since we know in advance about the miracle of forgiveness, we may be tempted to rely on this miracle and commit sins, and assume that later they will be eradicated and mitzvos will be placed in their stead. The Torah is telling us "Do not rely on miracles." The Talmud (*Yoma* 85b) tells us that one who thinks that he will sin now and later repent, will not be given the opportunity to repent. We cannot rely on miracles.

The Talmud (*Eruvin* 63a) told us that although a fire came down from heaven to ignite the wood upon the altar, it was nevertheless a mitzvah to bring a man-made fire and place it on top of the altar. We are taught not to rely upon miracles. Interestingly, the Talmud also tells us that the law was taught to us by Nadav and Avihu, the sons of Aharon. Subsequently, Nadav and Avihu entered the *Kodesh HaKadashim* with a strange fire-offering. They were not told to do so and placed their lives in jeopardy by entering the Holy of Holies. Were they relying on a miracle that they would be forgiven and that they would survive? The end of the story was that they were not forgiven and they did not survive. Their own fires consumed them. Ironically, they perished from the consequences of their own lesson

✺ THE MITZVOS OF PARSHAS VAYIKRA

*p*arshas Vayikra contains 16 mitzvos, mitzvah 115 through mitzvah 130, according to the reckoning of the *Sefer HaChinuch.*

≈§ IT'S THE THOUGHT THAT COUNTS – THE KORBAN OLAH

The 115ᵗʰ mitzvah in the Torah is to adhere to the laws of the burnt-offering (*korban olah*).
*"If a burnt-offering (**olah***) be his sacrifice..." (1:3).*

One of the unique aspects of the burnt offering was that no part of it was eaten. It was entirely consumed on the altar.

There are numerous reasons and occasions when a *korban olah* is offered. The very first sacrifice brought in the Temple each day was an *olah*. This was called the Morning *Tamid, or Tamid shel Shachar*. The day's service was concluded with a *korban olah*. This was called the Afternoon *Tamid* or *Tamid shel Bain Ha'Arbayim*. The *olah* was brought by every male Israelite on each of the three festivals. After a mother gave birth to a child, she would offer an *olah*. There are a number of sins that required an *olah* as atonement. Another unique aspect of the *olah* was that it could be a free-will offering, meaning that one did not have a reason to offer it other than that he wished to express his thankfulness to HaShem. One could also offer the *olah* as atonement for sins for which the Torah did not specify the atonement. The only other animal sacrifice that could be a free-will offering was the peace-offering, the *korban shelamim*. All other animal sacrifices could only be offered if it was required by the Torah.

The *olah* was the only sacrifice that could be offered by a non-Jew.

The Talmud (*Nazir* 45a) tells us that when a series of different sacrifices are to be offered, the *korban chatas* always comes first. Why then was the *korban olah* mentioned in this *parshah* before the *korban chatas*?

The *Kli Yakar* explains that every sin begins with an improper thought. That thought may or may not lead to a physically sinful action. A *korban olah* is offered as atonement for the thought. Since the thought itself is not a physical thing, the sacrifice was not eaten and taken into the physical body.

The *korban chatas* (sin-offering) is an atonement for the physical action that resulted from the thought. Therefore, the *korban chatas* was allowed to be eaten and taken into the physical body.

We can now understand why the *parshah* mentioned the *korban olah* before the *korban chatas*. Since every sin begins with the thought; therefore the *korban olah* is mentioned first. However, it is the physical action that is the more serious sin and therefore the *korban chatas* is actually offered first.

≈؏ SOUL FOOD – THE KORBAN MINCHA

The 116ᵗʰ mitzvah in the Torah is to follow the laws regarding the meal-offering, *mincha*.
"A soul who brings a meal-offering (mincha) to G-d..." (2:1).

The Torah mentions the meal offering, *mincha*, right after the *korban olah* to teach us that just as the *olah* can be a free-will offering, so too can the *mincha* be a free-will offering.

Rashi comments that only with regards to the free-will meal-offering does the Torah use the word "soul." With regards to the other types of free-will offerings, the Torah does not refer to the one offering the sacrifice with any noun at all. For example, with the previous mitzvah, the *korban olah*, the Torah simply stated, *"If a burnt-offering (olah) be his sacrifice..."* There is no reference at all to the person other than the pronoun "his."

Rashi gives an answer based on the Talmud (*Menochos* 104b). Who would usually be the one to offer a meal-offering? It would be a poor person who could not afford an animal. HaShem is telling us that the small gift of the poor is so treasured by Him that He considers it as though the poor man offered his very soul to G-d.

The wealthier citizens would bring money from home to Jerusalem and purchase their sacrificial animal from the market place. The poor man had little or no money. He would bring flour that he produced himself. Earlier that year, he plowed his meager field and dug the furrows. He planted the wheat seeds in early spring and tended his crops carefully. When the harvest season had arrived, he cut the stalks, and threshed the wheat, and winnowed the grains. With great toil he ground the seeds into fine flour. This flour was made with great effort and love and would help his family survive the year. The poor man put his life into that precious bit of flour and therefore G-d reckons it as though he was offering his very life.

The legend is told that when King Shlomo was about to build the Temple, he divided the work – the walls, the buildings, and the furnishings, among all the people. The wealthier citizens brought money and bought supplies and hired workers to do their part. The poor were given the task of building the Western Wall. They had no money to buy bricks and hire workers. They had to hew the stones from the quarries themselves. They chiseled the stones into large blocks and hauled them into place themselves. G-d treasured the work of the hands of the poor and, so, when it was time for the *Shechinah* to descend, it descended upon the Western Wall. A Heavenly voice went out, "*I shall never depart from this wall and never shall it be destroyed.*" And to this very day, the poor gather in the shadow of the Western Wall and beg for alms because it is in their merit that the Wall still stands there today (From Zev Vilnai's *Legends of Jerusalem*, page 177).

PASSING UP THE SWEETS

The 117ᵗʰ mitzvah in the Torah is the prohibition to add either yeast or honey to any meal offering.

"Any meal-offering (mincha) which you bring to G-d shall not be made leaven, for any yeast or any honey you shall not offer..." (2:11).

The *Sefer HaChinuch* says that the word honey includes any type of sweetening agent.

What is the reasoning behind this prohibition? The Rambam (*Moreh Nevuchim*, part III, chapter 46) says that it was the universal practice among idolatrous people to only offer leavened and sweetened items as an offering. The Torah wished to remove itself from being associated with such practices and therefore prohibited leaven and sweets from being offered on the altar.

The *Baal HaTurim* gives another reason. Yeast, which causes dough to rise, represents haughtiness. Haughtiness is one of the primary tools of the *yetzer ha'ra*. Honey is a powerful sweetener. It can make something which is bitter and harmful for a person seem to be a delicacy. So too, the *yetzer ha'ra* can make the most egregious sin seem palatable. Therefore, the Torah did not wish for yeast or honey to be offered on the altar.

The *Sefer HaChinuch* says that we can never truly fathom the reason behind any mitzvah. Even those mitzvos which seem logical to us, such as the prohibition against stealing, are truly beyond the ken of human understanding. Only those who are familiar with the kabbalistic mysteries can begin to grasp the significance behind any mitzvah. However, the *Chinuch* continues, in order that our paltry minds can have some vague idea as to what the mitzvah is about, our Sages give reasons. But, bear in mind, those reasons only scratch the surface of the depth of the mitzvah's significance.

With that said, the *Sefer HaChinuch* gives a "reason" for this prohibition. One of the most important character traits to develop is alacrity, a cheerful eagerness and quickness. Our father, Avraham, was not slack in performing G-d's commandment of the *Akeidas Yitzchak*. He rose up early in the morning to perform his Divine task. His love for G-d and his eagerness to do His will propelled him to rise up early that morning. One should not think that the day is long and the year is great. *"Do not say that when I'll be free, I'll learn. Perhaps you will not be free and will not learn (Avos 2:4)."* The Talmud (*Sotah* 49a) tells us that the great ability to be divinely inspired (*ruach ha'kodesh*) begins with the character trait of alacrity. The opposite of alacrity is laziness and procrastination.

Yeast and honey are the opposite of alacrity. Yeast in dough requires time to rise. It just sits there and waits for time to pass. Honey, because of its natural thickness, pours very slowly. It seems that it takes forever for honey from the bottom of an inverted honey jar to reach the mouth of the jar. Yeast is slow in time. Honey is slow in action. Being slow prevents one from achieving greatness. Laziness and procrastination prevents one from achieving his true potential. Laziness and procrastination cause sin and therefore yeast and honey could not be part of the meal-offering.

Orchas Tzadikim (chapter 15) tells us the secret to developing the trait of alacrity. The secret is to be focused. When one rises up in the morning he thinks of how much he has to do that day and that a little bit of extra sleep will give him the energy to carry out the day's tasks. Perhaps it is cold outside and the warmth of the covers should be enjoyed just a bit longer. If a person, upon awakening, thinks that it is now time to daven and come close to HaShem, if he can just focus on that thought and banish all foreign thoughts from his mind, he will be able to jump out of bed immediately. He must think only of coming close to his Creator and not think about the day's tasks or the frigid temperature. This requires training and practice but is well worth the effort. No one said perfection comes easily.

REALIZING YOUR POTENTIAL – SALTING THE OFFERING

The 118ᵗʰ mitzvah in the Torah is the prohibition to offer a sacrifice without salt.

Please see next mitzvah.

> *"Any meal-offering shall you salt it with salt, it shall not be lacking..."* (2:13).

The 119th mitzvah in the Torah is to salt all offerings.

This applies to animal sacrifices as well as to meal-offerings.

> *"...upon all your sacrifices you shall bring salt"* (2:13).

What is the significance of salt that the Torah not only made it a mitzvah to add salt to every offering but it also made it a prohibition to leave out salt?

Rashi (*Bamidbar* 18:19) tells us that a unique quality of salt is that it does not deteriorate, rot, or spoil. Salt therefore represents the concept of consistency, unchanging, faithfulness. The Torah refers to an everlasting treaty as a "salt treaty" (*Bamidbar* 18:19). The commitment between HaShem and Israel is an everlasting commitment. In order for this commitment to be everlasting, Israel must have the ability to be forgiven. Man, as an individual, sins. Israel, as a nation, sins. If our sins could not be atoned and forgiven, the relationship between us and G-d would have long ago been severed. Since atonement is achieved through sacrifices, and its primary purpose was to allow the relationship between us and our Creator to remain everlasting, it is only fitting the every sacrifice be accompanied with salt.

The Ramban (2:13) points out another unique quality of salt. Salt is a flavor enhancer. By adding a small bit of salt to any food, the salt brings out the hidden flavors that were dormant. Salt, therefore, represents the bringing forth of potential abilities.

Each and every person has the potential for greatness. A young child realizes this and, therefore, he aspires to become a great *talmid chachom* or a millionaire who will be charitable with his money. Perhaps he will envision himself as a great physician who will cure diseases or maybe he will become a famous explorer. But somewhere along the way to adulthood the dream disappears. What stops this potential for greatness and causes it to remain unfulfilled? Why are so few people able to achieve greatness? Sin covers up the potential. Sin distracts us from becoming what we could become. If sins could not be forgiven, then no one would be able to become great. It is through atonement, such as sacrifices, that sins are forgiven. After the atonement we can once again dream of realizing our potential. The realization of potential is symbolized by salt and therefore each offering was accompanied with salt.

Rebbe Yochanan and Resh Lakish both say: At the time when the Temple stood, the altar used to make atonement for a person; now a person's table makes atonement for him (*Chagigah* 27a). Rashi explains that acts of kindness, such as inviting guests to our table, atone for sins.

Rebbe Yochanan elaborates: Since the nations of Ammon and Moab did not invite the Israelites to join their table after the Israelites departed from Egypt, converts of those two nations are not permitted to join the Jewish congregation in marriage. Since Yisro offered hospitality to Moshe, Yisro's descendants became judges in the Supreme Court of Israel (*Sanhedrin* 103b).

Today, our hospitality is our offering to G-d. Our table is our altar resting in the sanctuary of our home. This equates our home with the Temple, and our table with the altar, and our food with the offerings. Since salt was an integral part of every sacrifice, we have the custom to dip the bread of *ha'motzai* into salt (*Ramah, Shulchan Orech* 167:5). There is a custom to dip the bread into the salt three times because the *gematria* of HaShem's name is 26, 3 x 26 = 78. The *gematria* of *melach*, salt, is 78 (*Ta'amai Minhagim*, paragraph 182).

≈§ OFFERING OF THE ERRING SANHEDRIN

The 120th mitzvah in the Torah is for a *Sanhedrin*, Supreme Court, that gave an incorrect ruling, to bring an offering.

"If all the congregation sinfully errs... the elders of the congregation shall place their hands on the head of the bull..." (4:13-15).

*T*his Mitzvah regards a prohibition that involved the punishment of *kares*, excommunicating the soul from the future world. If the *Sanhedrin* mistakenly allowed that prohibition and if most of the Israelite nation inadvertently committed that infraction, then each tribe must offer a special sin-offering. The individuals who actually committed the sin are not required to offer any sacrifice.

⌘ TO ERR IS HUMAN – KORBAN CHATAS

The 121ˢᵗ mitzvah in the Torah is for an individual who unknowingly transgressed a prohibition that involved the punishment of *kares*, excommunicating the soul from the future world; that individual must bring a sin-offering, a *korban chatas* *"If a soul sins in error... he shall place his hands on the sin-offering (chatas)..."* (4:27-29).

*T*he question that begs to be asked is why is any atonement required since the sin was committed unknowingly? It was a mistake and should not count as a sin at all.

The Ramban explains that this verse used the word "soul," *"If a soul sins in error..."* because we are dealing with sins that affect the soul in the future world. Just as one who drinks a potion of poison, whether it was done intentionally or accidentally, his physical body will be affected. So too if one committed a sin that involved *kares*, whether it was done intentionally or accidentally, his soul will be affected. Therefore, even a sin committed inadvertently requires a *kaparah*, forgiveness. The spiritual realm, in this sense, is no different that the physical realm. They both came from the same One Creator.

✺ IF AND WHEN

I n the portion that deals with the *korban chatas* and *kores*, the Torah (4:3) talks about the chaplain priest of the army who sins. The verse begins with, *"If the Kohen sins..."* Later, the Torah (4:13) talks about a Supreme Court (*Sanhedrin*) that errs and causes most of Israel to sin. The verse begins with *"If the congregation of Israel sins..."* Afterwards, the

Torah (4:22) talks about the leader of Israel who sins. The verse begins with, *"When a ruler sins..."*

The *Sforno* makes an interesting observation. The verse that talks about the chaplain and the *Sanhedrin* begin with the word "if." The verse that talks about the leader of Israel begins with the word "when." The *Sforno* concludes that it is fairly unlikely that the chaplain of the army would commit a sin involving *kares*. Therefore, the verse began with the word "if." It is even less likely that the entire *Sanhedrin* would issue an incorrect ruling involving *kares* and that, furthermore, most of the Israelites would commit that sin. That verse too begins with the word "if." However, when it comes to a leader of a nation, the enormous wealth and absolute power that accompanies that position invariably leads him to commit egregious sins. As Lord Acton (1834 – 1902) said, *"Absolute power corrupts absolutely."* Therefore, that verse begins with the words *"When a ruler sins..."* because it is inevitable.

When the Torah talks about the chaplain, the *Sanhedrin,* and the leader sinning, it must be talking about a case in which they confessed and admitted to their sin. Without confession the sacrifice cannot be offered. Rashi (4:22) comments that the verse that talks about the leader sinning begins with *"When a ruler sins..."* The Hebrew word for "when" is *asher* which is similar to the word *ashrei*, fortunate. Rashi continues that it is most fortunate for a generation whose leader is willing to publicly confess to a sin.

In our times there have been presidents and prime ministers that have committed sinful indiscretions. Rather than confess to the shameful act, they deny it. These politicians involve others and coerce them into lying on their behalf. We, unfortunately, can readily appreciate the words of Rashi that it is most fortunate for a generation whose leader is willing to publicly confess to a sin.

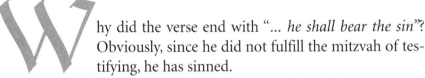

⇜ BEARING THE SIN
– THE MITZVAH TO OFFER TESTIMONY

The 122ⁿᵈ mitzvah in the Torah is for a witness to testify
"If he be a witness, whether he saw or he knew, if he does not tell, he shall bear the sin." (5:1).

hy did the verse end with *"... he shall bear the sin"*? Obviously, since he did not fulfill the mitzvah of testifying, he has sinned.

The Medrash (*Sifra*) explains the story behind this verse. A lender approached the borrower and asked to be repaid. The borrower denied having ever borrowed the money. There was a witness who saw the money being borrowed. The lender asked the court to subpoena the witness. The witness appeared before the court and testified that he did not see anything and he took an oath to that effect. Later, the witness confessed that he had lied and swore falsely. To atone for the false oath he must bring a sacrifice; however, the lender still will not be able to collect his money. As the Talmud (*Kesubos* 18b) tells us, "*Once a witness testifies, he cannot alter his testimony.*" Here too, since the witness has gone on record that he knows nothing about the matter, he cannot come to court again to alter his testimony. The lender will lose the money to which he was entitled and for that the witness must "bear his sin."

The lesson here is a great one. A sinner often not only harms his spiritual self, he harms others. Other people may be looking up to him as an example of a religious person. When they discover that the person sinned, they feel disappointed and their own faith is sorely tested. When the news media report that a religious man has committed a crime, it is a terrible reflection on the entire religious community. Members of the religious community feel a sense of shame. Members of the non-religious community mockingly point their finger at the so-called religious criminal.

Atonement can only do so much. It will allow G-d to forgive the sin. But, the damage done to other people, G-d does not forgive and for that "he shall bear the sin."

ⵥ A FATHER'S PAIN
– THE SLIDING-SCALE OFFERING

The 123rd mitzvah in the Torah is to bring a guilt offering called *oleh v'yoraid,* **a sliding scale.**
"He shall bring as his guilt offering to G-d for his sin... a lamb... and if his hand cannot afford a lamb, he shall bring as his guilt offering for that which he sinned two turtle-doves... and if his hand cannot afford two turtle-doves... he shall bring as his offering for that which he sinned a tenth of an ephah of flour as a sin offering..." **(5:6-11).**

*T*he sliding scale refers to the financial status of the sinner. A wealthier sinner will have to bring a more expensive offering than a poorer sinner.

Three different sinners have to bring this sacrifice. The first is a witness who was subpoenaed and falsely swore that he did not know anything about the case. He must bring an *oleh v'yoraid* for the false oath. The second is a person who was unclean, *tamei*, and either mistakenly ate sacred food or mistakenly entered the Temple precincts. He must bring an *oleh v'yoraid*. The third is one who made an oath to himself to do or not to do something and mistakenly violated his oath. He too must bring an *oleh v'yoraid*.

The Medrash (*Sifra*) tells us that the three sins are listed in the order of their severity. The most severe sin of the three is the witness who denied knowing testimony. The next severe sin is the *tamei* person who either ate sacred food or entered into the sacred precincts. The least severe sin is the one who violated his oath.

This presents a problem. Usually we determine the severity of a sin based on the punishment it incurs. Since a punishment is only carried out if the sin was done purposely, an examination follows of what the punishment would be for these three sins.

A *tamei* person who purposely ate sacred food or purposely entered the sacred precincts incurs the punishment of *kares*, his soul has no portion in the World to Come. This is the most severe punishment of the three. The punishment for one, who refused to testify, even if the sin is committed knowingly, requires no more than an offering. There is no punishment given, neither physically nor monetarily. This is the least severe sin of the three. The punishment for the sin of purposely violating an oath is *malkos*, lashes. *Malkos* is right in the middle of our severity scale. How can the Medrash say that the Torah listed the sins in the order of severity (witness, *tamei*, oath) since it seems obvious to us that it is not so (but rather – *tamei*, oath, witness)?

The answer lies in recognizing that we based our ranking on the only objective criteria available to us: the severity of the punishment. However, HaShem sets the standard and He has a different criterion for evaluating the severity of a sin. The witness who denied having knowledge of a loan is depriving the lender of his money and the lender will never be able to get it back as we explained earlier. In HaShem's book, a crime against a fellow man is the most severe crime. A *tamei* person eating sacred foods or entering a sacred area is a crime against G-d. That is the second degree of severity. A man who swore to himself to do or not to do something, and violated that oath is a crime against himself. That is the least severe of the three.

Why does HaShem consider a crime against a fellow man to be the most severe sin? Later in the *parshah* the verse says, *"A soul who sins and transgresses against G-d by denying his neighbor a security, or a loan, or a stolen item, or payment that is due to him..."* (5:21). The verse is listing one man's crime against a fellow man and yet the verse says *"A soul who sins and transgresses against G-d."* The Torah is telling us that a sin against your fellow man is also a sin against G-d. When a person injures someone's son, the Father feels the pain.

THE PROHIBITION OF SEPARATING THE HEAD OF A BIRD SIN-OFFERING

The 124ᵗʰ mitzvah in the Torah is the prohibition to completely sever the head of a bird sin-offering.
"And he shall cut the neck from the back but not separate." (5:8).

There are only two bird offerings – the bird burnt-offering (*olah*) and the bird sin-offering (*chatas*). The necks of the birds of both types of offerings were pierced by the thumbnail of the *Kohen* but the head of the *olah* was completely severed from the body whereas the head of the *chatas* was not completely severed.

What could be the reason for this prohibition given that this is the correct procedure for the olah? Perhaps one can be suggested in light of the *Kli Yakar* that was mentioned earlier. The *Kli Yakar* said that the *olah* atones for the thought of committing the sin. The *chatas* atones for the deed the thought brought about. Since the *olah* atones for the thought alone, the head of the *olah* was severed and made separate from the body. Since the *chatas* atones for the physical deed the thought caused, the head must remain attached to the body.

THE PROHIBITION TO ADD OIL OR FRANKINCENSE TO A MEAL SIN-OFFERING

The 125ᵗʰ mitzvah in the Torah is the prohibition to add oil to a meal sin-offering
"He shall not put on it oil..." (5:11).
Though a free-will meal offering had oil as one of its ingredients, the meal sin-offering contained no oil (Please see the next mitzvah).

The 126ᵗʰ mitzvah in the Torah is the prohibition to add frankincense to a meal sin-offering.
"...and he shall not place upon it frankincense..." (5:11).
Though a free-will meal offering had frankincense as one of its ingredients, the meal sin-offering contained no frankincense.

There are two types of meal-offerings. One was a **free-will** offering which was voluntarily brought as a gift to G-d (See Mitzvah 116). It consisted of flour, oil, and frankincense. The second was an obligatory **sin offering**. It consisted only of flour. Oil and frankincense were not allowed to be added.

Shimon HaTzadik was one of the last members of the Great

Assembly. He used to say: The world stands on three things – on the Torah, on the Divine Service, and on the practice of kindness (Avos 1:2).

Oil represents the wisdom of Torah (*Berachos* 57a). The sweet odor given out by the frankincense represents pleasant deeds. Flour is produced through great work and effort as we explained earlier. Flour represents work or the divine service. The **free-will meal offering** contained all three ingredients because the one offering it of his own free will is exhibiting all three things. The offering is not because of a sin; therefore, he must be a *ben Torah*. He obviously wishes to participate in the Divine Service because he is offering a *mincha*. Since he is giving the offering of his own free will, he must be a man of kindness and generosity.

However, one who brings a **meal sin-offering**, sinned and displayed behavior that was not indicative of a *ben Torah*. Therefore, his offering contains no oil. Most often a meal sin-offering is brought on account of a crime against his fellow man; therefore, he cannot be a man who practices kindness. The only thing we can say about him is that he is participating in the divine service by bringing his offering. Therefore, the meal sin-offering consists only of plain flour.

‎‎ THE PENALTY FOR THE UNAUTHORIZED USE OF SACRED PROPERTY

The 127ᵗʰ mitzvah in the Torah is to pay an extra fifth for the unauthorized use of sacred property.
"A soul who trespassed and sinned in error concerning the sacred property of G-d... he shall repay and add its fifth..." (5:15-16).

If one inadvertently benefited from sacred property, he must repay the Temple the value of that benefit plus an extra fifth. [Actually, he pays an extra one-fourth which will be one fifth of the total. For example, if he benefited $100 from sacred property, he must repay the $100 plus an extra one-fourth, which is $25. The total is $125. The extra $25 that he had to pay is one fifth of the total of $125.] In addition, he must bring a guilt-offering, a *korban asham*. An entire tractate in the Talmud is devoted to these laws, the tractate of *Me'ilah*.

◆§ KORBAN ASHAM TALUI

The 128ᵗʰ mitzvah in the Torah is the mitzvah of the sacrifice called *asham tolui*.
"If a soul that sinned... did not know..." (5:17).

The 121ˢᵗ Mitzvah was the mitzvah of the sin-offering, *korban chatas*. If one is not certain if he or she is obligated to bring a sin-offering, he or she brings a guilt-offering in its stead. That guilt-offering is called an *asham talui*, which means the "hanging" or "doubtful" *asham*. The procedures of the sin-offering and the guilt-offering were quite similar. The difference between them is that the blood of the sin-offering was placed against the walls of the altar above mid-height four times. The blood of the guilt-offering was placed against the walls of the altar below mid-height only twice. Both offerings were eaten by the *Kohanim* that were serving the day the sacrifices were offered.

◆§ THE GUILT-OFFERING – KORBAN ASHAM

The 129ᵗʰ mitzvah is the mitzvah of offering an *asham*

when required to do so.
"...and his guilt-offering (asham) he shall offer to G-d..."
(5:25).

I n the 121ˢᵗ Mitzvah we stated that if an individual unknowingly transgressed a prohibition that involved the punishment of
kares, excommunication of the soul from the future world, that
individual must bring a sin-offering, a *korban chatas.* Certain other
sins, which do not involve *kares,* are atoned with a guilt-offering, *korban asham.* [For the difference between a *chatas* and an *asham,* see
the preceding mitzvah.]

There are five instances when an *asham* is to be offered in addition to the above mentioned *asham tolui.*

1 – If one possesses property which is not his and in a court of
law he swore that he did not have it, he atones for the false
oath by offering an *asham.*

2 – One who inadvertently benefited from sacred property must
offer an *asham.*

3 – A nazirite who became unclean, *tamei,* must offer an *asham.*
(He must also offer an *olah* and a *chatas.*)

4 – A leper, *mitzorah,* who was healed, must offer an *asham.* (He
must also offer an *olah* and a *chatas.*)

5 – The last instance of *asham* is an interesting one. A female
non-Jewish slave cannot marry anyone. Therefore, she cannot possibly be guilty of adultery. However, the Torah does
allow her to live with a Jewish slave without the benefit of
marriage or she can live with a non-Jewish slave. A male
Jewish slave can either marry an Israelite woman or live with
a female non-Jewish slave. If a female non-Jewish slave is
freed by her owner, then upon freedom she assumes the status of an Israelite woman.

If a female non-Jewish slave was owned by two partners and
one partner freed his half, the woman is now half slave and
half free. She cannot marry a regular Israelite male because
she is half slave and a male Israelite cannot marry a slave. She

cannot live with a non-Jewish slave because she is half free and that half is considered an Israelite woman. An Israelite woman cannot live with a non-Jewish slave. She can only marry a Jewish slave because a Jewish slave can marry an Israelite woman and he can live with a non-Jewish female slave. If the Jewish male slave does marry the half freed female slave, she is considered only half married since only half of her is free. If she commits adultery, there is no death penalty because she is only half married. The penalty for her and the adulterer is for each to bring a *korban asham.*

The case of a half slave-half free person is an intriguing one. Can a half free man be included in the quorum for a minyan? Can he testify in court? Can he read the Torah in shul? There are dozens of other intriguing questions about the status of a half-Israelite which are discussed at length in the rabbinic literature.

◄§ RESTORING STOLEN PROPERTY

The 130ᵗʰ mitzvah in the Torah is for a thief to return the goods or money he stole.
"And he shall restore the stolen property that he stole..." (5:23).

Even if the owner gives up hope on the stolen item, the thief must still return it. However, if the thief gave the stolen goods to someone else after the owner gave up hope, the one who is now in possession of the stolen item may keep it and the thief must pay its value to the owner (*Baba Kamma* 115a).

Does that mean that one is permitted to buy stolen goods? The story is told of a sultan who issued two decrees. The first decree stated that one who buys stolen goods should be beheaded. The second decree stated that robbery was legal. All the people were very confused about the two decrees for surely it is more egregious to steal than to buy from a thief.

The sultan ordered all his people to come to the field outside the city. He scattered many shiny buttons on the ground. Shortly afterwards, many rodents came because they were attracted by the shiny buttons. The rodents took all of the buttons and ran off with them and stored them in their holes.

Later the sultan again scattered shiny buttons on the ground and once again the rodents were attracted by them. The rodents took all the buttons and ran to their holes. To the rodents' surprise, the sultan had sealed up their holes while they were going after the shiny buttons. The rodents had no where to put the buttons so they brought them back from where they had taken them and left them there. Then the people understood the wisdom of the sultan's two decrees (Based on *Vayikra Rabbah* 6:2).

As our Sages say: *It is not the rodent who steals but it is the hole* (*Gittin* 45a).

ﻬ **HAFTORAH VAYIKRA**

THE *HAFTORAH* IS FOUND IN *YESHAYAH* 43:21 – 44:23.

T he *haftorah* is part of the prophecy of Yeshayah in which he recites a lengthy poetic soliloquy by G-d. At times, G-d seems to be addressing the Children of Israel who have been exiled to Babylonia; at other times He seems to be musing to Himself. The lack of response from the Children of Israel adds to the dramatic impact of Yeshayah's vision.

The *parshah* of Vayikra introduced the concept of sacrifices as a means to achieve forgiveness for sins. In this soliloquy, G-d bemoans the fact that the Israelites during the latter years of the First Temple did not avail themselves of this opportunity. As a result, their sins were not forgiven and they were exiled. The *Yalkut Shimoni* (*Yeshayah* 43:14) comments that when the Jews were exiled to Babylonia, the *Shechinah* departed from the *Bais HaMikdash* and accompanied her children into the *galus*. G-d felt the pain of the Jews because He too was in exile with them.

In the beginning of the *haftorah* G-d recalls the birth of the Jewish Nation in Egypt and how He miraculously had delivered them from bondage. For forty years there were miracles following miracles, so many in fact that the Children of Israel were constantly praising G-d.

"This nation I formed for Myself; they recite My praise" (43:21).

G-d contrasts that time when the Jews spontaneously offered praise to G-d on a consistent basis to the final years of the First Temple. During those years, the Children of Israel not only did not offer thankfulness, but even in times of distress they did not call on G-d to save them. It was as though Israel had grown tired of their Father in Heaven and began to worship idols. (Rashi)

"But you did not call Me, O Yaakov, for you wearied of Me, O Israel" (43:22).

G-d employs sarcasm to arouse Israel, saying that perhaps He had overburdened them with the sacrifices. Actually, only two sacrifices were required to be brought on a daily basis. G-d caustically speculates that perhaps the meal-offering was too burdensome or that the fistful of frankincense that was offered had tired out the Temple priests.

"You did not bring Me the lambs of your burnt-offerings, nor did you honor Me with your sacrifices; did I overwork you with meal-offerings or did I weary you with frankincense" (43:24).

G-d bemoans the fact that since the Israelites were no longer offering sacrifices to atone for their sins, G-d was no longer experiencing the sweet savor of the burning altar. Instead, He was left holding nothing but the sins of Israel. G-d grew tired of holding the great weight of their sins. The sins fell to the ground and brought about the exile.

"You did not satiate Me with the fat of your offerings, you burdened me with your sins, you wearied Me with your iniquities" (43:24).

G-d is saddened by the fact that though it seems that the Jews grew weary of offering sacrifices to Him, they somehow found the strength to offer sacrifices to their various idols. The *Yalkut* (457) mentions the parable of a man who made a great feast and invited all the king's family and officers. The minor officials were only invited for dessert. The king was left uninvited. The King bemoaned, "I was not even invited for dessert!" So too G-d is saddened by the fact that though the Jews found the strength to offer sacrifices to all their many idols, they had no strength left to bring even a small offering to G-d. G-d calls out in despair, *"It is I and only I who can erase your sins"* (43:25). It is as if to say, "Why do you shamelessly expend your strength on those idols who cannot help you?"

There is a lesson here for us too. Somehow, we find the energy and strength to get through a long and tedious day. The work is difficult and the problems are taxing. Yet, we manage. When we come home at night, we lack the strength to learn even for a few minutes. To drive to shul for *Ma'ariv* is just too difficult. We have no strength left for G-d.

As the Medrash said, G-d was in *galus* with the Israelites. He felt their pain. G-d felt that for His own sake He had no choice but to gratuitously forgive His wayward children.

"For My sake, your sins I will not remember" (43:25).

Lest the Children of Israel think that G-d is about to redeem them because of their merits, G-d mockingly says that they should remind Him of those merits; perhaps He has forgotten them. G-d further says that He and His children should appear in court and let the judge decide if they merit redemption. G-d says that He will remain silent throughout the trial. Even so, the Children of Israel will be unable to prove their case. (*Malbim*)

"Remind Me! Let us appear together in judgment. You speak to vindicate yourselves" (43:26).

For much of the remainder of the *haftorah*, G-d expresses that He cannot comprehend how men could worship idols of their own creation. In spite of man's folly, G-d will forgive them. He will erase their mountains of sins as though they were a cloud dispersed by the wind. G-d pleads with Israel to return to Him even if they cannot find the strength to repent for their iniquities.

"I will wipe away your transgressions like a mist, your sins like a cloud. Return to Me. I shall redeem you" (44:22).

As always, the *haftorah* ends with an optimistic note on the future.

"Let the heavens sing glad songs on account of what G-d has done. Let the foundations of the earth shout for joy. Let the mountains and forests and woods break forth with song. For HaShem has redeemed Yaakov, and through Israel He will be glorified" (44:23).

TZAV

❧ PREPARING FOR MASHIACH

*"And G-d spoke to Moshe saying: Command ("Tzav")
Aharon and his sons saying 'This is the law (Torah) of the
burnt – offering on its burning pile of wood...'"* (6:1-2).

R ashi comments that G-d did not tell Moshe to speak to
Aharon and his sons but rather Moshe was told to command Aharon and his sons. Rashi explains that the word
"command" means to encourage someone to be enthusiastic and
zealous. Command also refers to mitzvos that apply then and
throughout the generations. Rashi concludes that this is especially so
when the mitzvah involves a loss of money.

This Rashi seems to be very difficult to understand. The verse is
talking about the laws of the burnt-offering, but those laws do not
apply throughout all generations. In our time we unfortunately have
no Temple in which to present our offerings. The laws of the burnt-
offering no longer apply. Also, Rashi concluded with the words *"this*

is especially so

when the mitzvah involves a loss of money." If an Israelite brought a burnt-offering to the Temple, Aharon and his sons performed the actual service. As a reward, the *Kohanim* were given the skins of the animal to sell. How did this involve a loss of money for the priests; to the contrary, they were given a reward? Also, if they were rewarded for their service, why did the *Kohanim* need encouragement to be enthusiastic and zealous?

The Medrash (*Vayikra Rabbah* 7:3) comments on the phrase, '*This is the law (Torah) of the burnt-offering*, that in our times when we are unable to offer sacrifices, Hashem regards the studying of the Torah's laws of the sacrifices and their lessons to be considered as though we actually offered the sacrifices.

Perhaps with this concept in mind we can understand the comments of Rashi. G-d knew that in the future, when the Temple would no longer be standing, the *Kohanim* would no longer be rewarded for their service; in effect this would represent a loss of money. Thus, they would not enthusiastically dedicate themselves to the study of the sacrificial laws. G-d told Moshe to encourage the *Kohanim* to study the laws throughout all the generations, even when they are no longer being rewarded, for the merit of studying the laws is tantamount to actually offering them.

Because of this concept, our Sages instituted that the laws of the sacrifices should be incorporated into the *Shachris* and *Mincha davening*. These laws, which are to be recited before the actual *Shachris* and *Mincha* are called "*Korbonos*." Unfortunately in our times the section of "*Korbonos*" has been relegated to the realm of "extra credit" prayers and is often skipped over. The Medrash (*Vayikra Rabah* 7:3) says that through the merit of the study of these laws we will see the rebuilding of our Holy Temple.

The story is told of the Chofetz Chaim that he had in the corner of one room a suitcase that was always packed. Each day, he would dedicate part of his time to the study of the laws of sacrifices even though they no longer applied. In addition, he would occasionally practice walking up and down a ramp. Someone once asked him about these matters and the Chofetz Chaim replied, "I firmly believe that Mashiach may come any minute. Should I not have a suitcase ready? Shortly after he arrives, the Temple will be rebuilt and I, as a *Kohen*, will be expected to know all the intricate laws of the '*korbonos*.' Shall I not begin studying them now? As a *Kohen*, I will have to go up the steep ramp of the *mizbayach* to offer the sacrifices. Shall I not strengthen myself now?"

Studying the laws and lessons of the *korbonos* is a reaffirmation of our belief that Mashiach may come at any time.

ENTHUSIASM IS CONTAGIOUS

T he first verse of the *parshah* contains one of the greatest motivational secrets known. I shall explain.

The *Chasam Sofer* says that Moshe was not aiming to encourage enthusiasm in Aharon and his sons but he wished to encourage the Israelites not to be lax in offering sacrifices even though they will incur a loss of money.

The obvious question is that if Moshe was supposed to encourage the Israelites, why did he command Aharon and his sons to be enthusiastic. He should have commanded the Israelites! But what is the best way to encourage enthusiasm among the Israelites, given their concern about the financial cost of the sacrifice?

Hashem told Moshe that he should make the *Kohanim* enthusiastic about their tasks. Enthusiasm is contagious. When the Israelites will see the passion with which the *Kohanim* perform their service, they too will become enthusiastic.

All of us wish nothing more than to have children who are dedicated and passionate about Judaism. How do we accomplish that? We must first develop and cultivate our own passion and enthusiasm for Yiddishkiet. As our children see and experience our enthusiasm, they too will become enthusiastic. Therefore, we must not only teach our children how to behave as Jews we must show them our own passion for the Torah way of life. That is how we can best assure that they will be the next link in our chain of tradition.

⋘ CLEANLINESS IS NEXT TO G-DLINESS

The 131ˢᵗ mitzvah in the Torah is the removal of the previous day's ashes from the altar.
"(*The Kohen*) *shall remove the ashes, which were a burnt-offering consumed in fire, from on the altar*" (6:3).

The *Kohen* was required to clean off the ashes from the altar in order to prepare the *mizbayach* for the upcoming day's service.

One may think that this mitzvah is actually a janitorial task and not very significant. This is very far from the truth as we shall see.

Those *Kohanim* who wanted to participate in this mitzvah had to rise up very early in the morning, immerse themselves in a *mikvah*, and wash their hands and feet from the laver. They had to don a special uniform and be ready by daybreak. At the crack of dawn, the *Kohen*, who was the overseer of the service, chose by lottery one priest from all those who had gathered to begin the mitzvah.

By the sun's early rays and by the glow of the fire on the altar, the lone *Kohen* would ascend the ramp with a silver shovel in hand. When he reached the top, he would scoop up some ashes and bring it down to the floor below. The ashes were placed not far from the ramp. The day's service had symbolically begun. Afterwards, all the priests who had readied themselves would rush up the ramp to help clean off the ashes.

The priests would heap the ashes into a great basin on top of the *mizbayach.* The basin was lowered to the floor below where other priests would carry the ashes outside the city walls and bury them so as not to be scattered by the wind or disturbed by the animals.

The importance of this mitzvah is demonstrated by the fact that only a *Kohen* was fit for the task. The *Kohen* had to be without a physical blemish *(mum)* just like a *Kohen* who performed the sacrificial service. Special priestly garments were worn for this task. Why did the Torah place such a great importance on this mitzvah?

My Rav, Rabbi Leibel Reznick, told me about one of his trips to Israel. He was once in Jerusalem and noticed a street cleaner coming up the road. He was pushing a large trash can on wheels with one hand and a broom and shovel in the other hand. He noticed that he was wearing a kipah. He was a religious Jew. His heart almost broke at the sight of a religious Jew having to degrade himself by becoming a street cleaner. He noticed that every so often he seemed to be whispering to himself as he pushed his can up the street. He assumed that he was bemoaning his luck at having to perform such a menial task. As he passed me by, he heard him whisper, "Ir hakodesh, ir hakodesh, (holy city, holy city)."

He understood that he was not grumbling about his luck at all. He was grateful for the opportunity to enhance the sanctity of our holy city. To him it was a privilege to clean the holy gutters. How many other Jerusalemites could say that they enhanced the holy city each and every day? How many of us could say that we ever enhanced the holy city?

Not only is cleanliness of a holy place important but our Sages also placed great importance to one's personal cleanliness:

R. Hiyya bar Abba also said in Rebbe Yochanan's name: Any scholar whose garment has a stain is unworthy (*Shabbos* 114a).

Mar bar Rabina's mother would make certain that her son wore freshly laundered clothes each day before going of to study (*Eruvin* 65a).

The angel appointed over livelihood is called Cleanliness (*Ne'kiyah*). The angel appointed over poverty is called Filth (*Nahvel*) (*Pesachim* 111b).

Perhaps the most famous of all quotes concerning cleanliness is the one made by Rebbe Pinchas ben Yair:

Zeal leads to cleanliness (of the body).

Cleanliness (of the body) leads to purity (of the heart).

Purity (of the heart) leads to abstinence.

Abstinence leads to holiness.

Holiness leads to humility.

Humility leads to the fear of sin.

The fear of sin leads to saintliness.

Saintliness leads to the holy spirit (ruach hakodesh).

The holy spirit (ruach hakodesh) leads to the resurrection of the dead.

The resurrection of the dead comes through Eliyahu of Blessed memory (Sotah 49b).

Rebbe Pinchas ben Yair is giving us the step by step program for self-improvement. The first step is to be enthusiastic and zealous. That was the very first lesson taught to us in this *parshah* (See preceding section – Preparing for Mashiach). This mitzvah is the second lesson that is taught to us, the lesson of personal cleanliness. The next lesson is that of purity *(taharah)*. The verse that tells us of the mitzvah about the cleanliness of the altar concludes with *"... and you shall carry out the ashes outside the camp to a pure (tahar) place"* (6:3). Carrying out the ashes, cleanliness, bring one to a place of purity. One cannot attain the level of a pure mind, heart, and intentions without first making certain that he is physically clean: both in body and in environment.

❧ "THE HUMBLE SHALL INHERIT THE EARTH"

(TEHILIM 37:11)

"Command Aharon and his sons saying, 'This is the law of the burnt – offering (olah) on its burning pile of wood'" (6:2).

 he Hebrew word for a burnt-offering is *olah* which also means "going upwards." Our Sages (*Vayikra Rabbah* 7:6) say that *olah* can also refer to one who is "uppity" or haughty. The verse can therefore be explained that one who is haughty deserves to be on the pile of burning wood.

Why did the Torah chose to condemn those who are haughty at this point? The Torah is about to mention the mitzvah of cleaning off the ashes from the altar. The Torah anticipates that some *Kohanim* would be very reluctant to "stoop so low" as to become "ash sweepers." Because of their haughtiness they will forgo this mitzvah. Therefore, it is here that the Torah expresses its condemnation of the haughty of spirit.

Why is it fitting that one who is haughty be punished with fire in particular? Fire is the source of heat. Heat rises. A haughty person raises himself above his fellow man and sometimes even above G-d. It is measure for measure that the haughty are condemned with fire.

The Medrash (*Vayikra Rabbah* 7:6) tells us that the generation of the Great Flood was comprised of haughty people and, thus, they were punished with a flood of boiling water. The residents of the city of Sodom were known for their arrogance and they were punished with fire. Pharaoh was so pompous that he proclaimed himself to be a god. He was punished with fiery hail. Haughtiness lies at the root of all sin.

The lesson of haughtiness is specifically taught here in connection to the mitzvah of raising up the ashes from the altar for another reason too. Our father, Avraham was known for his humility (*Chullin* 89a). He not only concerned himself with the hungry and tired wayfarers, but he personally attended to their needs. And how did Avraham regard himself? He proclaimed, "*Dust and ash I am*" (*Bereishis* 18:27).

Ash represents the humble, the meek and the downtrodden. And what does Hashem do with those who considered themselves to be like ash? "*From the ash-heaps He raises the needy*" (*Hallel, Tehillim* 113:7). The burning of the *olah* represented the burning downfall of the haughty. The lifting of the ash from the *mizbayach* represents Hashem's raising up the humble.

✃ THE SPARK OF G-DLINESS

The 132nd mitzvah in the Torah is to light the fire on the altar each day.
The 133rd mitzvah in the Torah is the prohibition to extinguish the fire.
"An eternal fire you shall light on the altar; it shall not be extinguished" **(6:6).**

T he following question is raised. Every day there was a mitzvah to bring two burnt offerings (*olah*): one in the morning and one in the afternoon. These two burnt-offerings had to be burned on top of the altar. Even without a special mitzvah to light the altar (Mitzvah 132) it would have been lit anyway in order to consume the burnt-offerings. Why did the Torah have to proclaim a special mitzvah to light the altar each day?

The Talmud (*Yoma* 45a) answers the question by explaining that there were three piles of lumber on top of the altar. One pile, the largest, was for burning the sacrificial offerings. A second pile was used as a source of embers for the incense that was offered twice daily. A third pile was only for the mitzvah of lighting the altar. Even though the large pile would have been lit anyway, for the burning of the sacrifices, there was a separate mitzvah to light the *mizbayach*.

There are still several questions which need to be answered:

1 – Why is there a separate mitzvah to light the *mizbayach*?

2 – Also, the Talmud (*Yoma* 21b) tells us that a fire came down from the heavens and ignited the altar on the very first day it was used. Why then is our fire needed?

3 – Why is it necessary for there to be two mitzvos concerning

the fire – one mitzvah to light it and a second mitzvah not to extinguish it?

4 – What did the three flaming piles of lumber on the *mizbayach* represent?

Let us begin by answering the last question first. What did the three fires represent? The fire of the pile that was used to consume the offerings represents man's duty to serve his Creator. When man does not fulfill this duty, he must atone by offering sacrifices on this pile.

The fire of the pile that was used for the burning of the incense represents man's obligation to serve his fellow man with kindness and charity. The sweet smell of incense permeates the air spreading its pleasantness abroad, representing a man's good deeds to others.

The fire of the special pile, which was used for the mitzvah of lighting the altar, the *Chasam Sofer* (*Parshas Tzav*) says, represents the spark of G-dliness that lies within each and every one of us. This spark of G-dliness is to be used by us to serve G-d and our fellow man.

Every person is unique. No two people are alike. Even with identical twins, each one has a unique personality. Each person has his or her set of talents and aptitudes. Each one of us is expected to add their talents and abilities to that spark of G-dliness. In that way we will create something new and different. Even though the altar was ignited by a G-dly spark, nevertheless, we must add to that spark our unique qualities.

Even if one does not add his or her unique spark to that fire there is still hope for the future as long as the fire of G-dliness continues to burn. If, however, one removes himself so far from spirituality that the fire of G-dliness goes out, there is no longer hope for the future. Therefore, there is not only a mitzvah to add to the fire, there is a prohibition to cause the fire to become extinguished.

THE ETERNAL FIRE

T he Medrash (*Vayikra Rabbah* 10:6) tells us that the fire atop the altar burned continuously for over one hundred years – thirty-nine years in the desert, fourteen years in the *Mishkan* of Gilgal, and fifty-seven years in Nov and Givon. In *Pirkei Avos* (5:5) we are told that among the miracles that took place during the 410 years of the First *Bais HaMikdash* was that the fire of the altar was never once extinguished by the rains.

The fire on the altar was truly a miraculous flame. The fire never flared up into a roaring blaze and never subsided into a faint glowing ember. The flame was the symbol of moderation.

The Rambam (*Dayos* 3:1-2) comments on the importance of moderation: A person may say, "Since envy, desire, and the pursuit of honor, and similar matters are an evil path and drive a person from the world, I should separate myself from them and move entirely to the other extreme." As a result he will not eat meat, or drink wine, nor marry, nor live in a decent home, nor wear proper clothes, but rather wear sackcloth and coarse wool and the like, as the pagan priests do. This too is a bad path and it is forbidden to follow such a way. Whoever goes in this path is called a sinner, for the Torah states regarding the Nazirite "*...and the priest shall make an atonement for him, for his having sinned*" (*Numbers* 6:11).

The Rambam continues: Our sages have declared: If the Nazirite, who abstained only from wine, requires atonement, how much more so does one who abstains from everything. Therefore, our sages directed man to abstain only from those things which the Torah denied him. A person should direct his heart and all his actions exclusively to the knowledge of God. Thus, one's resting, rising, and speech should all be directed towards this purpose. For example, when involved in business dealings while working for a wage, one should not think only about collecting money, but rather should do these things so that one will be able to acquire those objects that the body needs – food, drink, a home and a wife.

The Rambam is telling us the importance of balancing the spiritual realm with the material world. The two worlds can only co-exist if we moderate our approach to both of them. We are very aware of the dangers of one who becomes overly absorbed in material matters. He will lose sight of the more meaningful spiritual goals in life. Alternatively, we have seen quite clearly, in our times, the great danger of religious radical fundamentalism. Radical Moslems who are willing to live in caves, wear tattered rags, and solely devote themselves to the Koran are capable of murdering innocent people, using their own children as human bombs, and spreading terror and paranoia throughout the civilized world. Such is the danger of religious radicalism.

This theme of moderation is used by the Ramban (*Vayikra* 19:2) to explain G-d's command to Israel *"Be Holy!"* (*ibid*). Holiness is not achieved through a radical approach to religion. Holiness is achieved when one manages to balance religion and worldly needs through moderation.

This is the lesson of the flame of the holy altar. We must never become over zealous in our thoughts and actions and flare up nor should we become so indifferent as to become a mere glowing ember. Only through moderation will our flame continue to burn throughout the generations.

ONE KOHEN, TWO KOHANIM

As we explained above, the 132nd mitzvah in the Torah is to light the fire on the altar each day. Included in this mitzvah is the requirement to arrange fresh wood on top of the altar. Actually this was performed twice each day, once in the morning and once in the afternoon.

Concerning the morning arrangement, the verse says *"...and he shall arrange..."* (6:5). The verse implies that only one *Kohen* should do the arranging since it referred to "he" singular. Concerning the afternoon arrangement the verse says *"...and they shall arrange..."* (1:6). The verse implies that at least two *Kohanim* should do the arrangement since it referred to "they" plural. Why is there a difference between the two arrangements?

As we mentioned earlier, there are two types of mitzvos and obligations. One type is between a man and his Creator; the other type is between a man and his fellow man. The morning arrangement is done by a single *Kohen*, symbolizing those mitzvos that are between man and his Creator. Those mitzvos involve just the one man. The afternoon arrangement represents those mitzvos that are between a man and his fellow man. By the very nature of those mitzvos, at least two people are involved. Therefore, the afternoon arranging of the wood was performed by at least two *Kohanim*.

Why are the mitzvos between man and his Creator symbolized in the morning before those mitzvos that are between a man and his fellow man which are not symbolized until later in the day? The Talmud (*Berachos* 14a) tells us that to extend a greeting to your friend before davening is a lack of respect. One must "extend his greeting" to G-d before extending greetings to his fellow man. Therefore, the Torah is highlighting

this principle by directing a single *Kohen* to perform the morning arrangements and two *Kohanim* to perform the later arrangement.

TREE OF LIFE

*T*he question was presented earlier as to why the *Kohen* had to add a light to the altar each morning even though the fires were still burning. Perhaps we can suggest another explanation and insight.

Quite often the Torah and our Sages compare the Torah to a tree. For example, *"(Torah) is a tree of life to those who hold on to it"* (*Mishlei* 3:18). Why is the Torah compared to a tree which cannot think, communicate, and has no ability to move from its place. Would not some majestic animal, such as a lion, be a better representation of the Torah?

An animal is born very small compared to its mother. During its early months and years, the baby animal experiences a period of rapid growth. By late adolescence the growth ceases. The animal has achieved its maximum size and will remain that way throughout its adult life. A tree, on the other hand, always continues to grow. Each year the growth is marked by the formation of another ring in its trunk. A tree that ceases to grow will die.

The tree was chosen to represent Torah to teach us that we must always grow in our knowledge and commitment to Torah. Should one cease to grow, he will perish.

The Torah is also compared to a fire. *"From His right hand went forth a law of fire for them"* (*Devarim* 33:2). As long as fuel is added to the fire, it will continue to burn. When one ceases to add to the fire, it will begin to burn out. The fire is similar to the tree; both must grow or they will cease to exist.

This may also be the lesson of the fire on the altar. Though its flames are now burning, we must add to it. We must add the tree's wood to the fire; because, wood, like fire, must continue to grow or they both will die out. We too must never become complacent with our spiritual accomplishments. We must continuously add to them. As Hillel says in *Pirkei Avos* (1:13): *One who does not add causes it to cease.*

Without question, Judaism is a very difficult and challenging religion. As each day passes we learn of more and more requirements. Each day there are more spiritual challenges to be met. We must add our own "wood" and efforts to G-d's miraculous fire in order to attain self-fulfillment and to truly succeed in life.

✍ THE FAITH OF THE POOR

The 134ᵗʰ mitzvah in the Torah is for the *Kohanim* to eat from the remainder of the meal offerings.
"That which is left from it shall Aharon and his sons eat..." (6:9).

As a general rule, only a fistful of a meal-offering was burnt on the *mizbayach.* The reminder of the offering was consumed by the *Kohanim.*

The meal-offering was brought by the poor. It was a very humble offering as compared to an expensive animal offering. G-d wished to show how much he treasures the gift of the poor by only allowing the Temple priests to eat from it whereas many of the animal sacrifices could by eaten by anyone.

Why does Hashem treasure the poor? Charles Colson who was a White House Counsel to President Nixon, tells the following story:

> *A few years ago I took my two sons and my daughter to Peru. We met a man who lived in a hut atop a garbage dump. He had almost nothing in the way of material possessions—yet his eyes sparkled as we visited in his home. He had a quiet dignity. He was living in abject poverty—yet, he was a deeply religious man and his love for G-d was unshakeable. When we asked the man why he is so loving of G-d, he told us that he had fewer obstacles that stood in the way between him and the Lord. He had no one and nothing to trust except God.*
>
> *How amazing it was that such purity of love was found on that garbage dump in Peru.*

The sainted Baal Shem Tov more than once expressed his great to desire to have the unconditional love and complete faith in Hashem that the poor Jew has.

❦ THE POOR MAN'S BREAD

The 135th mitzvah in the Torah is that the *Kohanim* had to make certain that the *mincha* which they were eating was matzah and not *chametz*.
"...unleavened it shall be eaten in a holy place..." **(6:9).**

atzah is called "the poor man's bread" (*Pesachim* 116a). A temple priest is a man of superior social position. The *Kohen* may feel that it is beneath his dignity to eat "poor man's bread." Therefore, again, to show how much G-d treasures the gift of the poor, the *Kohen* was told to humble himself and partake of the poor man's bread. In addition, unlike many animal offerings which could be eaten anywhere within the camp of Israel, the poor man's offering could only be eaten within the confines of the Divine sanctuary.

❦ THE INAUGURAL MINCHA

The 136th mitzvah in the Torah is the mitzvah of the Inaugural Meal-Offering.
"This is the offering of Aharon and his sons which they shall offer to G-d on the day when he is anointed, a tenth of an ephah of fine flour as a continual meal-offering..." **(6:13).**

here seems to be a contradiction in this verse. The verse begins by referring to a meal offering that is to be brought once only *"on the day that he (the Kohen) will be inaugurated."* However, the text continues by saying that it is brought *"as a continual meal-offering,"* implying that it is to be brought on a daily basis.

Rashi explains that there are two different obligations being addressed in this *pasuk*. A simple *Kohen* was to bring this sacrifice only once, on the day he is to be inaugurated into the holy service. It served as an indoctrination offering. However, a High Priest, such as Aharon, had to bring this offering continually throughout the days and years of his service.

Since the High Priest had to bring this offering on a daily basis why is it referred to as an inaugural offering? In addition, why was he obligated to bring a humble meal-offering, usually associated with the poor? Why didn't the Torah require him to bring something more substantial, such as an animal sacrifice, to better reflect his lofty stature?

The position of the *Kohen Gadol*, High Priest, was a position of great honor and tremendous responsibility. It was the highest religious position that could be attained by a single individual. We can imagine that the very first day the *Kohen Gadol* was officially declared to be the High Priest; he must have trembled at having been chosen for such a position. He must have been overcome with humility and feelings of unworthiness. He must have felt determined to live up to the great expectations that everyone placed in him. But, as the weeks and months passed by, he became prone to a sense of comfort in his position. Perhaps he now felt deserving and worthy of the honor everyone was bestowing upon him. To prevent this from happening, the Torah decreed that each and every day the *Kohen Gadol* had to bring his inaugural humble meal-offering to remind him of the feelings and commitment he had that very first day. On a daily basis, the High Priest was reminded of his humble origins.

The following story will help elaborate this point. The story is told of a king who wandered into a nearby forest. He came across a simple shepherd wearing tattered clothing, sitting on the ground playing an enchanting melody on his flute. After engaging him in conversation, the king found the shepherd to be not only a gifted flute player but also to be exceptionally perceptive. The king invited the humble shepherd to join the palace staff and to be trained as a royal advisor. The shepherd humbly accepted the offer and returned with the king to the palace.

The talents and abilities of the shepherd were soon apparent. Within a short period of time, he moved up in the ranks and found himself in charge of the king's household. This, however, did not bode well with the other senior advisors. They became increasingly jealous and conspired to slander him to the king. "He is stealing from the royal treasury," they told the king. At first the king refused to believe them but after many repeated accusations the king agreed to pay a surprise visit to his favorite advisor's home to see if he was living way above his means.

On the morning of the surprise visit, the king and the senior advisers were totally taken aback at what they found. The house was very simple and unadorned with any lavish furnishings. The king was relieved to see this and was no longer suspicious that his trusted advisor was stealing from the treasury. As they were leaving, the royal entourage noticed a locked room. They asked the former shepherd to open the door. The shepherd was very reluctant but the king insisted. The senior advisors were certain that they had discovered where the shepherd was hiding his ill-gotten money. They asked the king to demand that the door be unlocked.

With great hesitation, the shepherd opened the door. Everyone rushed inside. To their amazement the room was bare. There were no furnishings; there was no money. Only two items rested in the middle of the floor, a flute and a pile of tattered clothing.

The king was very curious about the matter and asked the shepherd to explain the meaning of this room. The shepherd acquiesced. "From the day that I became an advisor to my gracious king, I was afraid that I would become arrogant and forget my humble beginnings. I therefore set aside this room where each and every morning I would go inside and put on my tattered clothing and play my flute. It is a constant reminder that I am nothing but a simple shepherd who has received great gifts from Gd and from the king.

We must never forget that each day is a gift from G-d. We must never take for granted our position in life. We must never forget our humble origins.

The 136th mitzvah is that the *Kohen Gadol* had to bring a *Mincha* offering twice a day (6:13). This is called the *Mincha Chavittin*. In addition to the regular daily offering (*korban tamid*) the *Kohen Gadol* had to bring this *Mincha* twice a day, in the morning and in the evening.

The reason for this *korban* is that the *Kohen Gadol* is the liaison between the Jewish people and G-d. It is he that entreats G-d in prayer on their behalf and through his prayers and service of his offerings that they find atonement. It is therefore fitting that he should have a special continual offering, like the continual offerings of the community. And just as those continual offerings were twice a day, he was obligated likewise to offer up his *Mincha* twice a day (*Sefer Hachinuch*).

A great and valuable lesson can be learned from this *korban*. Before one can take the liberty of criticizing our fellow man, we must be sure that our own affairs are in order. By his own offering, the *Kohen Gadol* demonstrated symbolically that, before asking his people to bring sacrifices, he himself had to take stock of his conduct and had to bring an offering to atone for his own transgressions. Consequently, the people will see that if someone so exalted as the *Kohen Gadol* felt it necessary to take stock of himself, they too must not hesitate to do the same.

✌ THE MEAL-OFFERING OF A KOHEN

The 137ᵗʰ mitzvah in the Torah is the prohibition for the *Kohen* to eat from the meal-offering that was brought by any *Kohen*.
"Any meal-offering of a Kohen shall be entirely consumed (in fire); it shall not be eaten" **(6:16).**

The *Kohen* led a conflicting life which he had to balance. On the one hand, he was told to eat poor man's bread to reflect the *Kohen's* appreciation of the humble Jew's contribution.

On the other hand, the *Kohen* had to live a higher standard of religious life. He could not become defiled (*tamei*). He was expected to dedicate himself to the furtherance of Torah and holy service. He could not afford to view himself as a simple Jew. To illustrate this balancing act that the *Kohen* had to perform, the Torah required him to eat the meal-offering of the poor Israelite but was not allowed to eat any meal-offering of a *Kohen*.

≈§ THE SIN-OFFERING (CHATAS)

The 138ᵗʰ mitzvah in the Torah is to follow the laws and procedures of the sin-offering.
"This is the law of the sin-offering, in the place where the burnt-offering is slaughtered you shall slaughter the sin-offering..." (6:18).

There is a difference of opinion between the Rambam and the Ramban concerning the counting of the mitzvos regarding *korbanos*. The Rambam counts each type of sacrifice as a separate mitzvah. Therefore, he counts the sin-offering as its own mitzvah. The Ramban considers all types of sacrifices to be included in one overall mitzvah called the mitzvah of sacrifices. Therefore the Ramban would not count this mitzvah of the sin-offering as a separate mitzvah. In order for the Ramban to achieve the required number of 613 mitzvos he had to count other mitzvos which the Rambam did not include.

It should be pointed out that though there is a disagreement between the Rambam and the Ramban, there is no practical difference between them. The Talmud (*Makos* 23b) tells us that all the mitzvos of the Torah amount to the number 613. The Rambam and Ramban merely disagree as to which mitzvos are to be counted in that exclusive list of 613. They both agree that, whether or not a verse in the Torah is counted in the number 613, all verses and laws must be kept.

The sin-offering, like the burnt-offering, was slaughtered north of the altar. Why did the Torah choose to say "*in the place where the burnt-offering is slaughtered, you shall slaughter the sin-offering.*" Why not simply state "you shall slaughter the sin-offering in the north."

In Hebrew, the word for north is *tzafon*, which also means hidden. The hiding of the matzah for the *afikomen* is called *tzafon*. What is the connection between the words north and hidden? In all the years of the traveling of the *Mishkan* and in all the years of the first and second Temple, the sun's rays never shone from the north, only the east, west, and south. This was due to the simple fact that the *Mishkan* and the Temples were always located north of the equator. On all points of the globe north of the equator the sun never shines from the north. Its rays are "hidden" from the north.

Rabbi Shimon bar Yohai (*Sotah* 32b) explains that the Torah phrases the slaughtering of the sin-offering by saying "*in the place where the burnt-offering is slaughtered you shall slaughter the sin-offering,*" to show that the Torah specially did not wish to make it apparent to others whether the animal being sacrificed was a free-will burnt-offering or a sin-offering that was the result of a transgression. Repentance for sin is a personal and private matter. It should be "hidden" from others.

This is also reflected in our prayers on *Yom Kippur* when we recite the confessional *vidui*. It is to be recited quietly, hidden from others. Any sense of shame that is felt should only be between the person and G-d. The Torah does not require nor does it seek public confessions.

This sensitivity encourages those that have fallen to rise up again and be able to face their fellow Jews without any shame.

✑ THE BURNT SIN-OFFERINGS

The 139ᵗʰ mitzvah in the Torah is the prohibition to eat any Sin-offerings (*chatas*) whose blood is sprinkled within.
"Any sin-offering whose blood was brought into the Ohel Moed to atone in the holy place shall not be eaten. In fire it shall be burned" **(6:23).**

As a rule, burnt-offerings (*olah*) were completely burned and not eaten. Sin-offerings (*chatas*) only had some of its internal organ burned and the remainder was eaten. However, there was a special group of sin-offerings that were completely burned and were not allowed to be eaten. The sin-offerings in this special group also had the unusual procedure that the blood was brought inside the *Ohel Moed* and placed on the golden altar. All other sacrifices had the blood placed only on the *mizbayach*.

Examples of this special group of sin-offerings that were burned would be the sin-offerings of *Yom Kippur*, the sin-offering of a *Sanhedrin* that erred, the sin-offering of the priestly chaplain of the army (See *Parshas Vayikra* for a more detailed explanation of these *korbanos*).

✑ THE GUILT-OFFERING (ASHAM)

The 140ᵗʰ mitzvah in the Torah is to follow the laws and procedures of the guilt-offering. (See *Parshas Vayikra* for a more detailed explanation of this sacrifice).
"This is the law of the guilt offering..." **(7:1).**

🪶 FROM THE HEART

The 141ˢᵗ mitzvah in the Torah is the mitzvah of the peace-offering (*shelamim*).
"And this is the law of the peace-offering sacrifice which one offers to G-d. If it be a thanksgiving-offering..." (7:11-12).

he peace-offering is a voluntary sacrifice which one offers simply out of a feeling of gratitude to Hashem. The peace-offering differs from all the other sacrifices mentioned thus far. All of the previous sacrifices – the burnt-offering, sin-offering, guilt-offering, meal-offering – were either totally burned on the altar or part was offered on the altar and the remainder was eaten by the *Kohanim* within the confines of the *Mishkan* or *Bais Hamikdash*. However, with regards to the peace-offering, part was burned on the altar, part was given to the *Kohanim*, and the rest was given to the one who brought the offering. He would then share it with whomever he wished. The meat could be eaten anywhere within the camp of the Israelites or, in the case of the *Bais HaMikdash*, anywhere within the walls of Jerusalem.

Another difference between the peace offering and the other offerings is the time limit for the eating. All the other sacrifices had to be consumed before daybreak of the following morning. The peace-offering could be eaten until sunset of the following day.

The Medrash (*Tanchumah Tzav* 4) explains how the peace-offering got its name. All the previously mentioned sacrifices were brought on account of some transgression. The peace-offering was brought under more peaceful circumstances. It was an expression of thanks. The peace-offering was shared by G-d, the *Kohanim*, and the Israelites. It united all three; unity is peace.

One type of peace-offering was the thanksgiving-offering, *todah*. The thanksgiving – offering was voluntarily brought because of one of four reasons:

Release from capture (*chavush*).
Recovery from life threatening illness (*yisurim*).

Return from a voyage (*yam*).

Crossing a desert, (*midbar*).

The first letters of the four Hebrew words spell out *chaim*, life.

Today, if one experiences one of these situations, in place of the thanksgiving-offering, the blessing of *Hagomel* is recited.

The thanksgiving-offering was very different from the other peace-offerings. The thanksgiving-offering could only be eaten until daybreak of the following day, unlike the other *shalomim* which could be eaten until sunset of the next day. In addition, the thanksgiving-offering was accompanied with 40 meal-offerings which had to be consumed before daybreak. Why did the thanksgiving-offering require so many meal-offerings? And, why was the time limit for eating reduced from sunset of the following day to daybreak?

The *Netziv* explains that since there was much sacred food to consume and so little time to consume it, the one who brought the thanksgiving-offering would have to invite many people to join him in a feast in order to eat the holy food. Naturally, at the meal the people would ask why the thanksgiving-offering was brought. In the course of the conversation, expressions of thankfulness to Hashem would be declared. It was those expressions of gratitude to G-d that were the primary purpose of this sacrifice.

Today, there are no sacrifices. In its place, when one wishes to express his gratitude to the Almighty, he prepares a festive meal and his dear ones are invited to the occasion. It is called a *seudas hodah*, a meal of acknowledgment. This is reminiscent of the thanksgiving-meal of which the *Netziv* spoke.

It is interesting to note that sacrifices that were to atone for sins were compulsory. Sacrifices that were expressions of thanks were voluntary. Imagine a mother and her child walking down the street and a kind man gives a candy to the child. The child accepts the candy but is silent. The mother turns to her child and says, "Say 'Thank you.'" The child looks up and says, "Thank you."

Was the child's thanks a true expression of gratitude? No, because his mother compelled him to say it. Likewise with regards to sacrifices that were expressions of thanks. It has to come from the heart and not because the Torah compelled him to offer it.

⋰ THE FORTY LOAVES

nother unusual factor about the thanksgiving-offering (*todah*) was that ten of the forty meal-offerings were *chametz*. As a rule, meal-offerings were not allowed to become leavened (See mitzvah 135). These ten meal-offerings were an exception to the rule.

Harav Shamshon Raphael Hirsch explains that the todah was brought on account of having risen above a dangerous situation. The leavened offerings represent this "rising." However, in spite of any feeling of exuberance he may be experiencing, he must remain humble. The other 30 meal-offerings which were matzah, represented humility. Matzah is called lechem oni, humble man's bread.

⋰ PEACE

> *"This is the law (Torah) of the peace-offering which one offers to G-d"* (7:11).

he Medrash (*Tanchumah*) says that the goal of all the laws of the Torah is to bring about peace and harmony between man and his Creator and man and his fellow. That is what the verse means when it says *"This is the law (Torah) of the peace..."*

Peace is so treasured by G-d that He took it as one of His names (*Berachos* 55b).

The very last thought that Rebbe Yehuda HaNasi expressed in his *Mishna* compilation is, *"G-d could not find a vessel that could contain blessing except peace."* The parable is told of an unfortunate man who was wandering in the desert dying of thirst. His luck took a turn for the better when he saw a well off in the distance. Excitedly, he ran to the well. He peered down into the narrow walls of the well and saw the cool, refreshing water. Unfortunately, he had no bucket to lower into the well to draw some water.

G-d is constantly bestowing blessings upon us; however, without a vessel to hold the blessing, it is all for naught. Rebbe Yehudah HaNasi is telling us that the name of the only vessel that can draw and contain the waters of blessing is peace.

The verse stated, "...*the peace-offering which one offers to G-d.*" The peace-offering is the only sacrifice that is directly referred to as an offering to G-d. We know that every sacrifice was an offering to G-d, but only with reference to the peace-offering does the Torah state it explicitly.

Perhaps the verse means that G-d will supply the water but we must supply the vessel. G-d will grant us blessings, but we must present to Him our vessel of peace in which to hold the blessings. "...*the peace-offering which one offers to G-d.*"

⏤ THE STYLE OF THANK YOU

The Medrash (*Vayikra Rabbah* 9:7) says that in the days to come, when Mashiach will rebuild the *Bais HaMikdash*, sin-offerings and guilt-offerings will no longer be offered. Only the thanksgiving-offerings will be brought. The Medrash continues, that in the days to come the *Shemoneh Esrai* will no longer be said except for the blessing of *Modim*, thankfulness.

The point that the Medrash is making is that in the days to come man will achieve a higher degree of spirituality. No longer will there be war, greed, envy, or transgressions. All of those will have gone "out of style." Though sin may one day go out of style, saying "Thank you" will never go out of style.

"WITH A MULTITUDE OF PEOPLE IS THE KING'S GLORY"

The 142ⁿᵈ mitzvah in the Torah is the prohibition to leave over meat from the *todah* after daybreak.
"And the meat of the thanksgiving-offering, on the day that it is offered it shall be eaten, he shall not leave over from it until the morning" (7:15).

This prohibition assures that the one offering the sacrifice will invite many people to join the meal to make certain that it is completely eaten within the time allowed. It was during that meal that he would publicly express his gratitude to Hashem.

The verse in *Mishlei* (14:28) reads, *"With a multitude of people is the king's glory."* The thought being expressed is that when many people participate in a mitzvah or join to merely witness the mitzvah, it is considered an honor to the King, Hashem. We find this concept mentioned many times in Rabbinic literature. The Rambam (*Bikurim* 4:16) mentions that the farmers of a geographical area in Eretz Yisroel would join together to bring their first-fruits to the Temple. They marched in a parade-like style. As they approached the holy city, all the craftsmen would cease their labors and come to witness the festivities. All of this was done in accordance with the concept of *"With a multitude of people is the king's glory."*

In the *Bais HaMikdash*, they would try to involve as many *Kohanim* as possible in the day's service in accordance with *"With a multitude of people is the king's glory"* (*Zevachim* 14b).

It is permitted to read the *Megillah* in the privacy of one's home; however, we all gather in shul to hear it read because *"With a multitude of people is the king's glory"*(*Mishna Brurah* 490:2).

Likewise with the *todah* sacrifice. The Torah wanted to encourage many people to participate in the *todah* meal and to hear the words of praise to Hashem. *"With a multitude of people is the king's glory."*

The 143rd mitzvah in the Torah is to burn any meat which was leftover after daybreak.

"That which remains over from the meat of the sacrifice... shall be consumed by fire" (7:17).

Though the 142nd mitzvah – not to leave over any meat past the end of the time limit for eating – is written in connection with the *todah*, it applies as well to all sacrifices which had a time limit for the eating.

Though the 143rd mitzvah – to burn all left over meat – is written in connection with the peace-offering (*shelamim*), it applies as well to all sacrifices which had a time limit for the eating.

IT'S THE THOUGHT THAT COUNTS

The 144th mitzvah is the prohibition to eat pigul.

"The one who offers it shall not think (an improper thought), it will become despised, the one who eats of it shall bear his sin" (7:18).

It is forbidden to invalidate a sacrifice with an improper thought. An improper thought that would invalidate a sacrifice is as follows: if the *Kohen* performing the service intends to burn the sacrifice after its proper time or intends to eat the sacrifice after its time limitation. The meat of the invalidated sacrifice, called *pigul,* is not allowed to be eaten.

The *Sefer HaChinuch* explains that sacrifices are to purify the thought process of man. Every transgression begins with a thought, the though to sin. His thought process was faulty. The offering will help rectify that deficiency.

Since the whole purpose of sacrifices is to improve the faulty thought process of man, a faulty thought in the offering of the sacrifice will invalidate it.

∙§ HOLINESS

The 145ᵗʰ mitzvah in the Torah is the prohibition to eat meat of a sacrifice that became *tamei*.
The 146ᵗʰ mitzvah is the Torah is to burn the meat of a sacrifice that became *tamei*.
"The meat (of a sacrifice) which touches any impure thing shall not be eaten..." (7:19)

The *Sefer HaChinuch's* explanation, that sacrifices are to improve the thought process of man, leads to the following thought. Improving one's mind is the path to purity and holiness. Therefore, if the man was in a state of ritual impurity, *tumah*, or if the sacrifice became impure, it could not be eaten. Holiness and purity are the antitheses of *tumah* and therefore they could not come in contact with each other.

∙§ LIFE AND ENERGY

The 147ᵗʰ mitzvah in the Torah is the prohibition to eat the abdominal fat of cattle, sheep, or goats.
The 148ᵗʰ mitzvah in the Torah is the prohibition to consume blood of any beast or fowl.
"Whosoever eats the abdominal fat of an animal which (could be) presented as a fire offering to G-d, the soul that eats will be cut off from his people" (7:25).
"Any blood you shall not eat..." (7:26).

The prohibition relating to abdominal fat applies to all domesticated kosher animals whether or not they were set aside to be a sacrifice. If so, why does the Torah make a connection between the prohibition of the fats and sacrifices when it writes, *"Whosoever eats the abdominal fat of an animal which (could be) presented as a fire offering to G-d..."*?

Likewise, the prohibition to consume blood applies to the blood of all animals and fowl whether or not they were set aside to be a sacrifice. That being the case, why does the Torah make a connection between the prohibition of blood and sacrifices when it writes,

"For the life of flesh is in the blood and I have given it to you to be upon the altar to atone for your souls..." (17:11).

In order to speculate upon a possible answer to these questions, we must understand the significance of blood and fat. In order for an organism to be able to function it requires two things: life and energy. If it has life but no fuel to energize it, the organism will instantly die. If it has fuel for energy but no life, obviously it will not function.

The Torah ascribes the source of life to the blood system. *"For the life of the flesh is in the blood"* (*Vayikra* 17:11). The body stores its fuel for energy in the fat. These two, blood and fat, were of such great spiritual importance, life and energy, that every animal sacrifice had its blood placed against the walls of the altar and had its abdominal fat burned on top. These two parts of the animal were reserved for sacred purposes and therefore the Torah prohibited them from being consumed by an individual.

◆ STOLEN WATERS

The Torah encourages us to be careful not to consume blood. *"Be strong, do not eat blood"* (*Devarim* 12:23). This seems a bit strange since most people find blood to be repulsive and would not consume it even if the Torah did not prohibit it. Why does the Torah have to reinforce the prohibition by inspiring us to be strong and resolute?

The story is told about a father who warned his son not to bite off the *pitum* of his esrog (so that it could be used for the mitzvah). Each day the father would remind his son not to bite off the *pitum.* The child could no longer contain himself and, when his father wasn't looking, he bit off the *pitum* of the esrog.

The point behind the story is that it probably would not have ever occurred to the child to bite off the *pitum.* The mere fact that his father told him not to, instigated his desire to do it. The same is true about blood. Possibly if the Torah did not prohibit it, we would not consider drinking it. It is repulsive. However, the Torah had to relate to us that it is a forbidden food. Now, it becomes a bit more tempting.

There is an expression found in *Mishlei* (9:17), *"Stolen waters are sweeter."* The *yetzer ha'ra* thrives on sins. To the evil inclination, sin is as sweet as honey. The fact that the Torah prohibits something makes it all the more tempting. Therefore the Torah encourages us to be particularly strong, regarding this prohibition, not to give in to the temptation.

≈§ THE GREATEST JOY

"And Moshe slaughtered and took from the blood..." (8:23).

"Moshe took... and burned (the offering) on the altar..." (8:28).

"And Moshe took the breast (of the peace-offering)... it was to Moshe a portion (to eat)" (8:29).

Until Aharon and his sons were consecrated into the priesthood, Moshe served as the High Priest. Therefore, as the verses above indicated, Moshe slaughtered the sacrifices, burned portions on the altar and was allowed the priestly portion of

the offering. Moshe was indeed the High Priest (*Zevachim* 101b).
However, G-d told Moshe that Aharon would also be a High Priest
and Moshe would serve as Aharon's assistant. As the verse indicates,
*"And Moshe brought Aharon and his sons and he washed them with
water and he put upon them the shirt..."* (8:6:7) (Medrash Sifra).

Throughout the forty years the Children of Israel wandered in
the desert, Moshe retained the title of High Priest (*Shmos Rabbah*
37:1). However, Moshe was only the Vice-High Priest. His brother
Aharon served as the supreme High Priest. Why was Moshe demot-
ed? The Medrash (*Vayikra Rabbah* 11:6) says that because Moshe
argued with G-d and was reluctant to serve as the one to lead the
Israelites out of Egypt, he lost his position of supremacy in the priesthood. Moshe's motives in expressing reluctance to be the leader of the
Israelites were honorable and clearly emanated from his unparalleled
humility before G-d. However we learn from here that Moshe's
humility should have stopped short of arguing with a directive from
G-d. Furthermore, we see that a spiritual leader must know when it is
proper to be humble and when it is detrimental to display humility.

In the verse quoted above, *"And Moshe slaughtered and took from
the blood..."* the cantilation (*trop*) above the word "slaughtered" is a
shalsheles. This cantilation note is found only four times in the Torah:

1 – When the three angels told Lot that Sodom was about to be
destroyed, Lot hesitated whether to leave or not. *"And he hesitated, and the (angelic) men grabbed his hand and the hand
of his wife and the hand of his two daughters, through the
mercy of G-d that was upon him, and they brought him out
and placed him outside the city"* (*Bereishis* 19:16). Above the
word "*hesitated*" is a *shalsheles*.

2 – Avraham wanted a proper mate for his son Yitzchak.
Avraham's faithful servant, Eliezer, thought that his master
would choose Eliezer's daughter as a mate for Yitzchak. Much
to the dismay of Eliezer, Avraham asked Eliezer to go to
Haran and seek there a mate for Yitzchak. Eliezer accepted
the task and prayed for his success. The verse says, *"And
(Eliezer) said: G-d, L-rd of my master Avraham, may (good
fortune) happen to me today and show kindness to my master*

Avraham" (*Bereishis* 24:12). Above the word "*said*" is a *shalsheles*.

3 – Potiphar's wife tried to seduce Yosef. The verse says, "*And he refused*" (*Bereishis* 39:8). Above the word "*refused*" is the third *shalsheles*.

4 – The fourth *shalsheles* is found here in *Parshas Tzav*, "*And Moshe slaughtered...*" Above the word "*slaughtered*" is the *shalsheles*.

A *shalsheles* is a vertical zigzagging line. It goes left, then right, left, right, left, right. It represents an inner conflict. In all four instances where the *shalsheles* is used, there was an inner conflict, a struggle with one's self. Lot could not decide whether to believe his angelic guests about the impending destruction of Sodom or not. Eliezer struggled with the fact that he wanted his own daughter to marry Yitzchak, yet Avraham wanted someone else. Yosef struggled with the influencing charms of the seductress. Moshe struggled with the disappointment that he would be relegated to second in the chain of the priesthood.

Interestingly, in three of the instances the *shalsheles* appears above the word after a resolution and decision was made. After Eliezer decided to do his master's bidding, he prayed for a successful mission. The *shalsheles* appears above his prayer. Yosef strengthened himself and resolved not to give in to temptation. The *shalsheles* appears above the word "refused." Moshe resolved to personally slaughter the sacrifices that would hail the inauguration of Aharon. Above the word "slaughtered" is the *shalsheles*. Only in the case of Lot is the *shalsheles* not above the resolution because there was no resolution. He had to be dragged out of his house in order to be saved.

The Torah marks the resolution of an inner conflict with a special cantilation, the *shalsheles*. It does not mark the resolution of a conflict with another person with any special cantilation. This shows us the great torment and struggle a person undergoes when he has to struggle with himself. The pain is great; but the joy that is felt when a resolution is achieved is equally great. As the Ramah, co-author of the *Shulchan Orech*, said, "*There is no joy like the resolution of doubt*" (*Shu"t* 5).

❧ BE INVOLVED

Rabah said: *Whosoever involves himself with the study of the Torah needs neither burnt-offering, nor meal-offering, nor sin-offering, nor guilt-offering* (*Menochos* 110a).

R abah's comment seems a bit strange. Many people who learn Torah do commit sins. What did Rabah mean?

If we look carefully at Rabah's choice of words we can find the answer. Rabah did not say whoever learns Torah or whoever studies Torah. He said whoever involves himself with Torah. The difference between study and involve is very clear. One studies in a detached manner. The one who studies and the material being studied are two distinctly different things. One who is involved becomes united with the subject being studied. They form a symbiotic relationship.

In life, there are those who diligently study Torah but do not have a deep personal relationship with Torah. This becomes evident through their behavior, or rather their misbehavior. They show little respect for their fellow Torah scholars and even less respect for their fellow Jew who may not be so scholarly. There are others who may have only an elementary knowledge of Torah but are very involved with that knowledge. They treasure it as though it was a diamond. They have an ongoing relationship with Torah. It is manifested in the way they honor Torah scholars and how they treat their fellow Jew – with compassion, kindness, and understanding. One who is totally involved in Torah sanctifies every moment of his life. He lives Torah. His every moment becomes an offering to G-d.

Each morning we recite a blessing for the study of Torah. It begins with "*Blessed art Thou, L-rd, our G-d, King of the Universe, who sanctified us with His commandments...*" It does not conclude with "...to study the words of Torah." Instead, it concludes with "...*to be involved with the words of Torah, la'asok b'divrei Torah.*"

Torah is not a subject to be studied. It is a way of life in which to be involved.

✑ KASHERING ONE'S SELF

"An earthen vessel in which (the sin-offering) is cooked shall be broken; if it be a metal vessel in which (the sin-offering) is cooked, it shall be scoured and washed." (6:21)

The walls of a pot absorb some of the food that is cooked in it. If sacred food is cooked in a pot, that pot will absorb some of the sacred food. Sacred food becomes forbidden after the time limit for eating has expired (*noser*); likewise, the absorbed food in the walls of the pot becomes forbidden. If that pot is later used to cook something else, the heat causes the forbidden food to be expelled from the walls of the pot and mix with the new food item. That will render the new food to be forbidden.

An earthen pot can never be totally cleansed of the forbidden food therefore it has to be broken so as never to be used again. A metal pot can be totally cleansed if it is scoured with hot water and cleaned. From here we derive the principle of *kashering* utensils (*Avodah Zorah* 34b).

Why did the Torah teach us the principle of *kashering* in connection with the sin-offering since it not only applies to all sacrifices but to all forbidden foods as well?

The *Kli Yakar* explains that the Torah is not only telling us how to *kasher* a utensil, it is also telling the sinner how to *kasher* himself. That is why the Torah mentions the law of *kashering* in connection with the sin-offering. Sometimes the sin becomes so ingrained in the sinner it is impossible to expunge all traces of the sin. The sinner must come before G-d with a totally broken heart and beg G-d for mercy. This is like the earthenware pot that has to be broken. Other times the sin is not so ingrained into the being of the sinner. The sinner can scour himself with repentance and cleanse the blemish from his soul. This is like the metal pot which can be cleansed if it is scoured and cleaned.

✒ HAFTORAH TZAV

THE *HAFTORAH* IS FOUND IN *YIRMIYAHU* 7:21-8:3, 9:22-23.

T his prophecy of Yirmiyahu is powerful in its rebuke of Israel on account of their great sins. It is a heartrending forecast of sadness and doom.

The *haftorah* first implores that more essential to Judaism than our devotion to G-d through sacrifices is our sincere observance of G-d's ways. *"Listen to My voice and I will be to you a G-d and you will be unto Me a people; you will go in the way I command you so that good will be unto you"* (7:23).

We demonstrated by the Golden Calf that Jews would need a regiment of sacrifices to achieve atonement for our failing to consistently follow in G-d's ways. The most important part of the sacrificial offering was the sincere thought of the one who brought it and the *Kohanim* who offered it. During the generation of Yirmiyahu, the Israelites and the *Kohanim* were not sincere. Their burnt offerings were to appease the false gods of idolatry. G-d mockingly says to them, *"Your burnt-offerings, bring instead peace-offerings which you can eat"* (7:21). Burnt-offerings were entirely consumed in fire as opposed to peace-offerings that were eaten. G-d wonders why they are wasting the meat of the animal on an insincere offering. If they would bring peace-offerings, at least then they could indulge in this otherwise empty act.

Yirmiyahu complains bitterly that idols have been erected in the holy *Bais HaMikdash*. It was supposed to have been the most sacred spot in the universe which proclaimed G-d's glorious name. Instead, it became a place of rebellion against G-d. *"They have placed their abominations in the house upon which My name is proclaimed; they contaminate it"* (7:30).

Nothing exemplifies the wayward spirit of the Israelites of that generation more than their dedication to *Molech*. Outside Jerusalem, there was a valley that ran along the western edge of the city. It was owned by the family of Hennom. In that valley the Jews built a great temple to the fire-god *Molech*. Fathers would bring their sons to the fire-god priests as an offering. The child would be brought into the inner sanctum of the temple and burned alive. Priests would beat loudly on drums, called *tofet*, to drown out the painful screams of the child. Such was the barbaric spirit of rebellion of Yirmiyahu's generation. The prophet foretold of the days to come when the valley, also called Tofet, would become a mass burial ground for all the victims of the Babylonian holocaust. *"It will no longer be called Tofet or the Valley of Hennom, but it will be called the Valley of Killing for they will bury in Tofet until there is no more room. The corpses of these people will become food for the birds of the heavens and for the animals of the earth"* (7:32-33).

Yirmiyahu continues, *"(The enemy) will remove the bones of the kings of Judah , the bones of its leaders, the bones of the priests, the bones of the prophets and the bones of the inhabitants of Jerusalem from their graves. They will be spread out under the sun and moon and all the heavenly legion, which they loved and worshipped ... not buried... but like fertilizer on the surface of the ground..."* (8:1-2). How truly remarkable was that prophecy. Of all the hundreds of thousands of Jews who were buried in ancient Jerusalem, the remains of not a single one has ever been found until this very day. A multitude of burial vaults have been discovered in modern times, many along the slopes of the Valley of Hennom, but not a single skeleton has been found. They all simply disappeared, like fertilizer upon the ground.

The Valley of Hennom was a valley of horrors. In better times it was the garbage dump of Jerusalem. Trash heaps were not permitted to be located in the holy city. All the refuse had to be brought outside the city walls and dumped in the valley. The stench of the valley was gut-wrenching. Fires were kept burning day and night to consume the trash and debris. In later years the fires of the trash became fires of the god *Molech* and the pitiful cries of children could be heard. Throughout ancient times, when a father wanted to show a wayward child what would become of a sinner in the next world, the father would bring the child to the edge of the valley. The acrid smell of the smoke, the flaring of the flames, and the nauseating smell of the rotting garbage taught many a child a lesson he would never forget. This Valley of Hennom, called *Ge'hennom* in Hebrew, eventually became the name of the netherworld where the wicked will reside.

Concerning the evil prophet, Bilaam, our Sages say (*Sanhedrin* 105b) that though he uttered words of blessing, his intent was to curse. The opposite can be said of the noble prophets of Israel. Though Yirmiyahu uttered words of curse, his intent was to bless. This lesson can be seen in the verse of doom, *"I shall eliminate from the cities of Judah and from the courtyards of Jerusalem the sound of joy, the sound of gladness, the sound of the groom and the sound of the bride, for the land will be in ruins"* (7:34). Although the scene depicted is a gloomy one, the words were altered slightly and were made into the joyous blessing recited at the conclusion of every Jewish wedding ceremony. *"Blessed art Thou, Hashem, our G-d, King of the universe...soon will be heard in the cities of Judah and from the courtyards of Jerusalem the sound of joy, the sound of gladness, the sound of the groom and the sound of the bride..."*

May we soon merit seeing the words of blessing hidden in all the prophecies and an end to the terror and horror of the *Galus.*

SHMINI

✍ AND WHAT WOULD G-D SAY?

"And it was ("va'yehi") on the eighth day (of the consecration of the Mishkan) that Moshe called to Aharon and to his sons and to the elders of Israel" (9:1).

The Talmud (*Megillah* 10b) tells us that a portion of the Torah that begins with the word *va'yehi* (and it was) is an indication that a time of woe lies ahead.

In every instance that the word *va'yehi* indicates that adversity looms in the near future, the same verse also indicates what the cause for concern was. The Talmud and the Medrash cite numerous places where this rule is applied. The *Megillas Esther* begins with *"And it was (va'yehi) in the days of Achashvayrosh, he is the Achashvayrosh who ruled from Hodu to Kush, one hundred and twenty-seven provinces."* The verse indicates the cause for the great concern about the adversity. Achashvayrosh was not the king of some small country. Had he been so, the decree of Haman would not have threatened all the

Jewish People. The fact that Achashvayrosh was the ruler of the entire Jewish world indicates how great the looming danger was.

The *Megillas Ruth* begins with, *"And it was (va'yehi) in the days when the judges ruled, that there was a hunger in the land."* The cause for concern was the fact that hunger was in the land of Israel and desperate times cause people to do desperate, and sometimes foolish, things. In this case it was the cause for the great benefactor of Israel, Elimelech, to abandon his country and his people and move to Moab.

The question, now apparent, is that our verse, *"And it was ("va'yehi") on the eighth day (of the consecration of the Mishkan) that Moshe called to Aharon and to his sons and to the elders of Israel,"* does not seem to indicate what the cause for concern was. What was the cause for concern?

The answer is found, not in what the verse says, but rather in what the verse does not say. After the birth of Moshe, portions of the Torah most commonly begin with *"And G-d spoke to Moshe **saying**."* Here, even though Moshe obviously was commanded, the verse, by omitting any reference to G-d, hints at the cause for concern. Nadav and Avihu entered the Holy of Holies without the permission of G-d; there was no commandment from G-d telling them to do so. That was the cause for concern about the tragedy that is about to unfold: the death of Aharon's two sons, Nadav and Avihu.

In learning lessons from the words of the Torah, we must pay attention not only to what the Torah says but also to what it does not say.

❧ LIVING IN THE PAST

I n the Medrash (*Esther Rabbah Pesichta* 11), we learn that while the word *va'yehi* (and it was) indicates adversity, the word *v'hayah* (and it will be) indicates joy. Why is this so?

The Medrash tells us that the words *va'yehi* (and it was) which indicates the past, and *v'hayah* (and it will be) which indicates the future, alone, do not indicate adversity or joy. The verse must also contain the word 'day' (or 'days'). Our verse says, *"And it was ("va'yehi") on the eighth* **day**..."

There are two types of people in our world. There are those that dwell on the past and there are those that look forward to the future. A verse that starts va'yehi and contains the word 'day(s)' perhaps is revealing that a preoccupation with the past is a woeful approach to life. Negating the opportunity of the future is a recipe for disaster. The verse that denotes joy has *v'hayah* and the word 'day(s).' Although we must learn from our past, our efforts must be focused on what the future holds in store. Setting our sights on achieving a wonderful future is a joyful approach to life.

[Note: in Biblical Hebrew *yehi* means "will be" and *hayah* means "was." With the letter *vav* at the beginning of the word, the meanings become reversed: *va'yehi* becomes "was" and *v'hayah* becomes "will be." This principle in Biblical grammar is known as the *vav ha'me'hapech*, the reversing vav.]

⤳ HE WHO LIVES IN A GLASS HOUSE...

"And (Moshe) said to Aharon: take for yourself a calf for a sin-offering... and to the children of Israel you shall speak saying: take for yourselves a goat for a sin-offering..." (9:2-3).

Why did Aharon's sin-offering consist of a calf and the children of Israel's sin-offering consist of a goat?

Rashi (9:2) explains that Aharon's calf was to be atonement for his part in the sin of the golden calf. The *Sifra* (9:2) says that the goat of the children of Israel was to be atonement for the sin of Yosef's brothers selling him into slavery. After the brothers had sold Yosef, they dipped his multi-colored coat in the blood of a goat and presented it to their father, Yaakov. This caused Yaakov to think that Yosef had been killed. The goat came to represent the selling of Yosef.

The *Pardes Yosef* asks why during the consecration of the *Mishkan* was an atonement required for the selling of Yosef. It is understandable that Aharon, who was just designated as the high priest, should offer atonement for his past indiscretion and involvement in the sin of the golden calf. But, what is the connection here to the indiscretion of Yosef's brothers?

The *Pardes Yosef* asks another question. How could Yosef's brothers, who were totally righteous men, commit such an egregious sin as plotting to kill their own sibling, the beloved one of their aged father? He explains that the brothers saw through prophecy that the first king of the divided kingdom of Israel would be the evil Yerovam ben Nevat. Yerovam would encourage the Jewish people to abandon the *Bais HaMikdash* and worship idols instead. The idols just happened to be golden calves. The brothers thought they could avert this future tragedy by killing the ancestor of Yerovam, who just happened to be Yosef. The brothers threw Yosef into a snake infested pit hoping that he would be killed. When they saw it was not the divine will that Yosef be killed, they sold him into slavery assuming that he would disappear among the nations of the world and not have a descendant worthy of becoming king of the Jews. The intentions of the brothers were to some degree noble and they did not require any atonement for that indiscretion.

The *Pardes Yosef* continues. It was amazing that the brothers saw the great flaw in Yosef's descendant who would induce others to worship idols; yet, they did not see the great flaw in their own descendants. The Israelites, their descendants, would induce Aharon to form the golden calf, which ironically became the symbol for Yerovam's idolatry. For that, the Israelites had to offer a sin-offering, a sin-offering for the selling of Yosef. The tribes could see the defect of their brother but they could not see their own defect: which was the very same imperfection.

The Talumd (*Kiddushin* 70b) says: whoever sees a flaw in others, sees his own flaw. This is an invaluable lesson in human psychology and the path to self-improvement. Two people can observe the same character flaw in another person. One observer is greatly annoyed at the flaw and is very critical of the friend. The other observer, who sees the same flaw, is not as disturbed and therefore does not offer any harsh criticism. He is gentle and more forgiving in his condemnation. What accounts for this difference?

Our sages explain the difference. The one who was very critical, saw in his friend a fault that he himself may have. However, he does not consciously see it in himself. Subconsciously, he knows that he has that same fault but has yet to deal with it properly. Therefore, in this self-imposed state of denial, he is critical of his friend.

The other observer realizes that he has the same flaw; however, he was able to face it and properly deal with it. Therefore, when he noticed it in his friend, it did not irk him very much. His criticism was toned down.

The first step in self-improvement is to be consciously aware of your own character flaws and weaknesses. That is not an easy task to accomplish. If you want to know what your weak points are and in what areas you need improvement, just see what faults others have that irk you. When you discover them, you will come to realize that those are your very same weaknesses. You can now head down the path of self-improvement.

✑ SKELETONS IN THE CLOSET

"And Moshe said to Aharon: come close to the altar and bring your sin-offering..." (9:7).

Rashi explains that Moshe had to encourage Aharon to assume the role of High Priest. Aharon was very reluctant. As Rashi phrases it, "Aharon was **embarrassed and afraid** to approach." Moshe explained to Aharon, that because he was embarrassed to approach, was the very reason he was chosen to be the High Priest.

The *K'sav Sofer* explains that Aharon was embarrassed and afraid. He was embarrassed because of his role in the sin of the Golden Calf and he was afraid that his role as High Priest would lead him to become haughty. Moshe convinced Aharon that it was because of his sense of shame that he was chosen to be the High Priest. Shame is the greatest expression of repentance (*Berachos* 12b). In addition, the shame that Aharon felt would prevent him from becoming haughty. Aharon knew full well what sin was like and how important atonement was.

Our Sages says (*Yoma* 22b), "*Any leader who does not carry a sack of rodents on his back will not be a successful leader.*" Or, to phrase it in more modern terminology, "Any leader that does not have skeletons in his closet will not be a successful leader." A leader must be aware of the indiscretions that he has committed in the past; he will then exhibit more understanding to those who commit indiscretions under his rule. He must know what it means to be human. Then he will be less likely to become haughty and, thus, have a greater chance at successful leadership.

✑ A TIME FOR HUMILITY AND A TIME FOR PRIDE

The *Pardes Yosef* sees a different explanation for Moshe telling Aharon not to be embarrassed and to assume his role as High Priest. Moshe was the personification of Torah. He received the Torah on Sinai and transmitted it to the Children of Israel. To be a master of Torah requires humility and Moshe was "*exceedingly humble, more than any person upon the face of the land*" (*Bamidbar* 12:3). The character trait of humility is what qualified

Moshe to be the law-giver.

The priesthood required a different character trait. The *Kohanim* were the aristocrats in Israel who were intermediaries between G-d and his nation. They were, in a sense, G-d's agents (*Nedarim* 35b). That position required a sense of nobility and, yes, some degree of pride. Therefore, Moshe told Aharon not to be overly embarrassed about assuming the role of High Priest and not to be too concerned about feeling a sense of pride. That was part of the requirement for the "job." Of course, Moshe knew that Aharon would be able to know the difference between carrying himself with dignity and pride and carrying himself with haughtiness.

In the preceding verse (9:6) Moshe told Aharon to perform the service. Aharon did not move. In this verse (9:7) Moshe tells Aharon to "*come close.*" In the next verse it says, "*And Aharon came close...*" Perhaps this is the source for what the Talmud (*Berachos* 34a) states: *If one tells you to daven for the congregation, hesitate. If you are told a second time, get ready. The third time, go.*

The Medrash (*Yayikra Rabbah* 11:6), was cited above in *Parshas Tzav* to teach us that humility, particularly for a leader, has boundaries. Interestingly, that Medrash points out that Moshe was not allowed to serve as the High Priest in the consecration ceremony because when G-d told him to go to Pharaoh, and tell him to free the Children of Israel, **three** times Moshe refused to go.

❧ DOWN BUT NOT OUT

Aharon was greatly saddened on account of his role in the sin of the Golden Calf. It was a great calamity and its ramifications were felt throughout the course of Jewish history. We would imagine that Aharon would have been so depressed that he would have spent the remainder of his life wallowing in his depression. However, that was not the case. Aharon rose above it. The sense of shame he felt for his failure became his source of strength. He was able to rise to new heights. It revealed Aharon's true character.

This is a profound lesson for anyone who has strayed from the path of Yiddishkeit. If they feel any remorse at all, they will feel guilty and depressed. They can either spend the rest of the life wallowing in the mire of their depression or they can use the experience to rise to greater heights. These are the challenges that test men's lives.

Though sin is wrong and distances man from G-d, ironically it also becomes the catalyst for his return. The occasion can be the fire furnace that tempers the metal of his spirit and gives him greater strength than he ever knew. Introspection and remorse brings man closer to G-d than he had been before.

Life is full of bumps and bruises but the true character of man is seen in how he rebounds from them. It is for this reason that Aaron was chosen.

"*Though the righteous will fall seven times, he will rise*" (Mishlei 24:17). The verse does not say that though he falls seven times he will **get up**, rather, it says that he will **rise**. Rav Hutner explained that it means not only will the righteous person do *teshuvah* when he falls and be able to stand up; he will be able to use the occasion to rise to greater heights.

On the 6th day of creation, man was created. The Torah says, "*And G-d saw all that He did and behold it was exceedingly good*" (*Bereishis* 1:31). On the other days of creation, the Torah says simply that it was "*good.*" Why here did it say "*exceedingly good?*" The Medrash (*Bereishis Rabbah* 9:7) tells us that Good is the *Yetzer HaTov* (the Good Inclination); Very Good is the *Yetzer Ha'Ra* (the Bad Inclination). How can the *Yetzer Ha'Ra* be **very** good? It is because through the *Yetzer Ha'Ra* we fall; and the process of rising after the fall is what makes us a greater person.

ᵊᵌ **FROM THE HEART**

"And Aharon lifted his hands towards the people and blessed them" (9:22).

Rashi says that this verse refers to the mitzvah for a *Kohen* to bless his fellow Jews, which we call *to duchen*. The word *duchen* means a platform and refers to the platform upon which the Temple priests stood when they blessed the people. The actual mitzvah is not counted until *Parshas Naso*, mitzvah 378. There, the Torah says, *"And so you shall bless the Children of Israel... May Hashem bless you and keep you..."* (*Bamidbar* 6:23).

The Gerer Rebbe (Rabbi Avraham Mordechai Alter) pointed out that though the *kohanim* are commanded to bless the Israelites, the Torah does not phrase it as an outright commandment. In our *parshah*, the Torah merely tells us that Aharon blessed the people. It does not state he was commanded to do so. In *Parshas Naso*, it tells us that when the *Kohen* blesses the people, these are the words they should say. Again, it does not say they are commanded to do so. The reason, the Gerer Rebbe explained, is because a true blessing must come from the heart. It cannot be something that is commanded. Therefore, the Torah did not phrase it as a commandment.

One of the great mysteries about the mitzvah of *duchening* is that though the mitzvah is supposed to be done each and every day, in *chutz la'aretz* (the Diaspora) we only *duchen* on Yom Tov. No reason has ever been given as to why this is so.

In our verse, the *Targum Yonassan* says, *"And Aharon blessed them from on top the altar and he came down from there with joy."* Perhaps the *Targum* is teaching us an additional lesson about blessings. Not only must it come from the heart, it must be expressed with great joy.

Perhaps this is the reason why the blessing of the priests is not recited each day in *chutz la'aretz*. The fact that we are here in *galus* seriously detracts from any possible expression of joy the *kohanim* could have. They therefore refrain from reciting the blessing.

However on Yom Tov, the mitzvah of *simchas* Yom Tov, rejoicing on the holiday, allows the *Kohen* to recite the blessing with joy.

ASSUMING PERSONAL RESPONSIBILITY

Rashi (9:23) tells us that after the consecration of the *Mishkan* was completed, the *Shechinah* still did not appear. Aharon said to Moshe, "It is because Hashem was angry with me, the Divine presence has not appeared."

Aharon took personal responsibility for what had happened. He blamed himself. He did not blame Moshe nor did he blame the Children of Israel. It was his entire fault.

What a remarkable lesson this is. It is instinctive that when something goes wrong we look for someone or something to blame. The fault never is with us; it is always someone or something else. We live in a society that has made assessing blame into an art form. If one carelessly spilled hot coffee on himself, the fault must be with the one who served the coffee. If one robs and steals, the fault lies with the society that had allowed the pangs of poverty to breed such desperation. If a child is disruptive in school, it must be a genetic disorder. After the 9/11 tragedy, Congress was looking for a scapegoat to blame. It was all George W. Bush's fault. It was America's fault for being so pro-Israel. It was all an Israeli plot. When we search for blame, we look in all the wrong places and often come to the most absurd conclusions.

Aharon did not seek to look in the wrong places. He found the fault within himself. That enabled him to remedy the situation. He and Moshe went into the *Ohel Moed* and together prayed. Immediately thereafter, the *Shechinah* descended.

As Cassius once put it, "*The fault, dear Brutus, lies not in our stars, but in ourselves.*" – William Shakespeare, Julius Caesar I, ii

✒ THE SIN(S) OF NADAV AND AVIHU

"And the sons of Aharon, Nadav and Avihu, each took a pan and placed a fire in them and put incense on top and they brought before G-d a strange fire-offering which He had not commanded them. A fire went out from before G-d and consumed them. And they died in the presence of G-d" (10:1-2).

The *Shechinah* had just descended upon the *Mishkan*. The glory of G-d was seen by all. A fire came down from the heavens and ignited the altar. It was an awe-inspiring moment. It was a time of great joy. Unfortunately, the joy was marred by the death of the two sons of Aharon, Nadav and Avihu. How did this come about? What was their great sin?

Numerous suggestions are given as to what was the sin of Nadav and Avihu. Here is a sampling:

1 – Nadav and Avihu decided a matter of *halachah* without first consulting Moshe (*Rashi*, quoting the Medrash).

2 – *"... each took a pan and placed a fire in them.."* Each one did it on his own. They didn't even consult one another (*Vayikra Rabbah* 20:8).

3 – They had just consumed wine before entering the *Ohel Moed* (*Rashi* 20:1).

4 – They were unable to find wives that would suit them (*Vayikra Rabbah* 20:10).

5 – They had no interest in fathering children (*Yevamos* 64a).

6 – Moshe and Aharon once walked along with Nadav and Avihu trailing behind them and all Israel following in the rear. Nadav said to Avihu, "When will these old men die so that you and I will be the leaders of our generation." But the Holy One, blessed be He, said to them, "We shall see who will bury whom" (*Sanhedrin* 52a).

7 – They offered a private fire-offering. There was no such sacrifice as a private fire-offering (*Sifra* 10:2).

8 – They gazed upon the *Shechinah* at the revelation at Sinai (*Vayikra Rabbah* 20:8).

9 – They entered the Holy of Holies without permission (ibid).

10 – They brought an offering that they were not asked to bring (ibid).

Harav Yaakov Kaminetsky explained that they were actually guilty of only one sin and that one sin caused all the others. What was that one sin? It was haughtiness. Everything they did and everything they said could be explained away. There was some rationalization for everything. However, it was the underlying spirit of haughtiness that caused their downfall. That was their one great sin.

When Nadav and Avihu decided a matter of *halachah* without first consulting Moshe, their ruling was correct (see *Eruvin* 63a), but, still, they should have asked Moshe their teacher (*Rashi,* quoting the Medrash).

They didn't even consult one another because each one in their own eyes knew they were right.

There was nothing wrong with entering the *Ohel Moed* after consuming wine. The prohibition was not taught until after their death.

They were very great men and understandably they felt that there were no suitable spouses for them.

They had no interest in fathering children because they felt it would detract them from their holy studies.

Moshe himself said that Nadav and Avihu were greater than Moshe and Aharon (*Rashi* 10:3). It is understandable how Nadav and Avihu could have said, "When will these old men die so that you and I will be the leaders of our generation."

It was true that there was no such sacrifice as a private fire-offering. It was true for the common Jew but they were not common Jews.

They were great enough to be able to gaze upon the *Shechinah* at the revelation at Sinai.

They felt they did not need permission to enter the Holy of Holies on account of their greatness.

They brought an offering that they were not asked to bring because they thought that they did not even have to be asked. They would take the initiative themselves.

Everything can be explained away, everything except their haughtiness.

HIGHER STANDARD

Why were Nadav and Avihu punished so harshly? In most cultures, leaders are given some leeway when it comes to wrong-doings. In fact, it is even expected. Politicians are allowed a certain amount of corruption without being held accountable. Union leaders are permitted a reasonable amount of graft. Religious leaders are granted a few moral indiscretions. However, in Judaism the opposite is the truth. The Talmud (*Baba Kamma* 50a) says, "*The Holy One, blessed be He, is particular with those around about Him even for matters as light as a single hair.*"

This may seem a bit unfair; however, consider the following illustration. A woman was standing in a candy store about to make a purchase. She saw a man walk in with his son. To her surprise, the man swiped a two-cent piece of candy and stuffed it in his pocket. The woman thought to herself why should she call it to the attention of the store owner and cause a scene, after all, it was only two cents. She resolved to remain silent. We know exactly what she was thinking and we may even be tempted to agree with her. Why make a big fuss over such a trivial thing. However, the man's son also saw his father swipe the two-cent piece of candy. He too saw his father stuff it in his pocket. What would you guess that the son was thinking?

The son considered his father to be his leader, his guide, his source of strength. He looked up to him. When he saw his father swipe the candy he will conclude one of two things – either his father is a crook and totally not deserving of his respect or he will think that stealing small stuff is okay. Either way, the father and the son both lose: and all for two cents.

Maybe now we can gain some understanding as to why G-d holds leaders up to a stricter standard of morality and justice.

✑ "A TIME FOR MOURNING AND A TIME FOR DANCING"

(KOHELES 3:4)

"And Aharon remained silent" (10:3).

U pon hearing the sad news regarding the death of his two sons, Aharon remained silent. When tragedy befalls a person, his first tendency is to ask G-d why did this happen? Aharon did not question G-d's justice. However, we would expect that at the very least he would have cried and mourned over the loss of his sons. Aharon did not cry. He remained silent. This day was a great and joyous day for the Jewish People. Aharon did not want to mar the occasion with his personal grief. And so, he remained silent.

There is a remarkable story regarding a *Rosh Yeshiva* in New York. Since I did not ask his permission to tell the story, I will not divulge his name. It was *Simchas Torah*. The *bochrim* in the *Bais Medrash* were dancing with the greatest of fervor. Their *Rosh Yeshiva* was singing and dancing with such joy, it inspired everyone. He was the conductor of this symphony of spiritual ecstasy. Around and around they danced, singing and shouting, for hours and hours. Unexpectedly, someone quickly entered the *Bais Medrash*, rushed over to the *Rosh Yeshiva* and called him aside. The fellow whispered something into the ear of the *Rosh Yeshiva*. The fellow departed. The *Rosh Yeshiva* paused for a few seconds and then returned to the dancing and singing. Until the early hours of the morning he continued to lead his symphony of celebration.

It wasn't until the next day that everyone found out what was whispered into the ear of the *Rosh Yeshiva*. He had a wonderful young daughter who brought him great joy. Unfortunately she was very ill. That night, the night of *Simchas Torah*, she passed away. The *Rosh Yeshiva* was heart-broken; however, he could not allow his personal tragedy to mar the joy of *Simchas Torah*. And the *Rosh Yeshiva*, like Aharon, was silent.

The Medrash (*Yalkut Shimoni Mishlei* 31:10) states the follwing story.

One Shabbos afternoon, as Rebbe Meir was learning in the *Bais Medrash*, a tragedy struck at home. Both of his sons passed away. His wife took the remains of her sons and brought them into a bedroom. She laid them on a bed and covered them with a sheet. When Rebbe Meir returned home that evening, he asked his wife as to the where-abouts of their sons. His wife replied that they went away to the *Bais Medrash*. She prepared the *Havdalah*. After *Havdalah*, again Rebbe Meir wondered where their sons were. His wife began preparing something for Rebbe Meir to eat and told him they would return soon.

After Rebbe Meir completed his meal, his wife posed the follow-ing question. "Someone loaned something to me that is quite pre-cious. I have had it for some time and I have become completely attached to it. Now the person wants it back. Must I return it?" Rebbe Meir responded in bewilderment, "Certainly you must return it to its rightful owner." She then led him into the room where her sons were. She removed the covering. When Rebbe Meir saw his two sons, he burst into tears. "My sons, my sons, my teachers, my teachers. They were my sons who honored me most dearly. They were my teachers for they brightened my eyes with Torah."

His wife then said, "Why do you say that they are 'My sons?' Did you not say that we must return something on loan to its master? *The L-rd giveth and the L-rd taketh. May the name of G-d be blessed*" (*Eyov* 1:21).

We have a tendency to accept G-d's judgment in those times when He bestows good fortune upon us but we question His judg-ment when good is taken from us. Our Sages tell us, "*We must bless Hashem for the bad as well as the good* (*Berachos* 54a). Just as we accept His judgment in times of our good fortune, we must also trust and accept His judgment in times of misfortune. If we realize that it comes from the all-knowing and all – loving G-d, then that knowledge makes the burden much easier to bear.

✍ RESPECT FOR THE POSITION

The 149ᵗʰ mitzvah in the Torah is the prohibition for the *Kohen* to perform the service with unkempt hair.
The 150ᵗʰ mitzvah in the Torah is the prohibition for the *Kohen* to perform the service with torn garnments.
"Let your hair not grow long and let not your garments be torn..." (10:6).
The 151ˢᵗ mitzvah in the Torah is the prohibition for a *Kohen* to leave in the middle of a Temple service.
"From the doorway of the Ohel Moed (Tent of Assembly) you shall not leave (during the service)" (10:7).
The 152ⁿᵈ mitzvah in the Torah is the prohibition to drink any intoxicating beverage before participating in the service.
"Wine and intoxicants you shall not drink... when you come to the Ohel Moed (Tent of Assembly)" (10:9).

These four mitzvos are to establish the decorum and responsibility that the *Kohen* must maintain with regards to his position in the *Mishkan* and *Bais HaMikdash*. The *Kohen* is the liaison between G-d and Israel. As such, the *Kohanim* are expected and commanded to honor their position with dignity.

One who is in mourning does not cut his hair. He wears torn clothing. In times of great sadness we do not think of ourselves and how we look or whether or not we are comfortable. The mourning takes us away from thinking of ourselves. Mourners cover the mirrors of their homes so as not to even see themselves. However, a *Kohen* must always think of himself and his responsibility when he is performing the service. His appearance and attire must reflect his position.

Obviously, a *Kohen* must respect the work he is doing. One who leaves in the middle of something is showing disrespect. Just as we do not leave the *shul* in the middle of the reading of the Torah, a *Kohen* does not leave the sacred area while the *avodah* is being performed.

A *Kohen* was not permitted to consume alcoholic beverages on the day he was serving. Alcohol impairs ones judgment. A *Kohen* has to be acutely aware of each thing he was doing. Just as we cannot drink and drive, he could not drink and serve.

We also derive from this verse that a judge or rabbi could not render any legal decision or decide a *halachah* after having consumed an intoxicating beverage.

The great Sage, Rav, would speak words of Torah during the Shabbos and Yom Tov meals. He would not allow those words to be made public. Since they were spoken after drinking the Kiddush wine, he feared that the wine may have affected his judgment (*Beitza* 4a).

✍ THE DUAL PERSONALITY OF WINE

"Come eat of my bread and drink of the wine which I have prepared" (*Mishlei* 9:5).

The more we learn about wine, the more confused we become. Is wine considered good or bad? What is the Torah point of view?

Based on the prohibition for a *Kohen* to drink wine or any intoxicant before performing the service, we get the impression that wine is not a beneficial substance. Many authorities even prohibit a *Kohen* from entering the *Mishkan* and *Bais HaMikdash* after drinking, whether or not he intends to perform any service. However, we find that many mitzvos can only be properly performed over a cup of wine: *Kiddush, Havdalah,* a *Bris,* a marriage ceremony, *Pidyon HaBen, Sheva Brochos,* etc. That certainly implies that wine has very positive qualities. Which is it: good or bad?

The obvious answer is that wine is good or bad depending on its use. The verse in *T'hillim* (104:15) hints at this dual nature of wine. It says, *"Wine makes glad the **heart** of man."* The Hebrew word heart is spelled L-V-V instead of the more usual L-V. Why is there an extra V (*vav*)? The Talmud (*Berachos* 54a) quotes the verse in Shema, *"And you shall love G-d with all your **heart**..."* The word heart is spelled with an extra V (*vav*). The Talmud tells us that the extra V teaches us that there is a theme of duality emanating from our heart. Not only should we serve Hashem with the *Yetzer HaTov,* the Good Inclination, but also with the *Yetzer Ha'Ra,* the Bad Inclination. In other words, the Hebrew word for heart, when it is spelled with two V's(*vavs*), refers to both the Good Inclination and the Evil inclination. In the verse, *"Wine makes glad the **heart** of man,"* the Hebrew word for heart is also spelled with two V's to teach us that wine can be a tool of the *Yetzer HaTov* and it can also be a tool of the *Yetzer Ha'Ra.*

The Talmud Yerushalmi (*Pesachim* 10:6) says that wine consumed as part of a meal or right before or directly after the meal is not intoxicating. Based on that statement, Tosfos (*Ta'anis* 17a) rules that a *Kohen w*ho drank wine as part of a meal may afterwards perform the service since the wine was not intoxicating. Every mitzvah that is associated with wine is also associated with a meal. If one limits his drinking to meals, especially a *seudas* mitzvah, the wine can make the feast a more pleasant and festive experience. It can be a tool of the *Yetzer HaTov.* Obviously, we are assuming that the wine is consumed in moderation.

One who drinks alcoholic beverages for its own pleasure, not as part of a meal, is indulging in abusive behavior. Even if the beverage is being consumed in moderation, it is still abusive behavior. It is a tool being used by the *Yetzer Ha'Ra* and can very well lead to inappropriate and dangerous behavior, not to mention alcoholism.

✍ THE ANSWER IS THE QUESTION

"And Moshe inquired, inquired" (10:16).

*T*his verse marks the halfway point of the words in the Torah. The first "inquired" is the last word of the first half of the Torah and the second "inquired" is the first word of the second half.

The Talmud, which is basically a legal commentary on the Torah, is replete with questions and answers, inquiries and resolutions. The very center, the heart, of Torah study is inquiry. Man is a very curious creature. Children freely allow their curiosity to roam. This leads them to discoveries about the world around them. The more they learn, the more curious they become. Questions, answers, questions, answers. Most people lose this marvelous sense of curiosity as they enter adulthood. Their intellectual growth stops. The curiosity has been banished to some unknown hinterland. This verse is telling us, "Inquire! Inquire!" Never stop. Continue to grow and develop intellectually and spiritually throughout your life.

As Aristotle, in his introduction to Metaphysics, put it, "*All men by nature have a desire to know.*" The quest for knowledge is an integral part of human nature. It should never be suppressed.

The first half of the Torah ends with the word "inquire" to teach us that true learning leads to more and more questions. Those questions lead to answers which in turn lead to more questions. It is a never ending pursuit. The answer always leads to a question.

Ben Bahg Bahg states in *Pirkei Avos* (5:22) "*Turn it over and over, everything is there.*" Torah contains it all. The solutions to all of life's problems are there but we must search, ask, study and review to find them.

The Jew has been blessed with an insatiable thirst for knowledge. The Torah obligates a father to teach his young child. Education is not only part of our religion, it is part of our culture. We instill in our youth the importance of striving to reach their potential. We equate success with knowledge. No wonder Jews have had enormous success in their endeavors. Though we are a mere 1/500th of the world population, Jews have been 20% of the Nobel Prize recipients. Jews have been recognized by the Nobel committee for their contributions in the fields of chemistry, physics, economics, literature, medicine – including physiology, immunology, endocrinology, epidemiology, in addition to their contributions towards peace. Jews have excelled in journalism, philosophy, philanthropy, and of course in business.

On the other hand, there have been notorius individuals who have reached fame through less desirable means, while abandoning the noble heritage they received from their ancestors. One of the more infamous successes of the twentieth century was Leon Trotsky (born Lev Davidovich-Bronstein). He attended a typical Russian "cheder" in his youth. The creed of faith was instilled in him during those tender years, yet he lost his way. He left the Torah of his fathers and forefathers and adopted a new faith, a new religion, called Socialism. "Religion will only cease to exist completely with the development of the socialist system," he boldly proclaimed. [Note: A great-grandson of Trotsky, in Eretz Yisroel, returned to a life devoted to Torah]

Ben Bahg Bahg is telling us that we must channel our drive for success through the path of Torah. A Jew who is successful in any endeavor, whether it is in business, education, medicine, or entertainment, if it was accomplished in the light of Torah, it will be a blessing for all of Israel. Those religious Jews who were accomplished in their chosen field of endeavor were always faithful to their people. They were men of charity and compassion. They supported community projects and yeshivos. Those Jews who abandoned their faith became self-hating Jews. Not only did they no longer identify with the Jewish People, they became successful Jewish anti-Semites.

≈§ LAWS OF KASHRUS

"Make yourselves holy, be holy, for I am holy, do not defile yourselves by (eating) any swarming thing that creeps upon the earth" (11:44).

*T*ell me what you eat, and I will tell you what you are. – Anthelme Brillat-Savarin (1755–1826), French jurist, gastronome

The remainder of the *parshah* deals with the laws of kashrus and the laws of purity (*tumah* and *taharah*) with regards to food.

Until this point, the Torah has told us about the construction of the Sanctuary, its consecration, its holiness, the holy service, the sacrifices, and the eating of the sacrificial meat. Lest you think that the eating of the *korban* was a very minor part of the service, the Talmud (*Pesachim* 59b) teaches us that if the *Kohanim* did not eat the meat of the sacrifice, then there was no atonement for the one who offered it. How do we understand that? The eating of the meat seems to be just a bonus for the *Kohanim* and not an integral part of the offering service.

The purpose of the mitzvos is to instill holiness into the earthly world around us. The most holy place in the world was the *Mishkan* that rested in the center of the camp of the Israelites. The holiest group of Israelites was the *Kohanim*. The holiest food eaten by the *Kohanim* was the sacrificial meat. Holy food, consumed by holy people, in a holy place. *"Holy, holy, holy, is the Lord of Hosts; the whole earth is full of His glory"* (*Yeshaya* 6:3) Bringing together these three holies, in turn, brings the glory of Hashem into this earthly plane.

It is the goal of each and every Jew to make his home a Sanctuary: where the presence of G-d can dwell. Each and every Jew must see himself as a Temple priest performing the Divine service. Each and every Jew must be certain to eat meat which is sacred. This last statement, sacred meat, is addressed in the remainder of our *parshah*. Some foods contain metaphysical impurities. They are called *tumah*, impure or unclean. We must remove ourselves from those food items. Which foods are they? They are the non-kosher foods.

Concluding the portion of kashrus is the verse quoted above (11:44). It is interesting to note that the verse uses the word "holy" three times.

⮜ WHY DID G-D CREATE ANTS?

hy did G-d create so many non-kosher animals, if we are prohibited from eating them?

There are several answers to that question. KingShlomo said (*Mishlei* 6:6), "*Go to the ant, lazy one. See her ways and become wise.*" Each and every creature, whether it is kosher or not, can teach us a valuable lesson. The Talmud (*Eruvin* 100b) tells us that if one observes any animal carefully, it can teach a person a virtue. "*Rebbe Yochanan said: Had the Torah not been given we could have learned modesty from the cat, honesty from the ant, chastity from the dove, and good manners from the cock.*" The cat buries its feces. The ant does not steal food from another. The dove is faithful to its mate. The cock crows gently to the hen before it mates.

Another answer is provided by the Mishnah (*Makkos* 23b). G-d created many non-kosher animals in order to increase man's merits. If a person, upon seeing a horse, thinks to himself that there goes an animal whose flesh I cannot eat, he is rewarded for the thought. We are rewarded even if we have no compelling desire to eat the horse. Just remembering that it is a forbidden food contributes to our reward in the future world. If we see a non-kosher animal and we have an urge to taste its flesh, we are given a greater reward for resisting the temptation. Haven't you ever wondered what a Big Mac tastes like? Learning self-control strengthens the mind and soul.

With regards to keeping kosher, the verse says, "*Make yourselves holy, be holy, for I am holy, do not defile yourselves by (eating) any swarming thing that creeps upon the earth.*" Keeping the laws of kashrus makes one holy. How so? The Ramban (19:2) explains that holiness is achieved through self-control. Self-control leads one to conduct himself with regards to his fellow man in an honest and sincere fashion. He will not desire to obtain money through illegal or nefarious means. Self-control will enable him to conduct himself in a manner so as not to offend anyone. These are all aspects of behavior that promotes holiness. Self-control leads to holiness which establishes a closer relationship between man and his Creator.

Another reason possibly lies in the fact that everything that was created serves a purpose. Every creature, kosher or not, has its role to play in sustaining creation. There is a Medrash called *Alpha-Beta Di' Ben Sira* that has many pages devoted to showing the importance of seemingly insignificant creatures. It records the story of King David who asked G-d why He created the spider. "The spider is such an ugly creature who weaves a beautiful web that is of no use to man." G-d told David that the day will come that he will kiss the spider.

Once, David was hiding in a cave from Shaul. After David was safely inside the cave, a spider came along and wove a large web across the mouth of the cave. Shaul approached the entrance to the cave and saw the spider's web. He thought to himself that no man had recently entered the cave for he surely would have destroyed the web. Shaul departed without going inside the cave.

When David realized what had transpired, he understood that the spider saved his life. As David was leaving the cave, he saw the spider. He bent down and kissed the spider. "Blessed is your Creator and blessed are you. How glorious is G-d's creation in which everything has a purpose."

We would like to know the purpose of every living creature. Unfortunately, the only easy way to really understand the importance of a creature is to remove it from its environment and see what happens.

During the Vietnam war, American troops stationed near the jungle were pestered and pained by the annoying mosquitoes. The army sprayed the area with pesticide to kill the mosquitoes. It seems that cockroaches feed off the carcasses of mosquitoes and since there were no more mosquitoes, the cockroach population decreased sharply. There was a lizard that relied on the cockroach as a source of food. With fewer cockroaches, there were fewer lizards. The feral cats that lived near the jungle fed off the lizards. Since there were no more lizards, the cats died off. That allowed the jungle rat population to grow unchecked by their former enemy, the cat. The rats multiplied at a prodigious rate. The abundance of rats had to compete with each other to find food. That emboldened the rats and they became very aggressive. The troops were no longer bitten by the mosquitoes but were gnawed at while they slept by the ferocious rats.

Everything serves a purpose, even the lowly mosquito. If there was no purpose for mosquitoes or spiders then G-d would not have created them. The mere fact that they exist indicates that they have a role to play in the universe. We exist: you and I. We each have an important role to play. Otherwise, G-d would not have allowed us to come into existence. The journey through life is to discover that role and to fulfill it.

✑ THE FINGERNAILS OF OUR ANCESTORS

Said Rav Yochanan, "*Better were the fingernails of the earlier generations than the intestines of our own generation. (And if you think that we are better than they, consider that) the Temple was rebuilt for them and it has not been rebuilt for us*" (*Yoma* 9b).

What did Rav Yochanan mean by his odd reference to fingernails and intestines? In the simple sense, the expression is meant to allude to the notion that even the least important part of our ancestor's bodies carries more spiritual value than the more important part of our own bodies. Why, though, did he mention specifically "fingernails and intestines" and not more obviously contrasting body parts such as heels and head?

The Vilna Gaon (*Kol Eliyahu* 201 & *Perush Al Kamah Agados*) offers a deeper explanation. The Torah gives the guidelines for determining which animals are permissible to be eaten. There are two signs which an animal must have in order to be kosher. The first sign is that the animal must ruminate (chew its cud). This is an internal sign since the stomach system is inside the animal. The second sign is that it must have split hooves. The sign of split hooves is external; it can be seen on the outside of the animal.

These two signs of a kosher animal indicate that the animal is not a beast of prey. Such an animal does not feed upon other animals but rather its eats the grasses and vegetation of the ground. A hunting animal does not chew its cud since meat is digestible without rumination. Once the prey is digested, the predator seeks new food, ever discontent and constantly ravenous. A ruminant, on the other hand, is content with whatever is already in its stomach. After partially digesting the food, the animal brings the food up to its mouth and chews again, thus helping to further satisfy its hunger. A hunting animal possesses claws with which to tear its victims apart. A kosher animal is satisfied with the food its Creator brings forth from the ground. It has no need for claws and thus it has hooves.

The Torah specifically mentioned four animals which have only one of the two signs of a kosher animal – the camel, the rabbit, the hare, and the pig. The first three all ruminate but do not have split hooves. They have the internal sign but not the external sign. The pig has split hooves but does not ruminate. It has the external sign but not the internal one. In spite of the fact that these four do posses one of the signs of being kosher, they are still completely unkosher.

The Medrash (*Vayikrah Rabbah* 13:5) tells us that these four animals are represented by the four great kingdoms that have subjugated the Jewish people: Babylonia, Persia, Greece, and Rome. The first three are represented, respectively, by the camel, the rabbit, and the hare; the fourth, Rome, is represented by the pig.

The first three non-kosher animals mentioned in the Torah only had the internal sign of kashrus. On the outside they displayed their claws. The first three kingdoms also had the internal sign; they believed in G-d and His Divine providence. But, on the outside they displayed their claws. They were like the beasts of prey, seeking wealth and self-aggrandizement at the expense of others. The Roman Empire, however, displayed all the external signs of commitment to spirituality. Externally they seemed quite civilized. They looked after human welfare and preached justice and human rights. Inwardly, though, it believed in nothing but self – worship.

After the destruction of the First *Bais HaMikdash*, the Jewish people were exiled among the first three of these four nations. When the second *Bais HaMikdash* was destroyed, we became subjugated to the Roman Empire. In light of the above Medrash, it is clear that Hashem chose our oppressors in a most befitting manner. The Talmud (*Yoma* 9a) says, "*Why was the First Bais HaMikdash destroyed? On account of the three cardinal sins: idolatry, sexual immorality, and murder. But why was the Second Bais Hamikdash destroyed since the Jews were busily studying Torah and performing Mitzvos? It was destroyed because they hated each other without cause. From this we learn that baseless hatred is as great a sin as idolatry, immorality, and murder all together.*"

The earlier generations suffered from serious evil in their external behavior: idolatry, immorality, and murder. Internally, in their hearts, they acknowledged G-d's kingship. Therefore they were exiled and subjugated by the kingdoms that only had the internal sign but lacked the external sign.

The later generations, in the time of the Second *Bais HaMikdash*, were like the pig. They had the external sign, they studied and did mitzvos, but they lacked the internal sign. In their hearts, they hated without cause. They loved only themselves. They were exiled and subjugated by Rome which also had the external sign but lacked the internal one.

This, the Vilna Gaon says, explains Rav Yochanan's comment about fingernails and intestines. The "fingernails" he mentioned allude to the "claws" (as opposed to cloven hooves) of the hunting animal. The fingernails represent the external sins of the earlier generations. The "intestines" he mentioned refer to the internal organs and represents the internal sins of the generation of the Second *Bais HaMikdash*. Rav Yochanan's comment can now be understood as follows, "Better one who behaves like a beast of prey, but whose heart longs for G-d, than the most sanctimonious of men, who, in his heart, worships only himself!"

[Based on Rabbi A. Feldman's translation in "The Juggler and the King," Feldheim, 1990 as presented by Rabbi Mordechai Kornfeld http://www.dafyomi.co.il/.]

✒ SOCIALLY REDEEMING VALUES

"And the swine because it has split hooves, completely split, but its cud it does not chew, it is unclean to you" (11:7).

The *Kli Yakar* asks about the odd wording in this verse. The swine has the external sign of kashrus. It has split hooves. It lacks the internal sign, chewing its cud. Why then did the verse say that it is unclean "because it has split hooves" – that it the sign of being kosher? It should have written it is unclean "because it does not chew its cud." This same oddity is found by all four of the mentioned non-kosher animals: camel, rabbit, hare, swine.

The *Kli Yakar* answers by referring to the Medrash (*Vayikra Rabbah* 13:5, quoted earlier) that says the four animals are personified by the four nations that subjugated the Jewish People. How did it come to be that, of all the nations of the world, only these four were able to conquer the Jews? The answer is that the Jewish people had very high moral and ethical standards. Though they may not have always adhered to them, they were their standards. All the other nations of the world were so barbaric and devoid of any redeeming social value that the Jews had no contact or interaction with them. The Jews could not relate to such barbarism. Thus, those nations had no influence on the Jewish People.

The Empires of Babylon, Persia, Greece, and Rome all had socially redeeming aspects. The Babylonians made great advances in mathematics. The Persian were great poets. The Greeks were known for their sculpture and art. Rome was known for their advances in philosophy. It was because of these social values that the Jews allowed themselves to have some contact with these nations. They could relate to and appreciate them to some degree. This contact led to the empires exerting great influence upon the Jews and, before they realized it, they were subjugated by these nations.

The *Kli Yakar* explains that it was the kosher sign of the swine that created the problem. The swine stuck out its feet and said, "Look! I'm kosher, I'm civilized. I will teach you many wonderful things." And the Jewish People allowed the swine in. Therefore, the Torah said that it is because of the kosher sign that they are a danger and are to be deemed unclean.

100% GLATT KOSHER

Another wonderful lesson taught to us by the unclean swine is that to be a kosher Jew, one must have the inner and the outer signs of a Jew. Dressing with all the external trappings of a fine religious person is not enough. Having the fanciest *tallis* and the nicest esrog alone does not make one a complete Jew. The swine also has the external trappings but a pig with a *kipah* is still a pig. One must be a Jew on the inside as well. He must be compassionate, kind, and considerate.

As Rabbi Yosef Breuer would say, "*One must not only be Glatt Kosher, he must also be Glatt Yosher* (straight and honest)."

One of the prohibited birds that the Torah specifically mentioned is the *chassida*, the stork. Rashi explains that the stork is called *chassida* because it acts with kindness in sharing its food with other storks. *Chassidah* comes from the word *chassid*, kind-hearted. One would think that a bird with a name like *chassida* would be kosher. Kindness is a very kosher trait.

In fact, the stork is not kosher. It is kind only to other storks. It will not share food with other species. In order for a Jew to be kosher, he must be kind not only to members of his own sect – whether it be Ashkenazi, Sefardi, Chassidush or any other type of grouping – he must extend kindness to everyone. True kindness knows no boundaries. It has no limitations or prejudices.

✌ THE MITZVOS

The 153ʳᵈ mitzvah in the Torah is to ascertain that the meat we are eating is kosher.
"These are the animals which you may eat from among all the animals that are upon the earth. All that has split hooves, completely split and chews its cud" (**11:2-3**).
The 154ᵗʰ mitzvah in the Torah is the prohibition to eat non-kosher meat.
"However, these you may not eat..." (**11:4**).
The 155ᵗʰ mitzvah in the Torah is to ascertain that the fish we are consuming is kosher.
"From that which is in the water, these you may eat. All that has fins and scales..." (**11:9**).
The 156ᵗʰ mitzvah in the Torah is the prohibition to eat non-kosher fish.
"All (sea animals) that have no fins and scales... from their flesh you shall not eat..." (**11:10-11**).
The 157ᵗʰ mitzvah in the Torah is the prohibition to eat non-kosher fowl.
"These abominations from among the fowl you may not eat..." (**11:13**).

The 158ᵗʰ mitzvah in the Torah is to ascertain that an insect is kosher, (assuming he desires to eat it).
"These you may eat from among the winged insects..." **(11:21).**

Rashi points out that we are no longer certain which insects are kosher and therefore we do not eat any. In addition, in western culture, eating insects, in general, is considered repulsive and there is little interest in determining which ones may be kosher. However, from a nutritional point of view, insects are very high in protein.

The 159ᵗʰ mitzvah in the Torah is to observe the laws of purity and uncleanliness (*tumah* and *taharah*) with regards to these creatures.
"And (the carcasses of) these (eight) are unclean (tamei) among the detestable animals that swarm the earth – the weasel, the mouse, the toad and its related species, the hedgehog, the lizard, the crocodile, the snail, and the mole" **(11:29-30).**

There are various opinions as to the exact translation of the eight creatures.

The 160ᵗʰ mitzvah in the Torah is to observe the laws of purity and uncleanliness (*tumah* and *taharah*) with regards to food items.
"All foods which may be eaten... can become unclean" **(11:34).**

The 161ˢᵗ mitzvah in the Torah is to observe the laws of purity and uncleanliness (*tumah* and *taharah*) with regards to animal carcasses.
"When an animal, which could have been to you a food, dies, whoever touches the carcass shall be unclean until the evening" **(11:39).**

The 162ⁿᵈ mitzvah in the Torah is the prohibition to eat swarming creatures.
"All swarming creatures that swarm upon the earth are

detestable and it may not be eaten" (11:41).

Swarming creatures, as defined by our Sages, are creatures whose abdomen is very close to the ground. This would include insects, rodents, snakes, worms, centipedes etc.

The 163ʳᵈ mitzvah in the Torah is the prohibition to eat those insects that were born inside the fruit but have subsequently been exposed to the earth.

"That which swarms upon the earth you may not eat of them" (11:42).

"Swarms upon the earth" refers to insects which fly about over the earth or insects that crawl upon the earth. Insects that are born inside fruits or vegetables are not prohibited because they are not exposed to the surface of the earth. However, once those insects come out of the fruit or vegetable, they are then exposed to the earth and are forbidden.

The 164ᵗʰ mitzvah in the Torah is the prohibition to eat creatures that swarm in the waters.

"Make not yourself detestable through any swarming thing" (11:43).

The Rambam (*Forbidden Foods* 2:12) explains that since this verse did not mention "earth," it comes to teach us about creatures that swarm in the waters of the rivers, lakes, and oceans. He defines those creatures to be anything that does not resemble a fish at all. That would include lobsters, clams, snails, jellyfish, etc.

The 165ᵗʰ mitzvah in the Torah is the prohibition to eat "creeping" insects.

"Do not defile yourselves with any swarming thing that creeps upon the earth" (11:44).

The Rambam (*Forbidden Foods* 2:12) says that this verse contains a special prohibition for insects that begin their life cycle feeding on decaying matter. The most common example would be maggots. The Rambam explained this to be the definition of the Biblical term *"creep"* which this verse used.

✑ HAFTORAH SHMINI

THE *HAFTORAH* IS FOUND IN *SHMUEL* II 6:1 – 7:17.

K ing David desired to build the *First Bais HaMikdash* in the holy city of Jerusalem. Anticipating that event, he had the Holy Ark brought from Baale-Yehudah to the capital city. A wagon was made especially to transport the Ark. The wagon was drawn by a team of oxen. The team was led by Uzzah and his brother. King David and 30,000 Israelites escorted the wagon on its journey. There was singing and dancing accompanied by musical instruments beyond counting. The joy and celebration were overwhelming. Suddenly, the team of oxen was startled and backed up. The wagon tilted and it seemed that the Ark was going to fall off. Uzzah grabbed the Ark to steady it. Uzzah fell to the ground next to the Ark: dead.

David blamed himself for the death of Uzzah. In this time of joy he forgot about the dignity of the Ark. How could he allow the Ark to be brought to Jerusalem in a wagon? The Ark was supposed to be carried on the shoulders of the Levites. How could he allow Uzzah and his brother to travel in front of the Ark. They had their backs to the most holy possession of Israel. How could he allow Uzzah to touch the Ark. No one was ever allowed to touch it. Even if it seemed that the Ark was about to fall, one may not touch the Ark. If necessity demanded, the Ark could carry itself. It did not need man's help (*Sotah* 35a).

This incident is found in *Shmuel* II, chapter 6. Coincidently enough the same chapter relates another incident that parallels the *haftorah*. The Philistines had captured the Holy Ark and brought it to their land. A plague broke out and the Philistine priests advised sending the Ark back to the Israelites. They fashioned a new wagon and placed the Ark in it. A team of oxen was hitched to the wagon and the oxen, without any guidance, brought the Ark back home to Bait Shemesh.

Many men of Bait Shemesh were curious as to what the tablets inside the Ark looked like. They opened the Ark to peer inside. Suddenly, a great death occurred among those men.

David should have taken lesson from that incident. If it was the

Divine will that oxen transport the Ark, then the oxen would have gone on their own accord down the proper route. They would not have needed Uzzah and his brother to guide them (*Malbim*).

The great joy of bringing the Ark to Jerusalem was marred by the death of Uzzah just as the joy of consecrating the *Mishkan* was marred by the death of Nadav and Avihu.

Unlike the consecration of the *Mishkan,* the procession stopped and the Ark was brought to the house of a Levite, Oved-Edom, for safe-keeping. It was kept there with honor and dignity for three months. The house of Oved-Edom was blessed on account of the Ark. Mistreatment of the Ark brings plagues and death. Proper treatment brings blessing.

After three months, the Ark was brought the rest of the way to Jerusalem. Again there was great joy and celebration. King David, wearing very simple clothing, jumped and danced as if he was a simple Jew. His wife, Michal, saw her husband acting like a commoner and was very displeased. She was the daughter of King Shaul and never once saw her father behave in anything less than a regal fashion. David explained to her that when it came to honoring G-d and His Ark, everyone was a commoner. Michal did not accept her husband's explanation. Michal was punished by G-d and though she had one child from King David, she would not give birth to another until the very day of her death. She died giving birth to her second son (*Rashi* 6:23 & 3:5).

At this point the *haftorah* ends according to the Sephardic custom. However, the Azkenazim continued the sequence of events.

The Ark was brought to Jerusalem. King David began preparing to build the *First Bais HaMikdash.* Nosson the prophet gave his blessing; but, it was not to be. G-d appeared to Nosson and told him to tell King David that he was not to build the *Bais Hamikdash.* That task would be left to his son Shlomo. G-d promised King David that He would be with Shlomo all his days and that a royal dynasty would issue forth from King David.

TAZRIA

❧ TO BE OR GNAT TO BE

"If a man does not act in a meritorious way, say to him, 'The gnat preceded you'" (*Vayikra Rabbah* 14:1, introduction to *parshas Tazriah*).

This *parshah* begins with the mitzvah of circumcision and the laws of impurity for a woman who gave birth. It then proceeds to outline the laws of *tzara'as*, commonly translated as leprosy. The preceding *parshah* concluded with the laws of impurity with regards to animals and animal carcasses. The question is asked why the laws regarding animals were written before the laws regarding man. Is not man more important than an animal?

Rashi (12:2) answers the question by stating that just as the creation of man took place after the creation of the animals so too are the laws regarding man recorded after the laws regarding the animals.

What does the creation of animals and man have to do with the laws regarding animals and man? Why should one follow the pattern of the other?

The Medrash (*Bereishis Rabbah* 1:1) says that G-d looked into His Torah and created the world. Thus, the Torah was the blueprint for creation. Everything in this universe has its source in the blueprint of Torah. There is a very real relationship between the creation and Torah. Since the creation of man was preceded by the creation of animals, the Torah's laws pertaining to man must be preceded by the laws pertaining to animals.

When the Torah teaches us that the order of creation is patterned after the Torah itself, it is conveying a very important lesson. When a man builds a house, first he digs the foundation, then he sets up the walls, and finally he puts on a roof. The most important part of a shelter is its roof. The least important part is the foundation. Yet, the foundation was dug first and the roof was put on last. From this we see that the more important part is made at the end. Man was created at the end of the six days of creation. Man was the climax of creation. He is the most important entity in the entire universe. He was instilled with abilities that nothing else in creation has. Man can think, reason, invent, create, decide, talk and communicate. Only Man can study Torah, follow its precepts, and derive all kinds of wonderful lessons and observations from its words.

The Evolutionists believe that everything evolved by chance. Creatures evolved by chance and those well-suited to survive in their environment did so; those ill-suited for survival in their environment did not. This is called the Spencerian theory of the "survival of the fittest." According to them, man is no more important than a gnat. Both evolved by chance. Both were well suited to survive in their surroundings. One is not more important than the other. From their perspective, one can be happy not be a gnat, but one can not claim superiority.

According to that philosophy, there is no compelling reason for us to behave better than a gnat: other than it creates a more comfortable society. There is no right or wrong, good or evil. There is only comfort and discomfort. Evolutionists think that it should be illegal to steal and murder, not because it is morally wrong or evil but, because it would not be a comfortable life knowing that someone could enter your home and legally take your possessions or even legally kill you. So, in order to live a more comfortable life-style, laws were created by man.

The Torah is teaching us that there is a sequence of importance in creation. Man is the most important thing. Following the pattern established in the Torah, our *parshah* details laws of impurity of man after having concluded these laws for animals. Man, creation, and Torah are inextricably bound together. There is right and wrong, good and evil. One who does not believe this and thinks everything evolved by chance, to him you can say, *"The gnat preceded you."* That lowly insect was created before you. You are less significant than the gnat.

The Medrash (*Tanchuma Pekudai* 3) says that a person is a universe in miniature. Just as the universe was conceived by G-d and culminated with the formation of a male, Adam, our *parshah* begins with the conception of a mother which culminated with the birth of a child.

ONE HUNDRED CRIES

"A woman who has seed and gives birth to a son, she shall be unclean seven days..." (12:2).

We can readily understand that uncleanliness is associated with death. The separation of life from the body is an unpleasant concept. The body loses all vitality and functionality. That a corpse is deemed ritually unclean is very logical. But, why is birth also associated with uncleanliness? The miracle of life is welcomed and treasured. Birth should herald a higher degree of sanctity rather than a state of uncleanliness.

The mitzvah that epitomizes *Rosh HaShanah* is the mitzvah of blowing the *shofar*. The *shofar* is blown at the beginning of the *Mussaf* prayers and at its conclusion. Altogether, we hear one hundred blasts of the *shofar*. What do these one hundred *shofar* sounds represent?

The Talmud (*Rosh HaShanah* 34a) tells us that the sound of the *shofar* is the sound of crying and moaning. On *Rosh HaShanah* we hear the *shofar* cry and moan one hundred times. In two places we find one hundred cries and moans. The *Tur Shulchan Orech* (592, quoting *Sefer HaAruch*) says that when the enemy general, Sisera, was killed in battle, Sisera's mother cried over his death one hundred cries. The Medrash (*Vayikra Rabbah* 27:7) says that the pain of childbirth causes the mother to cry out one hundred times. So, we find that one hundred cries are associated with death and with birth.

One of my Rabbis, Rabbi Leibel Reznick, explained that the *shofar* sounded at the beginning of the *Mussaf* service represents the cries of birth which are heard at the beginning of life. The *shofar* sounded at the end of the service represents the cries of death which are heard at the conclusion of life.

When the Children of Israel stood near Mount Sinai, they were forbidden to come near the mountain while the Divine Presence was there. The mountain was in a state of holiness. After, the Divine Presence departed, the mountain was no longer holy and there was no restriction to approach the mountain. How did the people know when the Divine Presence departed? The Torah (*Shmos* 19:13) says that the sound of a *shofar* was heard. That *shofar* signaled that the holiness had left.

Our Sages tell us that when a fetus is in its mother's womb, it is being taught all of the Torah by an angel. It is as though the fetus is at Mount Sinai receiving the Torah. It is in a state of great holiness. When the child is born, all the Torah taught to it is forgotten. The holiness has left. The mother cries one hundred times at birth. She thinks that it is because of the pain; but, in fact, her voice is the sound of the *shofar* signaling that the holiness is departing.

During the lifetime of a person, he is supposed to strive to regain that lost holiness. The mitzvos and good deeds that he does fill his soul with holiness. When he dies, that holy soul departs. Once again, the holiness has left and once again one hundred cries are heard.

On both occasions, birth and death, holiness has departed. It is the departure of holiness that causes the state of uncleanliness.

The Kotzker Rebbe also gives loss of holiness as the reason for impurity, but he adds another dimension. The verse (*Bereishis* 4:1) quotes Eve after the birth of her firstborn, *"I have acquired a male with G-d."* What did Eve mean when she said *"with G-d?"* She intimated that just as G-d is a Creator, He endowed woman also with the creative power to form another human being. During her pregnancy, she was like a partner with G-d. However, after she gives birth she is no longer on that lofty level of a partnership with G-d; thus, the impurity sets in. If one gives thought to pregnancy in the light of the mother forming a closer association with G-d, it makes the thought of an abortion all the more chilling.

The woman who gave birth immerses in a *mikvah* on the seventh day of uncleanliness; following sunset, the wife and husband are permitted relations. However she is not totally clean until she offers her sacrifices (12:2,4). During that time period, she may not touch or eat sacrificial meat. If the mother gives birth to a male child, the sacrificial meat will become permissible after 40 days. If she gives birth to a female child, her purification process will not be completed until after 80 days. Why does it take longer to become pure after the birth of a female child than after a male? A mother who is pregnant with a female fetus is a creator soon to give birth to another creator. Her bond with G-d is even greater. Therefore, when that bond of holiness ends, the state of impurity is greater.

◦§ BIRTH & DEATH

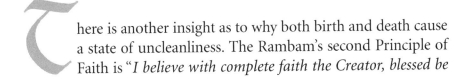

here is another insight as to why both birth and death cause a state of uncleanliness. The Rambam's second Principle of Faith is *"I believe with complete faith the Creator, blessed be*

His name, is unique and that there is no uniqueness that compares to Him in any way; He was, He is, and He will always be."

G-d is eternal, infinite. That is something so unique that it is beyond comprehension. We cannot imagine that G-d existed even before time was created. G-d had no beginning and has no end. He is above time. Everything in this world had a beginning and will have an end. Everything has a birth and will have a demise. Birth and death are the most remote concepts from G-d's uniqueness. Therefore, the Torah decreed that birth and death are so ungodly as to create a state of impurity.

✑ X & Y

"A woman who has seed and gives birth to a son..." (12:2).

The Talmud (*Berachos* 61a) explains the verse, "*A woman who has seed*" refers to a woman who has ovulated and has deposited the egg cell in the womb. The Talmud continues to relate that if the woman ovulated before the male sperm cell has reached the womb, then the child will be a male. If the sperm reached the womb before the woman ovulated, the child will be a female. Therefore, the interpretation of the verse is – *If a woman who has seed*, meaning she ovulated before the sperm cell reached the womb, she *will give birth to a son*.

That bit of medical information was written almost two thousand years ago and was not confirmed by medical researchers until quite recently. The medical science behind the Talmud's statement is as follows:

If a sperm cell carrying a Y chromosome fertilizes the egg, a boy will be conceived. If a sperm cell containing an X chromosome fertilizes the egg, a girl will be conceived. Studies have shown that Y chromosome cells are much more "aggressive" than X chromosome cells. However, the X chromosome cell has a much longer "life span" than the Y chromosome cell. If the woman has already ovulated, then the more "aggressive" Y chromosome sperm cell will fertilize the egg and the child will be a boy. If ovulation has not yet occurred, the sperm cells must "wait" until ovulation occurs. During this time, the short-lived Y chromosomes will have died out and the only cells left are the longer-lived X cells. The child will be a girl.

How remarkable it is that the Sages, who lived before the advent of the microscope, before cells were discovered, before chromosomes were known, knew that to be true. How did they know it? It was a *pasuk* in the Torah!

ABSENCE MAKES THE HEART GROW FONDER

"Unclean she shall be for seven days" (12:2).

Marital relations between a husband and his wife, who just gave birth, are forbidden. The *Netziv* (*Ha'amek Davar* 12:2) gives a beautiful reason for this *halachah*. The Talmud (*Nidah* 31b) says that one reason why marital relations are forbidden during the menstrual period is so that the couple will have the opportunity to renew their relationship. They will not take each other for granted. The fact that even physical contact between the two is not allowed will enable their longing and desire for each other to regenerate and grow. This helps to prevent the relationship from becoming stale.

During the months of pregnancy, the menstrual period ceases. Physical relations are permitted with no restrictions. Like any pleasure in life, unrestricted and unlimited pleasure will eventually lose its luster. When the wife gives birth, she is considered unclean. She and her husband must once again separate. The husband will once again long for his wife. The separation is beneficial for both husband and wife. It prevents their relationship from becoming habitual. It will aid the husband to regard his wife as dearly as he did when they were newlyweds. The Torah is giving the new father and mother the opportunity to once again revitalize their bond of love.

MAN'S DEEDS ARE FINER THAN HEAVEN'S

"And on the eighth day you shall circumcise the foreskin" (12:3).

In the teachings of Chassidus, we find an interesting reason why circumcision is performed on the eighth day. The number seven represents the physical world, which was created in seven days. Birth and the reproduction of species are natural occurrences that happen only in this physical world. Birth causes the mother to become unclean. Impurity and uncleanliness are concepts that only apply to this physical world of material substance.

The number eight represents the supernatural, that which is above and beyond the natural world, the realm of spirituality. Circumcision represents the idea that man is not born perfect. He must seek to improve himself spiritually. Since spirituality is symbolized by the number eight, the circumcision is performed on the eighth day.

The Medrash (*Tanchumah Tazria* 5) records that the evil governor Turnus Rufus asked Rebbe Akiva, whose deeds are finer, G-d's or man's?. Rebbe Akiva answered that man's deeds are finer. Turnus Rufus was astounded and asked if man can create heaven and earth. Rebbe Akiva pressed Turnus Rufus to ask what was really on his mind and not beat around the proverbial bush. Turnus Rufus agreed and proceeded to ask that if G-d is perfect, He must have created a perfect man. Why does a newborn need to be circumcised? Rebbe Akiva responded that he knew from the outset that this was Turnus Rufus's question. That is why Rebbe Akiva told him that man's deeds are finer than G-d's. G-d created an imperfect world. Our task is to finish G-d's work and improve it physically and spiritually. G-d created the fetus; yet it still requires the mother to sever the umbilical cord so that the child can physically survive in this world. Eight days later it is the task of the father to circumcise the child so it can survive spiritually in this world. G-d began creation; it is our task to complete it, both physically, through hard work, and spiritually, through the Torah and the mitzvos.

Circumcision represents the striving towards perfection through the Torah and the mitzvos.

❧ "THE SINS OF THE FATHERS ARE VISITED UPON THE CHILDREN"

(SHMOS 20:5)

"And when the days of her purification are completed for a son or a daughter, she shall bring... a young pigeon or a turtle-dove for a sin offering" (12:6).

The question has often been asked as to why a mother who gave birth must bring a sin-offering. What did she do wrong?

The Talmud (*Nidah* 31b) suggests that a mother who is undergoing the severe pains of labor will swear never to bear children again. It is for that sin of swearing that she must offer a sin-offering.

However, the *Ran* (*Nedarim* 4a) explains that the Talmud quoted above is merely *drush* (homiletics). Even if a woman is very certain that she made no such oath, she still has to bring a sin-offering. However, the Talmud cannot be totally ignored. Even when our Sages give a homiletic interpretation to a verse, though it may not be a totally accurate explanation of the verse, called *p'shat*, it does contain a kernel of truth as the true explanation. The key here is that there is a connection between the sin-offering and the pains of childbirth.

Why does a woman undergo such terrible pain while giving birth? The Torah itself provides the answer. After Adam and Eve ate from the Tree of Knowledge, they were punished. G-d told Eve, "*I will greatly increase your suffering and your childbearing, in pain you shall bear children*" (*Bereishis* 3:16). Eve's sin not only affected herself, it affected each and every descendant of hers. Every mother that gives birth is experiencing the punishment for the sin of Eve. Therefore, we can suggest that each and every mother brings a sin-offering to show that she suffered from the sin of Eve.

One may argue that this is simply not fair. Why should the children suffer for the sins of the parents? Whether it is fair or not really doesn't matter; it is a fact of life. For example, if a parent exposes a child to immoral, unethical, sinful acts, the chances are that the grandchildren and great-grandchildren will still suffer those effects. Of course, the converse is also true. A child that is raised in a nurturing, loving, Torah home will probably have children that are loving, caring, and adhere to the Torah and its mitzvos.

The mother who just gave birth is about to embark on the child-rearing experience. It is at this point that the Torah wants her to realize that her actions, both positive and adverse, will affect her children and their children for many generations.

✑ COMPASSION, EVEN TOWARDS BIRDS

"She shall bring... a young pigeon or a turtle dove for a sin-offering" (12:6).

T he *Baal HaTurim* makes a wonderfully amazing comment on this verse. First, he wonders why the young pigeon is mentioned before the turtledove. In every instance where pigeons and turtledoves are mentioned, (there are 10), turtledoves are mentioned first, except here. Why?

The *Baal HaTurim* explains that turtledoves choose a mate for life. Even after the spouse has died, the noble turtledove will not take another mate. This is not true of pigeons or any other bird. A woman who gave birth must bring a single bird for a sin-offering. The pigeon is mentioned first to encourage the woman who gave birth to choose a pigeon. That pigeon's mate will find another spouse when she realizes her mate has been taken away. It is better to take the pigeon than take a turtledove because the remaining turtledove would spend the rest of her days mourning the loss of her mate.

Perhaps, the *Baal Haturim* was implying that everywhere else, when two birds are required for the sacrifice, the one offering the sacrifice will bring a mated pair. In that way, both the male and female will be used in the holy service and neither one will be left behind to mourn. Since both turtledoves are used, the Torah mentions them before the pigeons in order to acknowledge their faithfulness to each other.

The Torah is teaching us that we must think of how our actions will affect all creatures, even animals and birds. We must be considerate of their feelings. The implication is obvious. If we must be compassionate towards birds, which were created to be of service to man, how much more so we must be compassionate towards man, who was created to serve his Creator.

⤙ THE MITZVOS

The 166ᵗʰ mitzvah in the Torah is for a mother who gave birth to observe all the laws of uncleanliness that

apply to her.
"If a woman who has seed gives birth..." (12:2).
The 167ᵗʰ mitzvah in the Torah is the prohibition for a woman who gave birth, and has not completed her days of purification, to eat sacrificial meat.
"She shall not touch any holy thing and into the Sanctuary she shall not come..." (12:4).
The 168ᵗʰ mitzvah in the Torah is for the mother to bring her offering when her days of purification are completed.
"And when the days of her purification are complete, for a son or daughter, she shall bring a year old sheep..." (12:6).

≈ "LIFE AND DEATH IS IN THE HAND OF THE TONGUE"

(MISHLEI 18:21)

"If a man will have on his skin a 'sh'es'-plague or a 'sapachas'-plague or a 'baheres'-plague..." (13:2).

Rebbe Samuel bar Nahmani said in the name of Rebbe Yochanan: Tzara'as ("leprosy") comes because of seven things – slander, the shedding of blood, vain oath, adultery, arrogance, robbery and envy (Arachin 16a).

This list of seven things seems very odd. How could the same punishment of *tzara'as* come because of slander or envy and also because of murder or adultery? Surely murder and adultery are much more serious a sin and should require a much greater punishment.

The Talmud (quoted above) shows how *tzara'as* is associated with all seven sins. The connection between *tzara'as* and murder is based on the incident involving Avner and Yoav. King David made peace with his former enemy Avner. Yoav, David's chief of staff, wanted Avner killed. Yoav sent messengers to tell Avner that David wished to speak to him. It was not true; Yoav merely wanted Avner in his presence so he could kill him. The messengers told the lie to Avner. When Aver came near the palace, Yoav killed him. When David heard what had transpired, he cursed the messengers that they should be afflicted with *tzara'as* (See II *Shmuel* 3).

In other words, those who were stricken with *tzara'as* for "committing murder" did not actually commit the murder. They were only complicit in the crime by telling the lie. It is obvious that the punishment for actually committing murder is much more severe than *tzara'as*. It is a capital offence. But, rather, the Talmud is describing the great potential harm of ill spoken words, words that can even lead to murder.

The connection between *tzara'as* and adultery is based on the incident involving Pharaoh and Sarah. Pharaoh wanted Sarah for a wife though she was already married to Avraham. Sarah was brought before Pharaoh and he spoke to her in a very lascivious manner. As a result, Pharaoh was afflicted with *tzara'as* (See *Bereishis* 12). Pharaoh did not physically commit adultery, only verbally. For that he was punished with this plague.

We see that when the Talmud said there are seven sins which are punished with this plague, all seven have the same one factor in common. All seven are not sins physically carried out with the hands or other external organs. All seven are sins commited by the tongue. All seven represent misspoken words. We call this *lashon ha'ra*.

The *Orchos Tzadikkim* (*chapter* 25) has a wonderful parable regarding *lashon ha'ra*:

> *It once happened that the king of Persia became ill.*
> *The royal physician told the ailing king that the only cure*
> *was the milk from a lioness. One brave member of the*
> *king's court volunteered to procure milk from a lioness. He*

asked the king for ten goats to take with him and then he set off.

Not long after, he came to the den of a lioness who was nursing her cubs. The first day he stood at a distance from the den and tossed the lioness one goat. The second day he came a bit closer and tossed the second goat. By the tenth day he was inside the den stroking the lioness. He was able to get milk from the beast and then began his journey back to the king's palace.

When night fell, he went to sleep and had a dream. In the dream all the organs of the body were arguing with one another. The feet said, "No one is like us for we brought the man to the lion's den." The hands argued that had it not been for them the man would not have been able to milk the lioness. The eyes claimed that had it not been for them the man would not have seen the lioness's den. And, so, all the organs argued and argued. The tongue spoke up, "Had it not been for me, the man would not have been able to volunteer to bring the milk." All the other organs banded together and mocked, "How dare you compare yourself to us, you slimy creature who wells in the saliva of the mouth." The tongue replied, "Soon the day will come when you all will admit that I am superior to all of you."

The man awoke the next morning and recalled the dream. Soon he was before the king. The king asked, "Were you successful?" The man replied, "Yes, my noble king, I was able to procure the milk of a dog." "A dog?" snapped the king. "I waited in agony until you returned and you brought back the milk of a dog? Off with his head!" shouted the angry king to one of his royal henchmen.

As the man was being carried off to be executed, the limbs began to bitterly protest to the tongue. "How dare you say that it was the milk of a dog? You are getting all of us executed, you worthless and spineless organ. The tongue replied, "If I save all of you, will you confess that I am your superior?" All the limbs agreed to the demand.

As the henchman was about to execute him, the man spoke up, "Please, my noble henchman, please let me appear before the king, There was something important I forgot to tell him. Afterwards, you may get on with your work." The henchman brought him before the king and said, "Your majesty, in all the confusion I forgot to tell you that in my humble village we refer to lionesses as dogs. The king was somewhat skeptical but drank the milk the man had brought back. The king was cured and the man was spared. All the limbs admitted that the tongue was their superior.

Moral: Life and death is in the hands of the tongue.

HE WHO HAS HIMSELF AS A PATIENT, HAS A FOOL FOR A DOCTOR

"And the Kohen shall see the plague..." (13:3).

Why does the afflicted person have to consult a *Kohen*? Why can he not decide for himself if it is the plague? *Tzara'as* comes because of character flaws such as gossip and envy. If this fellow was such a good judge of himself, how did he get into this mess in the first place? Why didn't he see those flaws and correct them? The eyes are located on the outside of the head. The person can see everyone, everyone except himself. Perhaps it would have been better to locate them inside the head so he could keep on eye on his tongue.

‎‏≈‎‏ THE SOUL OF HIS FLOCK

"And the Kohen shall see the plague on the skin of the flesh..." (13:3).

"And if the plague is greenish or reddish on a garment... it shall be shown to the Kohen ..." (13:49).

"The Kohen shall go and see the house and he shall look at the plague..." (14:36-37).

*T*zara'as can afflict a person, a garment, or a house. In all three cases the plague must first be seen and examined by a *Kohen* before a decision can be rendered if uncleanliness is present. Why did the Torah insist that a *Kohen* actually see the plague before rendering a decision? By all other questions in *halachah* one merely has to verbally convey the question to a rabbinical authority. The Rabbi does not have to see the dairy spoon that was washed with meat dishes to render a decision as to what course of action is to be taken. Also, why here is it necessary to have a *Kohen* examine the plague. Why not have one of the wise elders who has expertise in this area render the decision?

The Talmud (*Berachos* 28a) relates that Rabban Gamaliel head of the yeshiva in Yavneh had a series of debates with Rebbe Yehoshua. Throughout those debates, Rabban Gamliel was very abusive towards Rebbe Yehoshua. Because of that, Rabban Gamliel was removed from his position and it was given over to the eighteen-year old Rebbe Eleazer ben Azariah. On the same day that Rebbe Eleazer was appointed to be the head, another debate took place between Rabban Gamliel and Rebbe Yehoshua. The matter was voted upon and Rebbe Yehoshua's point of view prevailed. When Rabban Gamliel saw that Rebbe Yehoshua was held in such high regard by his colleagues, Rabban Gamliel decided to pay a personal visit to Rebbe Yehoshua at home. When he reached Rebbe Yeoshua's home, he saw that the walls of the house were covered with a thick layer of black soot. Rabban Gamliel remarked that he sees that Rebbe Yehoshua must have a very successful blacksmith business for himself which accounts for all the soot on the walls. Rebbe Yehoshua responded, "Woe to the generation of which you are their leader for you know nothing of the troubles of the scholars and their struggles to support and sustain themselves!" Rabban Gamliel said, "I apologize. Forgive me."

Rebbe Yehoshua did not have a thriving blacksmith business. He lived in poverty and squalor in order to be able to devote his time to Torah studies. Rabban Gamliel was a wealthy aristocrat. He had never seen poverty first hand. He assumed that a comfortable lifestyle was readily attainable. He did not understand the suffering and sacrifice Rebbe Yehoshua experienced in order to learn Torah. Had he understood Rebbe Yehoshua's great dedication, he would have appreciated him more and would not have abused him.

The *Kohanim* were the spiritual leaders of Israel. As the prophet Malachai said, "*The lips of the Kohen shall safeguard knowledge, the people shall seek teaching from his mouth, for he is the messenger of G-d*" (2:7).

These holy messengers of G-d were to dedicate their lives to the Divine service and to the teaching of Torah. Blessings were bestowed upon Israel through their actions and words. They had regulations as to whom they could marry that did not apply to other Israelites. They were not allowed to become defiled. They ate the holy *trumah* foods and shared the sacrificial meat. The Torah wanted to make certain that these spiritual shepherds came in direct contact with their flock and their homes. The *Kohanim* had to personally see anyone who was afflicted spiritually, whether it was the person, his garment, or his home. The Torah did not want any *Kohen* to make the same mistake as Rabban Gamliel.

The Talmud (*Shabbos* 88b) relates that when Moshe ascended to the Heavens to receive the Torah, the ministering angels argued against the Torah being given to mortal man. G-d told Moshe to defend his right to receive the Torah. Moshe explained that in the Ten Commandments there is a reference to the fact that the Israelites were enslaved in Egypt. The angels were not enslaved there. In the Ten Commandments it tells us to refrain from work on the Sabbath day. Angels do not work at all. The commandments tell us to honor our father and mother. Angels have no father and mother. Moshe continued to show that the purpose of the mitzvos is so that we can rule over the evil inclination, the *yetzer ha'ra*. Angels have no evil inclination. The Angels had no choice but to yield to Moshe's convincing arguments.

Why did the angels want the Torah? Didn't they realize it was not written for them? The answer is that the angels wanted the right to be the teachers of Torah to the world. Our Sages tell us that when a child is in its mother's womb, an angel teaches it the entire Torah. It is subsequently forgotten as soon as the child is born (*Nidah* 30b). Why are the angels such unsuccessful teachers? It is for precisely the reason that Moshe gave. If you do not eat and drink, you can not teach the laws of kashrus. If you have never experienced the love of parents, how can you transmit an appreciation and obligation to honor and respect parents? How can you transmit to others what you have never lived or experienced yourself? (Irving Bunim's *Ethics from Sinia*).

Rabban Gamliel was a great prince in Israel. He was almost on the same level of spirituality as an angel. But, angels do not make the best teachers because they do not know the trials and tribulations of their flocks.

As King Shlomo said, *"The Righteous knows the soul of his flock"* (*Mishlei* 12:10).

◆§ THE CURE FOR GOSSIP

> *"On the day that there appears in him raw flesh he shall be unclean and when the Kohen sees the raw flesh, he shall make him unclean"* (13:14-15).

The verse seems to contain a contradiction. The beginning of the passage indicates that the very day the signs of *tzara'as* appear he is unclean. The role of the *Kohen* would seem to be that of an expert who ascertains that indeed the plague is in fact a plague. If the plague appeared on Sunday and the *Kohen* was unable to examine it until Friday, once the *Kohen* determines that it was indeed *tzara'as*, it would seem logical to say that the man was unclean as of the past Sunday.

However, the end of the verse says *"When the Kohen sees the raw flesh, he shall make him unclean."* That indicates that it is the proclamation of the *Kohen* that makes the man unclean and not just the appearance of the plague. If the *Kohen* could not examine the flesh until Friday, then the man would not be rendered unclean until Friday. Which way is it?

Rashi (13:14) tells us that the second meaning is correct. The man is not considered unclean until the *Kohen* sees him and renders a decision that it is *tzara'as*. Why then did the verse tell us *"On the day that there appears... he shall be unclean?"* Rashi, quoting the Talmud (*Moed Katan* 7b), explains that the *Kohen* was not allowed to examine the flesh every day. There were certain days that examining the man were forbidden. Which days would that be? The days during festivals and during the seven day of a marriage celebration plagues were not allowed to be examined. The Torah did not wish to put a damper on those days of festivities.

That *halachah* seems quite strange. Imagine a festival or wedding feast in which someone realizes that there is a strong possibility that the food being served is not kosher. Would he decide to wait until after the festivities before consulting a rabbi in order not to put a damper on the celebration? Of course not! Why is it that with regards to *tzara'as* he is allowed to postpone consulting the *Kohen*?

It is well known that *tzara'as* appears on a person because he spoke *lashon ha'ra*. He spoke bad words about someone. Why does someone speak bad words about others? There are many reasons such as jealousy, hatred, revenge, etc. What they all have in common is that the speaker wishes to lower someone else's esteem so his own esteem by comparison will be raised. Why is he trying to raise his own esteem? It is because he is unhappy with himself. He has a poor self-image. One who is angry with himself is angry at others. Conversely, one who likes himself will like others. When the Torah says *"Love thy neighbor as thyself* (*Vayikra* 19:18)," the Torah presupposes that the person loves himself. He is told to then love others as he loves himself. One who has negative feelings about himself will have negative feelings about others. He will not be able to love others.

If one is in a happy mood, his negative feelings disappear. If honor is being bestowed on a person, he will be so happy as to think that everything is wonderful. All is well with the world about him. He will be very forgiving of the short-comings of others. A happy person will not speak *lashon ha'ra*. Since the signs of *tzara'as* indicate that the person is plagued with *lashon ha'ra*, and *lashon ha'ra* is only spoken when one is depressed and has negative feelings about himself, it is understandable why the *metzora* is not proclaimed unclean during a festival or wedding feast. During these times of joy he will not speak *loshan ha'ra*; he is not plagued with the evils of gossip. Therefore, the *Kohen* does not have to examine him at that time.

Tzara'as is a symptom of an inner feeling of unhappiness and dissatisfaction. A person must strive to resolve those issues and feel that he is accomplishing worthwhile goals. He must focus on what is important in life and work towards that end instead of tearing down others. Satisfaction, happiness, and joy are the psychological cures for the spiritual ailment of *tzara'as*.

The Hebrew word for plague is *nega*, spelled *nun, gimmel, ayin*. The Hebrew word for enjoyment is *oneg*, spelled *ayin, nun, gimmel*. The two words, plague and enjoyment have the same letters. The only difference is the placement of the *ayin*. *Ayin* is the Hebrew word for eye. One whose eye cannot see his own faults will see them in others. He will slander them and gossip about them. It will bring the plague on him. One who sees his own faults will seek to correct them. He will be more forgiving of others. He will have a life of enjoyment. How one views the outside world is a reflection of his inner self. The *Baal Shem Tov* is reported to have said, "*One who is good, sees good where ever he goes. One who is flawed sees flaws where ever he goes.*"

≈ɔ MANUFACTURER'S SUGGESTED RETAIL PRICE

"When you come to the land of Canaan, which I will give to you as a possession, and I will put a plague of tzara'as in a house of your possession. He that owns the house shall come and tell the Kohen saying: **Like** *a plague there seems to me in the house"* (14:34-35).

The Torah says that the homeowner should say to the *Kohen,* "Like a plague..." Rashi comments that even if the homeowner is a learned man and knows for certain that it is the plague, he should not pronounce it as though he was certain but rather as if he is uncertain.

The *Mizrachi* (14:35) gives several reasons why the owner of the house should make it seem as though he is uncertain:

1 – One should not state his opinion with an air of authority but rather it should be stated in a more humble form. After all, *tzara'as* comes because of *lashon ha'ra* and one speaks *lashon ha'ra* out of haughtiness and a feeling of superiority.

2 – It is up to a *Kohen* to proclaim a plague to be *tzara'as* or not. If the owner of the house were to definitively say "It is *tzara'as,*" he would be denigrating the role of the *Kohen.*

3 – If the homeowner is a learned man and he tells the *Kohen* that the house is plagued with *tzara'as,* the *Kohen* might feel compelled to proclaim it so even though he personally does not think it is true. And, the real decision is up to the *Kohen* and not the home owner.

4 – The *Maharal* (*Gur Aryeh* 14:35) gives another reason. He says that the house is not considered plagued until the *Kohen* personally examines the house and then proclaims it to be *tzara'as.* If the homeowner says to the *Kohen* that the house has *tzara'as,* it would be a lie since the *Kohen* has not seen it as yet. And, one of the reasons a plague afflicts someone is because of a lie. (See *Arachin* 16a)

These lessons are not simply recommended patterns of behavior.

The Rambam codifies the obligation for the homeowner to say "*Like the plague*" in his code of law (*HilchoTumas Tzara'as* 14:4). It is a *halachah*, a law.

Our Sages have often given us advice on how to behave properly. For some reason we do not take their words very seriously. We regard their words as though they were the manufacturers suggested retail price. We look at it with a smile and think it to be very unrealistic. We listen to the words of our Sages very carefully when it comes to the laws of Shabbos or to the laws of *kashrus* but their words regarding behavior are put into another class. They are second-class rules. The Rambam included the requirement for the homeowner to say "*Like a plague,*" in his code of law because proper behavior is *halachah*, just as Shabbos and *kashrus* are.

Rebbe Eleazer ben Azariah said (*Avos* 3:17): *If there is no Torah, there is no derech eretz. If there is no derech eretz, there is no Torah. Adherence to the halachos of the Torah are on the same level as derech eretz, proper behavior. They go hand in hand.*

❧ THE MITZVOS

The 169ᵗʰ mitzvah in the Torah is to follow the rules and regulations of the laws of *tzara'as*.
"*A man who has on the skin of his flesh a 'se'es'- plague...*" (**13:2**).
The 170ᵗʰ mitzvah in the Torah is the prohibition to shave the afflicted area.
"*The afflicted area he shall not shave...*" (**13:33**).

Since the plague comes as G-d's admonition that the person has sinned, it would be very impudent of him to try and remove it.

ᴈᴊ IT TOLLS FOR THEE

The 171ˢᵗ mitzvah in the Torah is for a person that is afflicted with *t'zaraas* to tear his clothes.
"The afflicted one who has the plague, his clothes shall be torn and his hair shall grow wild, he shall cover his head until his lips and cry out 'Unclean, unclean" (13:45).

Included in this mitzvah is for the afflicted to wear torn clothing, not cut his hair, cover his head with a hooded cloak, and call out to others that he is unclean.

Rashi points out that this mode of behavior is also the conduct of a mourner. One who is sitting *shiva* wears torn clothes, cannot cut his hair, and in days of old would cover his head with a hood so as not to let the world see his mournful, teary eyes. They would share with all who came their way the tragic loss that they had suffered. The Talmud (*Moed Katan* 15a) furthers the comparison of one afflicted with the plague to a mourner by stating that neither one is allowed to greet others nor should others extend the tradional greeting of Shalom to them. The Rambam in his *halachic* compendium (*Hilchos Tumas Tzara'as* 10:6) also points out the similarity between the man with *tzara'as* and the mourner. Just what is the connection between these two seemingly unrelated people?

We have mentioned in the past that all of Israel is one great spiritually organic entity. Each of us is like a cell or organ of that being called Israel. A *metzora* is one who spoke improperly about another person. The Talmud (*Arachin* 16b) tells us that he severed his relationship with the brotherhood of Israel and as a result he is placed in isolation. When a cell or organ has been severed from the body, it has lost its life-source and begins to die. Likewise, the *metzora* who severed his tie to Israel has been cut off from his spiritual life-source. Unless he repents his brash actions, he will suffer a demise of the spirit. It is for that the *metzora* mourns. He mourns for his own spiritual death and decay. He is mourning for himself.

"*A metzora is considered as though he were dead*" (*Rashi Bamidbar* 12:12).

❧ THE EMPORER'S NEW CLOTHES

The 172ⁿᵈ mitzvah in the Torah is to adhere to the laws regarding *tzara'as* of the garment.
"*A garment that has in it the plague... if it be greenish or reddish...*" (13:47-49).

*T*zara'as can also afflict garments. Why garments and not any other article a person may own? A garment reflects the image a person wishes to project.

Our first impression about a person is based to a great degree on how they are dressed. We can deduce many things about a person based on his attire. We may be way off the mark, but at least we made our assessment based on the image the wearer wanted us to see. One who speaks *lashon ha'ra*, whether he realizes it or not, is projecting an image of insecurity, haughtiness, envy, and insensitivity. To call to his attention the poor image the person is projecting, the plague strikes at the very thing that most projects his image, his clothing.

A person who is a *talmid chachom*, a righteous scholar, was expected to examine his clothing very carefully to make certain that there was no soiled spot or stain. He represents the Torah and as such he had to be dressed in a clean and presentable manner. One who is not a *talmid chachom* would not carefully examine their clothing every day. We can just imagine some fellow putting on his $250 Austin Reed trousers, $200 Sulka shirt, $300 pair of Bruno Magli loafers, and $800 Versace blazer and proudly walk down the street: not noticing the greenish plague-like spot on the back of his trousers. It's *tzara'as*! But, he doesn't notice it. Everyone else sees it but him. He comports himself as though he was an emperor but everyone else can see that the emperor has no clothes.

ᴥᷝ **HAFTORAH TAZRIA**

THE *HAFTORAH* IS FOUND IN *SHMUEL II* 4:42 – 5:19.

Aram was a kingdom to the north and east of Israel. Since the days of Yaakov and Lavan, Israel and Aram were bitter enemies. During one major battle at the time of the prophet Elisha, an Aramean archer, Naaman, took careful aim with his arrow and struck down the evil Israelite king, Achav. Israel withdrew from the battle front and Achav's son, Yehoram, was proclaimed king.

Naaman's fame quickly spread and he was made general chief of staff of the Aramean army. Unbeknownst to Naaman, it was not he who took careful aim of his arrow, but it was G-d who guided the arrow along its path into the heart of the Israelite king. Nevertheless, Naaman took great pride in "his" feat and became quite haughty and boastful. G-d punished the mighty Naaman, afflicting him with leprosy.*

During that battle, a young Israelite girl was captured and she was made to be a servant to the wife of Naaman. The young Israelite girl saw the distress of her mistress' husband and told him that in the land of Israel there was a prophet who could miraculously cure leprosy. Word was sent to the Israelite king, Yehoram, demanding that the king see to it that Naaman's leprosy was cured. Yehoram was distraught. He had no idea how to cure the dreaded disease. The prophet Elisha heard of the king's plight and volunteered to cure Naaman.

Naaman, with a great entourage, set off to see the prophet Elisha. Accompanying Naaman's group were wagons laden with 6,000 pieces of gold, ten talents of silver, and ten wardrobes of the finest clothing. All of this was to be the payment for the miraculous cure. When they came near to the prophet's house, Elisha sent his attendant, Gaichazi, with the instructions how to cure Naaman's leprosy. Gaichazi met Naaman and the mass of people who had escorted the general from Aram and told Naaman that he was to bathe in the Jordan River seven times. That would cure his affliction. Naaman thought that Elisha's attendant was mocking him. Naaman explained that in Aram there were rivers with waters more pure than the Jordan. He had bathed in them often but those waters did not cure him. Naaman felt that he was being made out to be a fool. Gaichazi urged Naaman to try the cure since it was not a very difficult matter. Naaman acquiesced.

After bathing in the Jordan seven times, Naaman's leprosy vanished. His skin became soft and subtle as when he was a youth. Naaman quickly came before Elisha and offered him the wealth that he had brought with him from Aram. Elisha refused payment. G-d had healed Naaman, not Elisha. Naaman was so overwhelmed with Elisha's G-d that Naaman pledged never to serve idols again and to become a faithful adherent to the seven Noachide mitzvos. Naaman filled one wagon with dirt from the land of Israel to bring back to Aram. From that holy earth, he constructed an altar to G-d.

The Talmud (*Arachin* 15b) tells us that the cure for *tzara'as* is humility. *Tzara'as* afflicts a person who is arrogant and egotistical. The only cure for that is to become humble. Most often, it is very difficult to simply make one's self humble. G-d has to do it for him. There is nothing more humiliating than to suffer from a plague that isolates the person from society. Naaman was extremely arrogant and as a result had to be completely humiliated. Let us examine carefully the humiliation of Naaman and what it took to break that egotistical spirit.

One, Naaman was afflicted with leprosy. Two, he had to rely on the word of a female slave for advice. Three, he had to ask his enemy, the Israelites, for help. Four, the prophet Elisha did not personally greet him but rather he sent his attendant. Five, he felt that Gaichazi was mocking him with the advice to bathe in the Jordan. After all that, Naaman's spirit of arrogance was finally broken.

The Medrash (*Yalkut Shemoni* 229) tells us that after Naaman's haughty spirit was broken he reached a spiritual level higher than Moshe's father-in-law, Yisro. Yisro believed that Hashem was greater than any other god. Naaman believed that there was no other G-d, besides Hashem.

The next *parshah* deals with the plague of *tzara'as* that can afflict a house. If the *tzara'as* of a house does not show signs of purity within two weeks, the house is dismantled and buried. Rashi (14:34) mentions a Medrash that says that the dismantling of the house is really a blessing that will reveal hidden treasures buried in its walls.

The question arises: if *tzara'as*, in all its forms, is a punishment for *lashon ha'ra*, spoken because of a superiority complex, then why this blessing?

The answer is very simple. Naaman was extremely arrogant and as a result he was punished with leprosy. As the story progressed he became more and more humiliated. In his new found spirit of humility, he discovered the great truth of life: that Hashem is the only G-d. Naaman had dismantled his house of arrogance and found within himself a great treasure, the greatest treasure of all: the truth of G-d's supremacy.

The great lesson for us is that all of G-d's punishments contain hidden blessings and treasures. First we must acknowledge that the punishment is just. Then we must correct our ways. From those ashes of despair will rise up a spiritual phoenix bringing us to a higher level of holiness.

METZORA

ᴗ҉ BUT IT'S TRUE!

"THIS SHALL BE THE LAW OF THE METZORA ('LEPER')..." (14:2).

O ur Sages say that the word *metzora* is a contraction of *motzai shem ra*, one who attempts to ruin the reputation of another through *lashon ha'ra* (*Arachin* 16b). One who tells bad things about another person, whether it is true or not, is punished with *tzara'as*. Saying the truth is no defense against the prohibition of *lashon ha'ra* if our motive is not pure (*Rambam Da'os* 6:2).

Moshe spoke the truth and was punished. Aharon spoke an untruth and was rewarded. When G-d told Moshe to tell the Children of Israel that He has not forgotten them and they will be redeemed from slavery, Moshe said, *"They will not believe me"* (*Shmos* 4:1). In fact, the Children of Israel did not believe Moshe, as it is written, *"And Moshe spoke to the Children of Israel but they listened not to Moshe"* (*Shmos* 6:9). Still, Moshe was punished with *tzara'as*, *"And when*

(Moshe) brought his hand away from his lap, behold his hand was white as snow with tzara'as" (*Shmos* 4:6). Aharon, on the other hand, spoke words which were not true. Whenever he saw two friends who had quarreled, he would secretly approach one of them and say that the friend regretted quarreling but was too ashamed to apologize. He would say the same to the other. Aharon would then bring them together and they would embrace each other and never mention the quarrel again (*Avos D'rebbe Nosson* 12:3).

We see that what you say is not as important as to why you say it. Moshe had no reason to belittle the Jewish People. His words were true, yet he was punished. Aharon spoke words that were not true and yet he is praised for it. The Talmud (*Kesubos* 17a) asks how a person should praise a newlywed bride who is deformed or handicapped. Hillel responded that one should sing, "A beautiful and gracious bride."

The Torah does say, *"Be far from falsehood"* (*Shmos* 24:7). However, Aharon and Hillel both felt that their words were based on a truthful angle. Aharon truly believed that the two friends deep down desired to make amends. Aharon spoke on behalf of what he strongly believed was in their hearts. Hillel too judged that the bridegroom must have regarded his new bride as beautiful and gracious. Aharon and Hillel spoke what they assumed to be the truth: though it may not have been totally accurate. Since it was for a good cause, it was classified as *lashon tov,* not *lashon ha'ra.*

QUESTION. A friend is about to hire a new employee. You personally know that the new employee is dishonest and has embezzled money from former employers. Can you tell your friend about the person he is contemplating to hire? **ANSWER.** One must always consider his motive before he speaks. When speaking about someone else, even if it is true, if it is for your own benefit, to make yourself seem more important or to relieve yourself of a responsibility, then it is *lashon ha'ra.* If it is for revenge, it is certainly *lashon ha'ra.* If your words are solely for the benefit of the one you are speaking to, then it is *lashon tov.* However, we must take great care not to embellish or exaggerate our words to make them more believable. Also, we must also have some degree of certainty that our friend will believe us: at least to investigate the matter. If we believe that our words will be totally dismissed, then we cannot speak about the prospective employee (*Chofetz Chaim* 1:10, 2:10). The truth is no defense.

✑ **THE RABBI AND THE PEDDLER**

he Medrash (*Vayikra Rabbah* 16:2) relates the following story. There was an itinerant peddler who went back around the towns in the vicinity of Sepphoris who would call out, "Who wishes to buy the elixir of life?" Curious crowds drew around him. Rebbe Yannai, who was learning in his room above the crowd, heard him calling out, "Who desires the elixir of life?" Rebbe Yannai called down to the peddler, "Do come up and sell me some." The peddler called back and said to him, "Neither you nor people like you require that which I am selling." The Rabbi pressed him and the peddler went up to Rebbe Yannai. The peddler took out a scroll of King David's *Tehillim* and showed the rabbi the passage, "*Who is the man that desires life? Keep your tongue from evil, depart from evil and do good*" (34:13). Rebbe Yannai responded, King Shlomo said likewise, "*Whoever keeps his mouth and his tongue, keeps his soul from troubles*" (*Mishlei* 21:23). Then Rebbe Yannai said, "All my life have I been reading this passage in *Tehillim* but did not know how to explain it until this salesman came and made it clear."

The Talmud (*Avodah Zorah*19b) records a similar story. Rebbe Alexandri was once calling out, "Who wants life, who wants life?" All the people came and gathered round him saying, "Give us life!" He then quoted to them, "*Who is the man who desires life and loves days that he may see good? Keep your tongue from evil and thy lips from speaking deceptively, depart from evil and do good, seek peace and pursue it.*" One may say, "I kept my tongue from evil and my lips from speaking deceptively so now I can go to sleep." Therefore the verse tells us, "*Depart from evil and do good.*"

The *Kli Yakar* poses a series of questions based on these two incidents.

1) The Medrash identifies the salesman as an itinerant peddler. Why was that important to know? If we had thought that he was a shopkeeper hawking his goods, it would have made little difference in the point of the story.

2) Why did the Medrash say that the peddler went "back around the towns" instead of more simply "around the towns?"

3) Why is it important for us to know that the story took place in the vicinity of Sepphoris?

4) Why did the peddler only offer his "elixir" for sale whereas Rebbe Alexandri was willing to give his advice out for free?

5) Why did the peddler call his advice an "elixir" and Rebbe Alexandri did not refer to his advice by that term?

6) In the story of Rebbe Alexandri, the entire crowd chanted, "Give us life," yet in the story of the peddler no one in the crowd seemed to be interested in the peddler's product except Rebbe Yannai.

7) What did Rebbe Yannai mean when he said, "All my life have I been reading this passage in *Tehillim* but did not know how to explain it until this salesman came and made it clear?" What was so difficult to understand about that passage?

8) Why did Rebbe Yannai quote the verse from Shlomo's *Mishlei*?

9) What did Shlomo want to teach us in that verse in *Mishlei*? Not to speak *lashon ha'ra*? David, in his *sefer Tehillim,* already taught us that.

10) What did the peddler make clear to Rebbe Yannai, he only quoted the verse?

The *Kli Yakar* introduces the answer with a dispute found in the Talmud (*Arachin* 15b). One opinion states that one who slandered his friend should repent by occupying himself with Torah and conduct himself with humility. The other opinion says that one who has already slandered cannot atone for the sin.

The peddler, who was really a preacher, sided with the opinion that one who already slandered can atone for his sin by occupying himself with Torah and conducting himself with humility. The peddler himself had spoken *lashon ha'ra* and was atoning for his sin by going around speaking on behalf of the mitzvah of abstaining from gossip. By playing the part of a peddler, he was acting in a humble manner and was occupying himself with teaching Torah. How do we know that he had committed the sin? The Torah calls a gossiper a "peddler." "*A gossiper (peddler) shall not go among your people*" (*Vayikra* 19:16). Just as a peddler goes from place to place talking to all the people, so too a gossiper, he goes from place to place telling his slanderous tales to whomever he finds.

The Medrash used the phrase that the peddler went "back around" to tell us that the peddler was repenting and atoning for his sin. The Hebrew word for "going back" is *chozer*, which is also used to describe one who committed a sin and wishes to atone so he can "go back" to his former status.

The Medrash mentions that the story took place in Sepphoris; in Hebrew this means "birds." A *metzora* brings birds as part of his atonement. Rashi (14:4) tells us the reason he offers birds is because a gossiper is also called a "chirper," one who endlessly talks even when he has nothing good to say. In the towns around Sepphoris, *lashon ha'ra* was prevalent. Some say that is how the town got its name. They were chirpers.

The peddler was addressing people who already committed the sin of tale-baring. They were spiritually ill and needed an elixir, a medicine. Since they had already sinned, the atonement would not come easy. It would "cost" them. Just see what it took for the peddler to atone for his sin. He had to wander from place to place, away from family and friends, constantly admonishing the people. Obviously he was not making money off of his "sales." Who knows what poverty he had to endure? It is little wonder that no one in the crowd took him up on his offer of life.

What did Rebbe Yannai find so difficult about the verse? And, what was it that the peddler taught him? The difficulty Rebbe Yannai encountered arose from comparing the verse of David in *Tehillim* to the verse of Shlomo in *Mishlei*. Shlomo phrased his verse in the third person, meaning that he was talking in general terms and not to any specific person. "**Whoever** keeps **his** mouth and **his** tongue, keeps **his** *soul from troubles.*" David began his verse in the third person but then he switched it to the second person, as if he was addressing someone in particular. "***Who** is the man that desires life? Keep **your** tongue from evil, depart from evil and do good.*" That is what Rebbe Yannai found perplexing. Furthermore, what was Shlomo telling us in his verse that his father, David, had not already said in *Tehillim*?

The peddler was teaching Rebbe Yannai that even one who has sinned by speaking *lashon ha'ra* could atone for the sin. How so? By doing what he was doing: going around and gathering crowds and offering them advice. That is why David began his verse in the third person just like the peddler himself was calling out in the third person, "**Who** wishes to buy the elixir of life?" When the crowd drew near, he addressed them directly in the second person, "*Keep **your** tongue from evil, depart from evil and do good.*"

David was telling how to atone for speaking *lashon ha'ra*. Shlomo, his son, was giving different advice. Shlomo was saying that it is better to avoid the sin in the first place. That is why Shlomo phrased it in the third person; he was talking in general and not to any specific group or person.

Rebbe Alexandri sided with the other opinion that one who has already spoken *lashon ha'ra* cannot atone for his sin; therefore, he did not refer to his advice as an elixir, a medicine. He was advising people how to avoid speaking slanderously. The people Rebbe Alexandri was addressing would not have to atone and it would not "cost" them. Everyone was very interested in Rebbe Alexandri's free advice.

✺ G-D'S GIFT OF SPEECH

here are three aspects to a human – the body, the intellect, and emotion. Speech requires the physical body-the tongue, larynx, lips, palate and teeth. It also requires the intellect to choose the words that will express the emotion the person is feeling. The function of speech is to unite these three aspects of the human and to communicate it to the three aspects of another human. When one speaks improper words, he is uniting the three human elements to create a sin.

Our Sages (*Kiddushin* 40b) say, "*The three-strand rope is not easily broken.*" It means that when we bring these three elements together – body, intellect, and emotion, the results have great strength. They can apply equally to doing mitzvos as well as to doing *avairos*.

When G-d created man, the Torah says "*And G-d breathed into him the breath of life (Bereishis 2:7).*" The *Targum Onkylos* translates it to mean that G-d breathed into man the ability to think and speak. Rabbeinu Saadya Goan in his *Emunah V'Da'os* (*Beliefs and Opinions*) writes that G-d created nature. Most things that we see are part of this natural world. Trees grow, clouds move, animals reproduce, all such natural things that happen today are only possible because G-d created these natural forces during the days of creation. G-d is not directly doing that today; it is only the product of that which he did almost 6,000 years ago.

There are two exceptions to these natural phenomena: man's ability to think and his ability to speak. Nature did not endow us with the ability to reason and communicate; G-d did. The *Zohar* (beginning of *Tazria*) says that at the moment of inception G-d "personally" gives that particular fetus the potential to think and speak.

We are all familiar with the story of the *Maharal's golem*. The *Maharal* created a humanoid out of clay and brought it to life. It was to be the protector of the Jewish ghetto in Prague. The *golem* was unable to speak. It was a mute who lacked normal intelligence. Why couldn't the *Maharal* create a *golem* who could speak and think normally? The answer is that the creation of life itself is part of nature. All animals naturally procreate. Scientists can now create life in a test tube, in vitro fertilization. The *Maharal's golem* could breathe, eat and walk because these are natural abilities. However, thinking and speaking are not part of nature. Those are divine gifts bequeathed by G-d to a new born child. The *golem* did not receive those gifts and thus was unable to communicate and did not possess normal human intelligence.

Thought and speech are G-d's gift to every person. We should treasure those divine presents and use them wisely. When a person speaks slanderously he is using those gifts to do evil. What could be more blasphemous than taking G-d's gift to us and using it against His other children?

THE MIRACLE OF TZARA'AS

The disease of leprosy is a supernatural one, not a physical one. Our Sages tell us that *tzara'as* afflicts a person because he spoke *lashon ha'ra*. If that is the case, we should all be going around with white spots and hair falling out; who among us has not spoken damaging words?

Tzara'as was an affliction. It was a plague. It was an unwelcome omen of castigation. But, it was also a wonderful miracle. Can you imagine when we did something wrong and had forgotten all about it that an angel came down and whispered into our ear, "Pssst. Don't forget to atone for that sin you committed." We would be ever so thankful for the reminder. We would be happy to realize that our guardian angel was indeed watching out for our best interests. Well, that is what *tzara'as* is. It is a not-so-gentle reminder that one must atone for the sin of *lashon ha'ra*.

After the destruction of the Second *Bais HaMikdash*, the level of spirituality decreased greatly. We were no longer worthy of that miraculous reminder. Therefore, we should not rejoice and think that the plague has been cured and that *tzara'as* is no more. Quite the contrary, it is reason to be sad. No longer is our guardian angel tapping on our shoulders and whispering precious warnings in our ears.

When I was younger, I asked a Rebbe of mine whether or not we get punished for our sins in this world? His response was, "Only if you are lucky." The people who were stricken with *tzara'as* were the lucky ones. Those are the people who G-d deemed worthy enough to be warned in this world so they could correct their ways here and enjoy the splendor of the World to Come. We should only be so lucky.

⤳ TZARA'AS IS ONLY SKIN DEEP

"*A JEW WHO SINS IS STILL A JEW*" (*SANHEDRIN* 44A).

The plague of *tzara'as* only afflicted surfaces. It could appear on the surface of the skin, on garments, and on the walls of a house. This is to show us that when a Jew commits a sin, it is only on the surface. Deep down inside he is still a committed Jew.

There are cases when a Jewish husband is compelled to divorce his wife. What if he refuses? The *Bais Din* (Jewish Court) can use any coercive measure at their disposal, even physical force, to compel the recalcitrant husband to give his consent to the divorce. In general, using coercion to get an agreement is not considered a valid agreement. Why here, in the case of divorce, is the coerced consent valid?

The Rambam (*Gerushin* 2:20) gave a well known response to that question. A Jewish husband who is compelled to divorce his wife, such as a *Kohen* who is married to a divorcée, deep down wants to comply with the *halachah*. His Jewish soul is committed to keeping the Torah and its mitzvos. It is only the surface *yetzer ha'ra* that is refusing. When coercive measures are applied to the man, the cowardly *yetzer ha'ra* clams up. When the man says that he will consent to the divorce, it is his true Jewish self that is speaking.

Rabbi Yosef Dov Ber Soloveitchik once said that this is the lesson of *tzara'as*. *Tzara'as* is a plague that coerces the person to repent. Such repentance is considered valid because the plague only afflicted the surface *yetzer ha'ra*. Deep down, the person always remains a committed Jew.

When we see someone who has left the path of Torah, it may be natural for us to think of him in a disapproving and critical manner. But, that will not win him back. It will only keep him further away and entrenched in his beliefs. If we keep in mind that underneath that façade of a sinner lies a committed Jew, we are tempted to help him and, perhaps, with kindness and diligence, we can help him find his way back into the fold of his brethren.

❧ MEETING HALF-WAY

"This shall be the law of the metzora on the day of his purification; he shall be brought to the Kohen. And the Kohen will go to the outside of the camp..." (14:2-3).

There seems to be a contradiction in the verse. First it says that the *metzora* is brought to the *Kohen* and then it says the *Kohen* will go outside the camp where the *metzora* was. Which way was it? Was the afflicted brought to the *Kohen* or did the *Kohen* go to the afflicted?

A similar contradiction is found in the verse that we sing in *shul* on Shabbos after the Torah scroll is return to the ark. *"Return us to You, Hashem, and we shall return, renew our days as of old"* (*Eichah* 5:21). First the verse says that Hashem should return us, implying that Hashem should make us do *teshuvah*. Then the verse says that we shall return, implying we are doing *teshuvah* of our own accord.

The answer is that the *metzora* had to meet the *Kohen* half – way. The *Kohen* would come to the edge of the camp and the *metzora* had to come from wherever he was to meet the *Kohen*. Throughout the days of the *metzora's* suffering with the plague, the *Kohen* would talk to him: admonishing the afflicted one to repent. In order to become healed, the *metzora* had to meet the *Kohen* half-way. The *metzora* found it difficult to repent by himself.. He could conjure up all sorts of reasons why the sin of *lashon ha'ra* was not so terrible. After all, all he did was speak a few words. It's not like he really did something. The words were even true. You can't punish someone for speaking the truth, can you? And, if the words were not true, it will soon be evident that it was not true and everyone will disregard the slander. Therefore, the *Kohen* had to help the *metzora* to do *teshuvah*. He had to show him the serious nature of his offense. But, the *Kohen* also could not do it alone. He could not cure the plague unless the *metzora* truly repented.

Likewise, we say to Hashem that we alone cannot repent without Your help; we cannot return by ourselves. Our sins are so many that we cannot even recall them all. We are so accustomed to sinning that we no longer regard them as sins. Please, help us. *"Return us to You, Hashem."* We also realize that Hashem cannot make us do *teshuvah*. It must come from the heart – our heart. We say to Hashem, give us a little help; then we will meet You half-way and complete the *teshuvah*, *"...and we shall return."*

✍ FLYING ABOUT

> *"And he shall take for a purification two live kosher birds... one bird the Kohen shall command to slaughter ... and the bird which is alive... he shall let go into the open field"* (14:4-7).

hy did the *metzora* have to bring two birds to the *Kohen* if one was going to be set free?

Earlier, we mentioned that there is an opinion found in the

Talmud that says one cannot fully atone for the sin of *lashon ha'ra*. This requires some explanation. The Rambam (*Hilchos Teshuvah* 1:1) writes that repentance atones for every sin. What is so different about the sin of slander that one opinion says that repentance cannot help fully atone?

The *Chovos HaLevavos* (*Shar HaChaniah* 7) writes that one who slanders the reputation of another, forfeits to the victim all the mitzvos that the slanderer had previously done. In addition, all the sins of the victim are transferred to the slanderer.

We can now begin to understand why a slanderer cannot fully atone for his sin. Since he now has all the sins of the one he defamed, he is responsible to atone for those sins as well but he doesn't even know what those sins are. How can he atone for them?

Why is the punishment for slander so great? In the early 1980's, the United States Secretary of Labor under Ronald Reagan was Ray Donovan. He was accused of accepting bribes for favors. The press took great glee in vilifying Mr. Donovan and after a very lengthy trial, he was found innocent. As Donovan was leaving the courtroom, he turned to the reporters and said, "What office do I go to, to get my reputation back?"

Rebbe Shimon says: *There are three crowns – the crown of Torah, the crown of the priesthood, and the crown of royalty. The crown of a good reputation is greater than any of them* (*Avos* 4:13).

One who ruins someone's reputation has ruined a man's life work. It is not possible to repay it. If one murders another, the murderer has deprived the victim from continuing his quest to enjoy life, to do mitzvos, and to build his reputation even further. But, his reputation up until that point has not been damaged. It remains in tact. In that respect, slander is worse than murder. The slanderer has robbed someone of everything they had worked for in the past.

There is another aspect to *lashon ha'ra* that makes it such an egregious sin. When one speaks *lashon ha'ra* to another person, the other person will tell it to someone else who in turn will pass it along even further. The misspoken words now take on a life of their own and will go from person to person and from place to place. Even after the one who spoken *lashon ha'ra* has repented for his sin, the sin is still out there continuing to spread. It can never be taken back.

Perhaps that is why *tzara'as* is deemed a plague. Like a plague, it is highly contagious and is passed on from person to person. Even if the first person who had the plague is cured, the disease is still making its rounds affecting others and inflicting its damage.

We can now suggest what is symbolized by the live bird that is released. The *metzora* who spoke improperly of others has atoned for his sin. His affliction has been healed. He has offered a chirping bird as a sacrificial atonement. However, the Torah wants to make certain that the *metzora* realizes that his words are still out there flying around doing their damage. The atonement cannot be complete. Therefore the *Kohen* is instructed to release the second bird and let it fly about to show that the chirper's words are still flying about.

✍ SECOND HAND SMOKE

*T*zara'as can afflict even a child. The verse says, "*A person (adam) who has a 'se'es'-plague on his skin... (Vayikra 13:2).*" The usual expression in the Torah is the word "man," *ish*. Why does the Torah use the word "*person*" in connection with a *metzora*?

The answer is that *ish*, a man, excludes a minor. For example, the Torah says that "*When an ish (man) digs a pit...*" (Shmos 21:23), and the pit causes damage, the one who dug the pit is liable for the damages. This is only true if the one who dug the pit is a responsible adult. It does not apply to a minor. The word *ish* comes to exclude the minor.

The word *adam*, a person, includes even a minor. Since *tzara'as* can afflict even a minor, the Torah used the word *adam* instead of *ish*. In fact, there are discussions in the Talmud (*Nedarim* 31b) concerning a new born with *tzara'as*. The obvious question to be asked, given that the plague afflicted those who were guilty of slander, is as follows: how could a newborn have *tzara'as* if he cannot even speak as yet?

Rabbi Samson Raphael Hirsch explains that the Talmud (*Arachin* 15b) says that *lashon ha'ra* afflicts three people – the one who speaks, the one who listens, and the one being spoken about. It is obvious that slander hurts the one being spoken about. It also hurts and damages the soul of the one who speaks it. In addition, it also deeply affects the one who hears the slander.

A newborn, of course, cannot speak *lashon ha'ra*. It cannot even understand *lashon ha'ra*. But if it is exposed to *lashon ha'ra*, it can still suffer its ill-effects. Amazingly, the damage contained in these words entering one's ear is not contingent on the comprehension of those words. Just think of *lashon ha'ra* as second hand smoke. No clear thinking adult would expose his infant or child to the harmful effects of second hand smoke. Yet, many clear thinking adults do expose their infants and children to the harmful effects of *lashon ha'ra*.

✑ FRENCH FRIES FOR THE SOUL

The Mishnah (*Nega'im* 3:1) says that the afflicted person is not considered to be fully cured and clean until the *Kohen* announces verbally, "Pure" (*tahor*). Just as the plague appeared because of the word of mouth, so to it can only be removed by word of mouth. *"Death and life are in the hands of the tongue"* (*Mishlei* 18:21).

It is interesting to note that the verse does not say *"life and death"* but rather *"death and life."* Why is the negative placed before the positive?

The tongue has a natural partiality towards that which is harmful. We all know the first rule of good nutrition. If it tastes good, it's bad for you. The taste buds of the tongue have a natural preference for tastes that are detrimental. If it were totally up to our tongue, we would feast on a daily junk diet of milk chocolate, fat saturated donuts, French fries, ice cream, and several helpings of hamburger. We must train our tongue to graciously accept in our palate foods, which are more healthful. The same is true with speech. We have a natural inclination to say things that are harmful and unpleasant. Some people are so anxious to tell over bad news that they can hardly contain themselves. Saying something nice does not seem to come naturally. Remember your mother's golden rule: if you don't have something good to say, then say nothing. We said nothing. Good does not come naturally to the tongue. We must train our tongue to articulate words that are beneficial to the one we are speaking about, the one spoken to, and, most of all, ourselves. Because the tongue has a natural proclivity to that which is harmful, death is mentioned before life

✑ THE PURIFICATION OF THE METZORA

The 173ʳᵈ mitzvah in the Torah is to follow the procedure for the purification of the *metzora*.
"This shall be the law of the metzora ..." **(14:2).**

The purification of the *metzora* is more complex and takes much longer than the purification and atonement of any other sinner. This gives us some idea as to the severity the Torah attaches to the sin of *lashon ha'ra*.

The purification of the *metzora* is performed in three steps.

STEP 1:

   A – After the signs of the plague have disappeared, while still outside the city, a *Kohen* brings a pottery bowl and places therein some spring water. The *Baal HaTurim* (14:5) says that ocean water is not fit for the purification process. Fresh spring water is healthy; saline ocean water is poisonous. The purification process is to restore the spiritual health to the body and not to poison it. In Hebrew, spring water is called *mayim chayim*, the water of life.

B – One of the two birds brought by the *metzora was* slaughtered above the bowl of spring water. We mentioned before that one who speaks *lashon ha'ra* is compared to a chirping bird. Children are taught to sing, "Sticks and stones may break my bones, but names can never harm me." The Torah teaches us that there is nothing further from the truth. An injury caused by sticks and stones can be healed. The pain will go away. The effect of being called an insulting or slanderous name may never go away. The pain can last a lifetime. Even in adulthood, most of us can recall some insult hurled at us by a teacher in elementary school. The blood of the slaughtered bird represents the great harm done by *lashon ha'ra*. Cruel words can spill blood. The tongue can be guilty of murder (*Arachin* 15b). Sticks and stones may break my bones but names can tear at my soul. "*It is better to cast yourself into a fiery furnace than embarrass your friend*" (*Berachos* 43b).

C – The dead bird was buried in the place where it was slaughtered. No one was allowed to eat or benefit from that bird. Just as *lashon ha'ra* does not benefit anyone, not the speaker, not the listener, and surely not the one spoken about, so too the "chirper" was buried without benefit to anyone. "In the future, the animals will approach the snake and say, 'We bite to kill to have food to eat. Why do you bite and kill even if you derive no benefit?' The snake will respond, 'And what benefit does man receive when he kills with the bite of an evil tongue?'" (*Arachin* 15b).

D – A small board of cedar wood, a clump of hyssop, and a hank of scarlet wool are brought. The hyssop and cedar board are bound together with the end of scarlet wool. These were placed near the wing tips and tail feathers of the live bird. What does all this represent?

Cedar is a tall, large and imposing tree. It represents arrogance and haughtiness: the very root of the problem of the one who spoke *lashon ha'ra*. Hyssop is a low growing herb and represents humility, the opposite of haughtiness and pride. We tend to think in terms of absolutes. Pride is an absolute character flaw and humility is an absolute positive character trait. This is not necessarily so. A person is expected to have some pride in the way he dresses and conducts himself. One must wear clean clothing. He should not appear unkempt. However, he must not flaunt his mode of dress or appearance but should present a good image to the world. After all, he represents the Jewish people. One must not be humble to the extreme that he will not speak up when he sees an injustice. Both pride and humility have their time and place. The scarlet wool binds them together to show that each trait has its value. The scarlet wool in Hebrew comes from the word meaning "a worm." The scarlet dye was produced from the worm (*Coccus ilicis*) which infested the seeds of a species of oak tree (*Quercus coccifera*). The worm is a very lowly creature. The oak is also a mighty tree. The lowly worm and mighty oak live together in a symbiotic relationship producing a beautiful scarlet dye. The *metzora* is expected to take a lesson from these three things and keep his pride in check.

The live bird, as we mentioned earlier, represents the *lashon ha'ra* that continues to fly about long after the *metzora* has repented for his sins. The wings and tail feathers of the bird are the organic instruments of flight.

E – All four – the cedar, the hyssop, the scarlet wool, the live bird, were all dipped into the bloody spring water. They were flicked towards the back of the right hand of the *metzora* seven times. The bird was then released. Why the back of the hand?

An open palm represents "receiving." A receiver wants things and feels entitled to things. Haughtiness and pride give a person the illusion that he is entitled to gifts, honor, prestige, acknowledgments. The back of the hand represents giving. The *metzora* must picture himself no longer as a receiver but as a giver.

F – The *metzora* is completely shaved of all bodily hair. He immerses in a *mikvah*. Afterwards, he may enter into the city. However, his purification is not yet complete. The next step of purification will be performed seven days later. What is the significance of shaving the *metzora* and his immersion in a *mikvah*?

The purification of the *metzora* represents a rebirth. He is a new person with a new chance at life. Before an infant is born, it is completely surrounded by the embryonic fluid in the mother's womb. The fetus is devoid of bodily hair. The shaving of the hair and the total immersion in the *mikvah* re-enacts the moments prior to birth.

During the first day of creation, the universe was unformed and void. It was in its embryonic stage. The Torah describes the earth as completely covered by water, its embryonic fluid, so to speak. Just as the mother completely surrounds and protects the fetus within the fluid, so too the verse describes that *"the spirit of G-d hovered around the face of the deep"* (*Bereishis* 1:2). The *metzora* now has a new chance to merit G-d's protection.

STEP 2:

On the seventh day, the *metzora* is once again completely shaved and immersed in a *mikvah*. The *metzora* has now reached a stage of purity so that he will no longer defile vessels that he touches; however, he still may not touch sacrificial meat until the third step of purification has been completed.

The purification of the *metzora* represents a rebirth, a new creation. Just as the creation of the world took seven days to complete, the rebirth process of the *metzora* also took seven days to complete. Why did the *metzora* have to re-enact the rebirth on the seventh day? Why could he not simply wait until seven days passed by?

Creation can be divided into two parts. The first six days represent the creation of the physical world. All the material needed for the physical world was created from nothingness on the first day. Over the course of the first six days, G-d finished the physical creation by refining the material and setting everything into place (*Rashi Bereishis* 1:14, *Malbim Bereishis* 1:1).

The seventh day, Shabbos, was the day of a new creation, a spiritual creation. Rashi (*Bereishis* 2:2) tells us that tranquility, inner peace, was created on Shabbos.

The *metzora* was physically healed of his plague on the first day of his purification. That was the day of his physical rebirth. However, spiritually, he was still defiled. Not until the seventh day was he spiritually reborn and free of defilement. The seventh day of the *metzora's* purification represents the seventh day of creation.

> **The 174ᵗʰ mitzvah in the Torah is to shave the bodily hair on the seventh day of purification.**
>
> *"And on the seventh day he shall shave all the hair..."* **(14:9).**
>
> **The 175ᵗʰ mitzvah in the Torah is for the** *metzora* **to immerse himself in a** *mikvah* **on the seventh day.**
>
> *"...and he shall bathe his flesh in water so that he becomes clean"* **(14:9).**

The Sages extend this mitzvah to include all those who require immersion as part of a purification process, for example, one who came in contact with a corpse. This cleansing of his body is not to be construed as an act of physical cleanliness, but rather as an act of spiritual dedication to show that he has become pure not only in body but in mind.

STEP 3:

The following day, the eighth day of his purification, the *metzora* came to the *Bais Hamikdash* with three sacrifices: a burnt-offering (*olah*), a sin-offering (*chatas*), and a guilt-offering (*asham*). He also brought a flask of oil.

After the guilt-offering was slaughtered, some of its blood was touched to the right ear-lobe, right thumb, and right toe of the *metzora*. Some of the oil was also touched to those three places. Afterwards, the remaining oil was poured on the head of the former *metzora*. The purification process is now complete.

The Talmud (*Kesubos* 5b) wonders what the purpose of the ear-lobe is. It answers that if one is about to hear *lashon ha'ra* he should stuff the ear-lobe inside the ear so that he will not be able to hear it. The Talmud then wonders why the fingers are shaped like pegs. Again it answers that if one is about to hear *lashon ha'ra* he should place his fingers in his ears so as not to hear it. The question now arises why do we need both ear-lobes and peg-shaped fingers? Either one would suffice to block out the ill-spoken words.

I would like to suggest the following. The ear-lobes can only be used for your own ears. If you are about to hear something that is not allowed to be heard, you can place your ear-lobes insides your ears. Your fingers, however, can be used to place in someone else's ears. Who is it that would be most motivated to place their fingers in someone else's ears so that they will not hear the *lashon ha'ra*? It is the one being spoken about. He would like to prevent the listener from hearing words that will damage his reputation.

The Talmud (*Arachin* 15b) says that gossip harms three people: the speaker, the listener, and the one being spoken about. What do those three parts of the body – the ear, the thumb, and the toe, represent? The ear-lobe represents the listener. The peg-shaped finger represents the one being spoken about. The toes of the feet represent the gossiper himself. The Torah refers to a gossiper as a "peddler." Just as a peddler goes around hawking his merchandise, so too the gossiper goes from person to person spreading his rumor mongering. The toes represent the feet of the peddling gossip.

The blood touched to the three bodily parts represents the harm done to the three victims of gossip. Pure oil is then touched to the very same areas to teach that just as ill-spoken words harm those three people, kind words can benefit the same three people. Oil, which was used as fuel to shed light, represents the ability of words to enlighten.

Only after all of these lessons are learnt is the *metzora* completely purified.

> **The 176ᵗʰ mitzvah in the Torah is to follow the procedure of purification of the eight day.**
> *"On the eighth day..."* (14:10-31).
> **The 177ᵗʰ mitzvah in the Torah is the laws regarding a house that has the plague of *tzara'as*.**
> *"I will place the plague of leprosy in a house of your possession"* (14:34).

See the *haftorah* to *Parshas Tazria*.

THE MITZVOS

T he remaining five mitzvos in this *parshah* pertain to states of impurity that are the result of an emission from the male and female reproductive organs. It is beyond the scope and intent of this book to detail their myriad *halachos* and their intricacies.

The 178th mitzvah concerns the adherence to the laws of impurity of a *zav*, commonly mistranslated as gonorrhea.
"Any man who flows from his flesh a flow, he is unclean" **(15:2).**

The *Sefer HaChinuch* (178) explains that just as the plague of *tzara'as* comes as a result of speaking *lashon ha'ra*, a man becomes a *zav* as a result of overindulgence in his pursuit of his sensual desires.

Sensual desires and pleasures are important elements in creation. Without a desire for food, man would starve or, at the very least, suffer from malnutrition. G-d created the world in such a manner that mankind would have pleasure in eating so that he will be healthy. However, we are taught not to indulge in this pleasure merely for its own sake. The pleasure we derive from food should be turned into a sense of appreciation for G-d's great beneficence. Eating is always preceded and followed with a blessing. Whenever possible, the pleasure for food is centered on a *seudas mitzvah*, a feast related to a mitzvah. The pleasure we derive from the gastronomical delights and the social interaction is turned into a spiritual experience that can elevate the soul to a higher plateau.

The greatest desire the human has is the sexual drive. Without it, man would not procreate. Without this physical drive few people would have an interest in producing children because children do not provide any instant gratification. *"Not for emptiness was (the world) created; to be populated it was made"* (*Yeshaya* 45:18). Man's physical instinct compels him to produce offspring and thus enable the purpose of creation to continue. However, as important as this desire is, it should not be used merely for self gratification. It is to be viewed and experienced as a bond of love between husband and wife. It is an experience that can be externalized and become a loving bond between man and his Creator.

When a man becomes a *zav*, G-d is telling him that he is using this physical drive merely for self gratification and not for its intended purpose.

The 179ᵗʰ mitzvah in the Torah is for the purified *zav* to bring his sacrifices to the Temple.

"When a man has become clean from his flow, he shall count seven days for his purification and wash his clothes, and wash his flesh in flowing water and he shall be clean. On the eighth day he shall offer two turtle-doves or two young pigeons..." (15:13-14).

The 180ᵗʰ mitzvah in the Torah is to adhere to the laws of impurity regarding a man who had an emission of seminal fluid.

"A man who issues forth a seminal discharge shall wash all his flesh in water and he shall be unclean until that evening" (15:16).

The 181ˢᵗ mitzvah is for the husband and wife to adhere to the laws of *nidah*.

"A woman who has a flow of blood..." (15:19).

A woman, during her menstrual period is termed a *nidah*. During this time, all physical contact between the wife and her husband is forbidden (See mitzvah 207). This mitzvah is to counterbalance the mitzvah of a *zav*. A *zav* taught us not to over indulge in the pursuit of one's sexual pleasure. Overindulgence, besides being sinful, can lead to total disinterest. One who constantly eats a much desired food soon comes to loathe it. To prevent the intimate bond between husband and wife from becoming stale and distasteful, the Torah regulated when the union can take place.

The laws regarding family purity (*taharas ha'mishpacha*) teach husband and wife how to relate to each other emotionally, intellectually, physically and spiritually. They contain the groundwork of the Torah's definition of interpersonal marital relationships through love, mutual respect and self-control. Self-control teaches us to sanctify the physical world. It paves the way for husband and wife to relate to one another as loving human beings rather then as objects for self gratification.

> **The 182ⁿᵈ mitzvah in the Torah is to adhere to the laws of *zavah*.**
> *"A woman who has a flow of blood many days not in her* **(expected)** *time..."* **(15:25).**
> **The 183ʳᵈ mitzvah in the Torah is regarding the offering, by a woman with an irregular discharge, when she recovers.**
> *"If she ceases her flow, she must count seven days for herself, and afterwards she can be purified"* **(15:28).**

A woman who has her menstrual period far from her expected time is termed a *zavah*. A *zavah* has rules and regulations very similar to a *zav*. In fact, the Medrash (*Vayikra Rabbah* 19:3) wonders why the Torah repeated so many of the laws of *zav* in the *parshah* of *zavah*. The Torah could have combined the two and made them into a single mitzvah. The Medrash answers that the Torah understood full well that certain laws would be embarrassing and unpleasant to discuss in a public forum, such as the laws of *nidah, zav and zavah*. Had the Torah been more brief it would be less embarrassing. However, the Torah expects us to treasure each and every letter of each and every word with respect and holiness. If we treat the Torah that way then we will not suffer from any unpleasantness or sense any embarrassment. Therefore the Torah discusses it in detail rather than in an abbreviated manner.

That Medrash mentions how very important it is to value each and every letter in the Torah. In the *Shma*, we say, "*Hear O' Israel, Hashem, our G-d, Hashem is One.*" The last word in the *Shma* is the Hebrew word *echad*. The very last letter is a "*daled.*" The letter "*daled*" and the letter "*raish*" look very similar. The difference between them is a speck of ink in the upper right portion of the letter "*daled.*" Without that speck of ink, the "*daled*" becomes a "*raish*" and then that last word would become *acher*, meaning "another one." The *Shma* would then read, "Hear O' Israel, Hashem, our G-d, Hashem is another one." That would be blasphemous. It implies there is more than one

G-d, the very antithesis of the true *Shma*.

If the Torah chose to elaborate on a certain portion, we should not approach it with a feeling of shame or embarrassment. Each and every letter is a precious gift and the more letters we have the more precious gifts from G-d we have.

◄ੀ **HAFTORAH METZORA**

THE *HAFTORAH* IS FOUND IN *MELACHIM II* 7:3-20.

In the haftorah to *parshas Tazria* we read about the Aramean general Naaman whose leprosy was miraculously healed by the prophet Elisha. Naaman offered Elisha payment for this cure of his leprosy but Elisha refused to accept anything. However, Elisha's attendant, Gaichazi saw this as an opportunity not to be missed. Gaichazi ran after Naaman and told the Aramean general that Elisha had changed his mind and needed a measure of silver and a suit of clothing for two new students who had recently arrived. Naaman suspected that Gaichazi was not telling the truth and asked him to take an oath. Gaichazi swore falsely that his master asked for the measure of silver and suit of clothing. Naaman gave Gaichazi two measures of silver and two suits of clothing. Gaichazi took the silver and clothing and hid it in his house.

When Elisha heard what had transpired, he was very upset. Elisha had refused payment in order to make a *kiddush Hashem*, to bring glory to Hashem's name. Gaichazi undid that noble deed. Elisha placed a curse on Gaichazi that Gaichazi and his three sons, who were complicit in the deed (*Radak*), would be afflicted with the leprosy that Naaman had. Before Gaichazi had even left Elisha's presence, he had turned white as snow (from *Melachim II* 5:20-26).

All of this took place in the capital city of northern Israel, Samaria. Gaichazi and his three sons were forced to live outside the city as required for those who are plagued with *tzara'as*.

At this time, the army of Aram besieged Samaria. The devastating hunger was unimaginable. Food was so scarce that the head of a donkey sold for 80 pieces of silver. A half-gallon of pigeon dung cost 5 silver pieces.

A woman appeared before the king, Yehoram, and complained, "My friend and I each had a son. Our sons have perished from the famine. We agreed to a plan that we would eat the flesh of our sons: my son today and her son tomorrow. We have already eaten my son but she refuses to give over her son to be eaten." The king was so distraught at hearing this he pledged to behead the prophet Elisha that very day. Elisha could have prayed that the famine be stopped and yet he did not do so.

When Yehoram appeared before Elisha, the prophet proclaimed, "*At this time tomorrow, a four – gallon measure of wheat will sell for a mere shekel.*" The king's captain, who was standing there, said in disbelief, "*Even if G-d opens the windows of heaven, this cannot happen.*" Elisha replied, "*Tomorrow you will see it with your own eyes but you will not eat from it*" (*ibid* 6:24-33).

The *haftorah* of our *parshah* opens on the following morning. Gaichazi and his three sons were outside the city of Samaria. They were faint with hunger. Gaichazi said that they couldn't remain where they were; they would starve to death in a short time. They could not go into the city because there was no food there either. Their only choice was to surrender to the camp of Aram and plead for mercy.

The four lepers approached the great camp of Aram but not a sound could be heard. G-d had caused the sounds of a mighty army to be heard in the camp and the entire army fled in terror, abandoning everything. Gaichazi and his sons came to the first tent and saw food and drink. They helped themselves to their hearts' content. They also found gold, silver and clothing, which they hid for themselves. They began going from tent to tent gathering the spoils and hiding it. Not until later did it occur to them that they should tell Yehoram that the enemy siege was over and that food was plentiful.

The king found the words of the lepers to be true. People streamed outside the city to gather the great surplus of food and valuables that the enemy army had abandoned. In the mad rush to get out of the city, the king's captain was crushed to death. That day the price of a four-gallon measure of wheat sold for a mere shekel.

Parshas Metzora began with the plague of *tzara'as*, which comes on account of ill-spoken words. The underlying cause of those words of jealously is due to a feeling of pride and arrogance. Pride gives us the illusion that we are entitled to the power, possessions, and prestige which others possesses. Pride feeds the lustful soul. The character flaw of lustfulness was brought out in the end of the *parshah*, in the mitzvos of a *zav* and a *zavah*. Gaichazi was certainly guilty of ill-spoken words. He swore falsely to Naaman. What was Gaichazi's motive? He wanted the silver and clothing for himself. He desecrated the name of G-d for the gain of a few ounces of silver and some cloth. As a result, Gaichazi and his sons were afflicted with *tzara'as*.

Did they learn their lesson? Obviously not. When they discovered that the camp of Aram had been abandoned, their first reaction was to gather gold and silver for themselves though their fellow Jews were still starving to death. This shows how great the power of lust can become.

The Talmud (*Sanhedrin* 90a) tells us that Gaichazi has no portion in the world to come. Gaichazi was a great Talmudic scholar (*Yerushalmi Sanhedrin* 10:2). He was the principle disciple of the great prophet, Elisha. Yet, he chose to give up his greatness for a few measures of pleasures in this world.

We must stop and reflect about ourselves. We are certainly permitted to enjoy the pleasures of this world. We all dream of a nice home and a nice automobile or two. The *Orchos Tzadikkim* (*Shar HaGa'avah*) tells us that one must live and dress according to the blessings that Hashem has bestowed upon him. However, the nice home must be used as a place of assembly for scholars: such as parlor meetings. Our nice automobiles must be used to enable us to do mitzvos. We should utilize our vacations to renew our spirits and energy to serve Hashem. Are we sometimes guilty of surrendering our chance for greatness and eternal bliss for a few ounces of silver and a suit of clothing? If we use our blessings merely for our own gratification, we are no better than Gaichazi who hid the gold and silver for himself, even at the expense of Jewish lives. We must stop and reflect about ourselves, not only on *Yom Kippur*, but each and every day. We must keep the lesson of Gaichazi in front of our eyes.

ACHAREI MOS

✑ THE KING IS DEAD

"And G-d spoke to Moshe after the death of the two sons of Aharon when they drew close to G-d and they died" (16:1).

This *parshah* is replete with mitzvos. One of the first mitzvos is the Temple service of *Yom Kippur*. The question is asked why the *parshah* introduced the mitzvah of *Yom Kippur* with a reference to the death of the two sons of Aharon. In addition, the verse seems to indicate that the sin of Aharon's sons was that they "drew close to G-d." We have always been taught that coming closer to Hashem is the greatest spiritual goal there is. Why does the Torah regard it as a sin?

In mid-nineteenth century San Francisco, there lived a wealthy gentleman by the name of Joshua Norton. Norton lost all of his wealth and was reduced to living in a squalid rooming house, working in a Chinese rice factory. His fall from the upper echelon of society took its toll on Norton's mind. He began to fixate on the ills of the government and came to the irrational conclusion that what this country needed was an emperor.

Since there was no one more qualified to serve in the capacity of emperor as himself, Norton proclaimed himself to be Emperor of These United States of America. The local newspapers picked up the story and light-heartedly published Norton's proclamation. Norton bought himself a second-hand military uniform, complete with medals, ribbons, and gold trim. His first official act as emperor was to abolish all political parties and he drew up a rambling, incoherent new constitution. Norton printed new currency for The Imperial Government of the United States.

All of his friends and former business associates played along with Norton's illusion of grandeur. Norton freely dined at the finest restaurants and rode public transportation without paying the fare. He levied taxes on businesses, 25 cents yearly for small businesses in his neighborhood and three dollars for sprawling enterprises. Norton often tried to negotiate multi-million dollar loans for his empire from his former business associates and gladly settled for a 50-cent piece.

The emperor reigned for 20 years. In the winter of 1880, Norton passed away. Reportedly, over 20,000 people attended the emperor's state funeral. The mourners included all classes of society, from industrialists to the pauper, from clergyman to the pickpocket, from well-dressed ladies to those who lived in poverty. The Headlines of the San Francisco Chronicle read *LE ROI EST MORT*, The King is Dead.

To a certain extent, we are all like Joshua Norton. His intentions were noble but delusional. We too live under the illusion that we are emperors of our personal realm, or at least captain of our ship. We all think we know what is best and proper for our realm. We go through life living this illusion and G-d plays along.

Nadav and Avihu, the two sons of Aharon, also thought they knew what was best. They thought that the best way to achieve closeness to Hashem was to enter the *Kodesh HaKadoshim* and offer their own devised incense-offering. They died in the Inner Sanctum believing they were right. The Torah defines how we are supposed to achieve a close relationship with G-d. We cannot invent such actions ourselves; even great tzaddikim, with the stature of Nadav and Avihu, are not able to innovate their own brand of lofty conduct.

Yom Kippur gives us the chance to pause and analyze what we have done over the past year and the direction in which we are headed. We are forced to think about our relationship with G-d. Is it according to His terms or according to ours?

Acharei Mos and the next *parshah, Kedoshim* are often read together on Shabbos. The combined *parshiyos* are called *Acharei Mos – Kedoshim.* This has become the source for an expression: *Acharei Mos Kedoshim* – after death is holiness. It means that after a Jew passes away, at the funeral service eulogies are delivered saying what a great and holy man or woman the deceased was. After death, everyone suddenly becomes holy. Was it true? Not necessarily. But so often, during one's lifetime, a person truly believes upon superficial reasoning that he or she is a holy person doing the will of G-d. Had they paused and sincerely introspected on Yom Kippur, then they might have come to grips with their flaws. Then they could have embarked on a course of self-improvement which can yield precious rewards. We must strive to resist living an illusion in which we are much like a self-anointed king. A Jew's funeral should not elicit the same reaction as that highlighted by the mocking headline of the San Francisco Chronicle: *LE ROI EST MORT.*

ATONEMENT AND LOSS

The Talmud (*Yerushalmi Yoma* 1:1) asks why was the death of the two sons of Aharon, which occurred two weeks before Passover, mentioned in connection with *Yom Kippur?* The Talmud answers that just as *Yom Kippur* atones for sins, so too does the death of the righteous.

The *Yerushalmi* is bringing out an important aspect of atonement. Atonement involves a loss. We know that giving charity is an important element in atonement. *Teshuva, tefilah, v'tzadaka ma'avrin es ro'ah ha'gezayrah: repentance, prayer and charity remove the evil decree.* On *Yom Kippur* we abstain from all sorts of pleasures – such as eating, drinking, and washing. These lost pleasures assist in the atonement process. The greatest loss that Jews can suffer is the loss of righteous men. Those who truly feel the loss in the depths of their heart will harness that feeling of loss and reflect on their own lives. They will feel compelled to better themselves. In that way, the death of the righteous can help atone for sins.

◄§ YOM KIPPUR AND THE TORAH

n the 6th day of *Sivan*, Moshe ascended Mt. Sinai to receive the Torah.

On the 17th of *Tammuz* he descended with the Tablets. He saw the Israelites sinning with the Golden Calf. Moshe broke the tablets.

On the 19th of *Tammuz*, Moshe ascended Mt. Sinai to plead on behalf of the Children of Israel for forgiveness.

On the 29th of *Av*, Moshe descended and told the Israelites that they were forgiven.

On the 1st of *Elul*, Moshe ascended Mt Sinai to receive the Torah.

On the 10th day of *Tishrei*, *Yom Kippur*, Moshe descended with the second set of Tablets. *Yom Kippur* thus became the Day of Atonement.

The question to be asked is that if the Children of Israel were forgiven on the 29th day of Av, then should not that have been the date ordained as the traditional Day of Atonement? Why was *Yom Kippur* set aside for atonement?

The sin of the Golden Calf was a major tragedy. It was a sin that cannot even begin to be measured. All the nations of the world were offered the Torah. They rejected it. G-d did not hold that against them. It was quite understandable that they did not want to be held to such a high standard of conduct. However, the Children of Israel proclaimed, "We will do it! We will listen." They obligated themselves to uphold the Torah. Yet a few weeks later they trampled on its precepts. The other nations did not pledge to keep the Torah. The Israelites did. The Children of Israel were now regarded as worse than any other nation in the world. When their sin was forgiven on the 29th of *Av*, the nation of Israel was then on par with the other nations. However, they did not achieve their former status as G-d's chosen people until the received the Second Tablets on *Yom Kippur*. *Yom Kippur* was the day that the atonement of the Jews was thorough and complete

Rabban Shimon ben Gamliel (*Tannis* 26b) makes a rather peculiar comment concerning *Yom Kippur*. He says that *Yom Kippur* was a day of great joy and matchmakers were hard at work on that day. The oddity is that we know *Yom Kippur* to be a very solemn day. It is ushered in with the hushed tones of *Kol Nidrei*. Sobbing can be heard over the voice of the chazzan. Why did Rabban Shimon ben Gamliel say that it was a joyous day and why were matchmakers hard at work that particular day of all days of the year?

Our Sages compare the receiving of the Torah to a marriage. G-d was the groom, the Children of Israel were the bride, and the Torah was the marriage contract. Originally, the marriage was to take place on the 17th day of *Tammuz* when Moshe brought down the Tablets. However, the sin of the Golden Calf marred the occasion. The marriage was called off. At first it seemed that it would never take place but on the 29th of *Av* Moshe informed the Jewish nation that the marriage would take place on the 10th day of *Tishrei*, on *Yom Kippur*.

It is the union between G-d and his nation that makes *Yom Kippur*, despite its solemnity, a day of joy. It was also deemed a "lucky" day for matchmakers. What better day to try and match up a bride and groom than on the day G-d, the groom, was matched with His bride, the Children of Israel.

The Children of Israel at Mt. Sinai were able to acknowledge the dual aspect of *Yom Kippur*, solemnity and joy. However, we find it very difficult to observe both facets of the holy day. The Sages, how-ever, have enlightened us by pointing out a connection between *Yom Kippur* and *Purim*. On both days the prayers of the Jews were answered. Both days involved a lottery. There was Haman's lottery to choose a day of destruction. And, in the Yom Kippur service there was a lottery to see which goat would be sent to *Azazel* to be destroyed. The names of the two holidays underscore the affinity of these two occasions – *Yom Ki***purim** (*Yom Kippur*) and *Purim*. The solemnity of the day is commemorated on *Yom Kippur* and the joyous aspect is cel-ebrated on *Purim*.

✒ YOM KIPPUR AND THE POINT OF CREATION

The 184ᵗʰ mitzvah in the Torah is the prohibition to enter the Holy of Holies.
"(The High Priest) may not come at any time to the holy place within the curtain before the covering of the Ark which is upon the ground so that he may not die..." **(16:2).**

The only person who was permitted to enter the Holy of Holies was the High Priest and only on *Yom Kippur* and only to do the Divine service on that day.

Why was such a great restriction placed upon entering the Holy of Holies?

The Medrash (*Bereishis Rabbah* 3:4) says that the creation of the universe began from the Holy of Holies. The primordial light was fashioned from the earth of the Holy of Holies. Another Medrash (*Tehillim* 92:6, *Pirke D'Rebbe Eliezer* 29) says that Adam was created from the ground of the Holy of Holies. We can see that the Holy of Holies represents creation: the creation of the universe, the creation of enlightenment, and the creation of Man.

Creation is a hidden process. The most creative physical process is the creation of a human being. That process begins with a very private and concealed act between a husband and wife. According to *halachah*, one is not permitted to watch animals copulating. Even with regards to vegetation we see that there is a hidden aspect. The seed takes root and germinates below the ground, out of sight. This perhaps explains why the Holy of Holies was kept hidden during the course of the year.

The *Zohar* (*Shmos* 31:18) says that the stone for the First Tablets came from the Holy of Holies. The Torah was also created, so to speak, from the Holy of Holies. On *Yom Kippur,* the High Priest, who represents Mankind, enters the Holy of Holies where the Holy Ark with the Tablets rested. Man and the Torah were once again united at the very point from whence they were created.

On the floor of the Holy of Holies was a large rock. It was called the "*evan she'siyah,*" the foundation stone. It was from this Rock that the world was formed. When the Temple was built, there were different levels of holiness in different areas. The closer the area was to the *Kodesh HaKadoshim,* the holier the area. Entry into the outer courtyard was prohibited to those who were defiled, "*tamei.*" Entry into the main Sanctuary was prohibited not only to those who were defiled, but also to non-*Kohanim.* Entry into the main section of the Sanctuary, the Holy of Holies, was permitted only to the High Priest and only on *Yom Kippur.* Only the holiest *Kohen* was permitted to walk into that room and only on the holiest day of the year when he was experiencing the highest degree of spirituality.

Today we are not yet worthy of having a rebuilt *Bais HaMikdash.* On *Yom Kippur,* we no longer have a High Priest to pray for us before the Throne of Glory. Each one of us has to serve as his or her own high priest. Our *shul* has to serve as our Holy Temple. Through fasting and fervent prayer we try to makes ourselves worthy of actually envisioning ourselves in the Holy of Holies in the *Bais HaMikdash* that still stands in the heavenly realm above. But the rock, on the Temple mount below is still there, defiled by its captors and enclosed by the Dome of the Rock. It still retains its holiness and, according to *halachah,* no one – Jew, Arab, or Christian, is allowed to walk there. The rock of creation is beckoning us to return to Hashem so it can be restored to its former glory.

⁀ഃ TWO GOATS

The 185ᵗʰ mitzvah of the Torah is for the High Priest to perform the service of *Yom Kippur.*
"From the congregation of Israel (the High Priest) shall take two goats for a sin-offering..." (16:3).

art of that service was to take two goats. They had to be very similar in appearance, stature, and value. Lots were drawn to see which was to be offered as a sacrifice to G-d and which was to be cast over a cliff to *Azazel.*

In May of 1940, refugees flocked to southern France seeking passage to Lisbon, Portugal via Spain, in hopes of finding a ship there to take them far away from the battle-fields and death-camps of Europe. In order to cross the frontier, the refugees needed Portuguese entry visas; but the Portuguese government instructed its consul general in Bordeaux to refuse entry visas to all refugees, especially to Jews. The consul general in Bordeaux at the time was Aristides de Sousa Mendes. All passage across the Spanish border came to a sudden halt and some ten thousand Jews remained stranded in Bordeaux.

One night, while Aristides de Sousa Mendes was walking in Bordeaux, he met Rabbi Chaim Krieger. Rabbi Krieger was a refugee and he and other Jews were preparing to spend the night in the street near the main syna-gogue. Mendes invited the Rabbi to the consulate for the night and offered to listen to the rabbi's account of the suf-

fering of the Jews. After the rabbi finished his unbelievable tales of persecution and extermination, Mendes announced that he was ready to grant entry visas to anyone who asked. Later, Rabbi Krieger recounted what followed:

"I sat with him a full day, without food and sleep, and helped him stamp thousands of passports with Portuguese visas. Mendes did not eat or sleep a whole day until late at night. During this short time, he issued several thousand visas, until the Nazis approached Bordeaux and we were forced to flee to Spain."

When Mendes returned to Lisbon, the Portuguese government was furious at his insubordination. Mendes was dismissed from the Foreign Ministry and all his retirement benefits were cancelled. Mendes was branded by the government as mentally unstable. As a result he could not find any means of gainful employment. With a family of twelve children, Mendes's life savings quickly disappeared. His wife was ill, his children were hungry, and he was despondent. The Hebrew Immigrant Aid Society (HIAS) helped to mitigate his and his family's suffering.

Years later, Mendes was asked about his ordeal. Mendes replied that he had no regrets. "If thousands of Jews can suffer because of one Catholic [Hitler], then surely it is permitted for one Catholic to suffer for so many Jews. I could not act otherwise. And I accept everything that has befallen me with love."

The Jewish community of Lisbon supported him financially in the years before his death, in 1954. In 1996, he was recognized by Yad Vashem as one of the Righteous Amongst the Nations.

On Yom Kippur, two identical goats are placed side-by-side. Lots are chosen. One is marked "To Hashem," the other, "To Azazel." The goat marked for Hashem is sacrificed by the High Priest to expiate the sins of the Jewish people and its blood was sprinkled in the Holy of Holies. The other goat was led into the wilderness, thrown off a cliff, its bones smashed on the rocks below.

Identical people from the same cities in Nazi Europe, with the same educations, the same religious backgrounds, the same experiences—yet, with very different destinies. One's lot fell to Hashem; the other's lot fell to Azazel. One's lot marked him for G-d, a rescuer who made amends for the sins of his people, destined for holiness, a person prepared to sacrifice himself and his family for the sanctification of G-d's name. The other lot marked for Azazel, a person who bowed before the demonic evil of the wilderness, who led his culture and his country to a barren land, cut off from all morality and civilized behavior. His destiny was to be smashed against the rocks of history; his legacy was scattered by the four winds.

The holocaust brought out the worst in man; it brought out the best in man. Many gentiles risked their lives and the lives of their families to take in Jews and protect them. Goodness challenges us in ways that evil does not. Compared to Eichmann, I am a saint. But compared to Mendes, how do I measure up? Would I have unlocked my door? Would I have taken into my home a sick man, a pregnant woman, a frightened family? Would I have kept them for days, weeks, months, years, knowing that discovery would mean imprisonment, torture and death for me and my family?

We are created in the image of G-d. Goodness is our moral mandate. Let us hope and pray for the day when all mankind will cast its destiny with G-d. "Goral echad laHashem." One destiny with One G-d – the G-d of love and mercy. The G-d of Israel.

WITH PERMISSION OF THE AUTHOR, RABBI HAYYIM KASSORLA

❧ THE KITTLE

*"And Aharon shall offer a bull for a sin-offering for himself and he shall make atonement for himself and for **his house**..."* (16:11).

I n the *Bais HaMikdash*, the *Kohen Gadol* wore special white linen garments to reflect the purity and sanctity of the day. The custom now is for married males to wear a special white garment on *Yom Kippur*, called a *kittle*. From the phrase *"for his house"* the Talmud (*Yoma* 13a) derives that a High Priest must be married in order to perform the *Yom Kippur* service. *"His house – that means his wife."* Just as the *Kohen Gadol* had to be married, only married males wear the *kittle*.

On *Yom Kippur* each Jew has a chance to emulate the angels. Angels are garbed in white; he is garbed in white. Angels do not eat; he does not eat. Angels stand; he stands. On this Day of Atonement, a Jew dedicates his thoughts to his soul and not to his body. *Yom Kippur* provides a chance for a person to put his life into proper prospective without being shackled by his physical desires. The Jew has a chance in this state to review his past actions and his position in life and to rectify the wrongs that he has done. The intrinsic holiness of the day provides man the chance to gain pardon for his sins.

*"For on this day atonement shall be made for you, to cleanse you from all yours sins **before G-d**, you shall be cleansed"* (16:30). The verse is teaching us that *Yom Kippur* will only absolve those sins which are between Man and his Creator. Sins that were committed between Man and his neighbor can only be forgiven if the sinner asks forgiveness from the person who was wronged (*Yoma* 85b).

A NEW YORK MINUTE

On *Yom Kippur* we refrain from wearing leather shoes to makes ourselves more humble before G-d. The spirit of humility adds to the special aura of holiness of the day. On *Yom Kippur* we are like angels dressed in white, immersed in prayer, and shod with simple canvas shoes or sneakers. But a critical test comes the moment *Yom Kippur* is over. After the blast of the *shofar* is heard, what is our reaction? Do we experience a heartfelt hope that the *shofar* is heralding the dawn of a new year: a year of dedication to G-d, to man, and to our families? Or, do we dash off to fill our empty stomachs? Do we hesitatingly leave the *shul,* reluctant to depart from the holiness of the day? Or are we out of there in a New York minute?

Yom Kippur tests man's dedication to G-d. It tests his self-control. It tests his ability to retain that dedication and self-control even after *Yom Kippur* is over. Is our *Yom Kippur* only one day a year or are we able to take the spirit of the holy day with us into the rest of the days of the year?

INNOVATIONS

"And he shall place the incense upon a fire before G-d..." (16:13).

A unique aspect of the *Yom Kippur* service was the offering of incense in the Holy of Holies by the High Priest. This offering was the very same one that the sons of Aharon, Nadav and Avihu, brought that caused their death. Nadav and Avihu sought to be innovative. They thought of this offering by themselves applying their great level of reasoning. Though their reasoning may have been correct, they were not commanded to bring the offering. They did not consult Moshe or their father Aharon. Innovation, even if well intended, must be brought about with the consultation and consent of the great spiritual leaders of Israel.

During the time of the Mishnah and Talmud, there was a renegade sect of Jews called the *Tzidokim,* or Sadducees. They did not believe in the Oral Law but rather they believed in their own interpretation of Jewish law according to the dictates of their intellect. A great debate arose between the Sadducees and the Rabbis. The Rabbis said that the incense must be placed on a fire inside the Holy of Holies. The Sadducees said that the incense must be placed on the fire outside and brought into the Holy of Holies already burning. "Does the royal baker prepare the meal in the presence of the king or is it prepared beforehand and then brought to him?"

The reasoning of the Sadducees may have been well founded; however, they sought to bring about a change in the *Yom Kippur* service without seeking the approval of the Rabbis. The Rabbis decreed that though the view of the Sadducees may be valid, their opinion may not be followed because of their rebellious spirit.

In every generation, the Jewish People have had their "Tzidokim," those who sought to introduce novelty into Judaism from what they have seen "outside the Holy of Holies". They seek to imitate the secular world and introduce "improvements," "adjustments" and "modernizations" into the inner sanctum of Israel. The Torah Sages of every generation fight a constant and bitter battle against these "improvements." That is not to say that the Torah is stuck in a bygone age. On the contrary, the Torah speaks to each generation on every aspect of life; sometimes involving itself in the finest minutiae of science, in order to express how the halachah views all that pertains to the modern world. But that view is extrapolated from the inward essence of the Torah, not grafted on from the outside. The Torah addresses the modern world, not in terms of compromise or appeasement, not through pandering to the ideolo-

gy of the hour, nor to the dictates of the fashions of the world at large. Rather it views the world through intrinsic principles enshrined in immutable criteria.

(Rabbi Yaakov Asher Sinclair)

✦ OUR MOTHER, THE SHECHINAH

"And he shall make an atonement in the Sanctuary for the uncleanliness of the Children of Israel, because of their transgressions, all of their sins, so he shall do in the Tent of Assembly that dwells with them in the midst of their uncleanliness" (16:16).

Rashi explains the phrase *"that dwells with them in the midst of their uncleanliness,"* to mean that though the Children of Israel are unclean the Divine Presence still dwells in their midst.

The *Zohar* explains that the *Shechinah,* the Divine Presence, is likened to a woman, a mother. While it may be that the father and the mother love a child equally, when the child soils itself, a father may choose to ignore it and leave the unpleasant task for later, preferably for someone else. The mother, on the other hand, will not ignore it. Rather, she rushes to aid her child. She gently washes it, changes its clothing, and gives the infant a loving kiss.

Similarly, G-d dwells amongst the Jewish people even if they are unclean. And, when the Jewish People are ready, G-d Himself comes and cleanses His precious nation. Because the *Shechinah* exhibits the maternal instinct, it is likened to a mother.

✍ CHARITY BEGINS AT HOME

"And he shall atone for himself and for his household and for all the congregation of Israel" (16:17).

The High Priest seeks to atone for the sins of the Jewish People. This verse teaches him the proper sequence of the people for whom he wishes to atone; first is himself, then his family, and then the rest of Israel. This sequence is quite understandable and can be extended to life in general. There are those who are so dedicated to providing for their family's need that they neglect their own health and wellbeing. The Torah is teaching us that we must attend to our own spiritual and physical needs first. If we are not in a perfect state of health, spiritually and physically, we will be of little use to others.

There are altruistic and selfless individuals who respond to the needs of the Jewish Community. They freely give of their time but at whose expense: their families. Some men spend so much of their free time doing for others that their families hardly see them. A wife needs a husband. Children need both a mother and a father. There is the famous story of a man well known for his kind deeds who became lost one night walking back from visiting some sick people. He stopped a young lad to ask of him directions back to his house. The lad looked up and asked, "Father, you don't recognize me?"

The Torah tells us that a man should first attend to the needs of his family. They are his primary responsibility. After that, he should see how he can benefit the community at large.

✌ TWO KIDS

At the conclusion of the Passover Seder we sing the traditional "*Chad Gadya.*" The refrain is: *One kid, one kid, that father bought for two zuz, one kid, one kid.* A question that has bothered me a long time has been that since it was only one kid, why do we constantly repeat the phrase and say "one kid, one kid?" And, what does the kid, a young goat, represent? What do the two *zuz* represent?

In the Temple service of *Yom Kippur*, the *Kohen Gadol* had two goats placed before him. They were identical in appearance, stature, and value. One was sent off to the wilderness to be cast to its death. The other was offered on the Altar as a sacrifice to Hashem. What do these two goats represent?

Goats are firmly identified with Eisav. When Eisav was born, the verse describes him, *"He was ruddy, and completely (hairy) like a coat of goats' hair"* (*Bereishis* 25:25). When Yaakov had to disguise himself as Eisav, Yaakov covered himself with goat's hair (*Bereishis* 27:16). Yaakov had to bring food to his father that Eisav would have brought. Yaakov brought goat's meat to him (*Bereishis* 27:9). Eisav lived in the mountainous area called Seir (*Bereishis* 36:8). *Seir* in Hebrew means goats. When Yaakov sent a series of gifts to Essav, the first gift consisted of 200 goats (*Bereishis* 32:15).

Yaakov and Eisav were twins. In their youth they were identical in deeds (*Rashi Bereishis* 25:27). Their potential for greatness was equal. Yaakov chose to use his talents and abilities for the pursuit of Torah. Eisav chose to use his potential for sin and evil. The two goats of *Yom Kippur* were also identical. They represent the two choices we have in life: the choice of Yaakov or the choice of Eisav. One will be a sanctification of Hashem's name on the holy Altar. The other will be thrown off a cliff in a wasteland: a waste of life.

G-d gives us life. He gives us gifts of talents and abilities. He gives us opportunities. We should not squander these gifts and opportunities. We should not waste our lives. Throughout our lives we are confronted with choices. Some of these choices may have major consequences. Where to go to school? Who should we marry? Where should we live? Often we have to make difficult decisions and we are not certain which to choose. We make a mental lottery and randomly choose one way and we hope the best. The two goats were randomly chosen to see which should be for Hashem and which for *Azazel*. Though it did seem to be random, during the forty years that Shimon HaTzaddik served as High Priest, the lottery always determined that the goat to his right was the one for Hashem (*Yoma* 39a). Though it seemed to be a random lottery, he always chose the "right" one. G-d guided his hand to the correct lot. On *Yom Kippur*, we too pray that throughout the year, may Hashem guide us in making the right decision.

"One kid, one kid, that father bought for us." We have but one life to live but there are two different paths. Our heavenly Father gave us this precious gift of life. How are we to know what choices to make as we go through life? We will be confronted with threatening cats, dogs, sticks, fire, and, ultimately, the Angel of Death. Which way to choose? The answer is contained in the Two Tablets, in the commandments of the Torah. If we try our best to adhere to the Torah's precepts, our choice will always be the correct one. The "*two zuz*" are symbolic of the Two Tablets.

It is remarkable how a simple seemingly childish Passover rhyme can contain such wonderful philosophical lessons.

⊰ THE GREAT UNIFIER

The 186ᵗʰ mitzvah is the prohibition to slaughter a sacrifice or to offer it outside the main *Mishkan* or Temple grounds.
"If to the doorway he does not bring to offer the sacrifice to G-d, before the Mishkan, spilled blood it will be considered for that man..." **(17:4).**

◄ THE DOMESTICATED MAN

"Since the life of the flesh is in the blood, I have given it to you (to be placed) upon the Altar to atone for your lives... and he who hunts the flesh of the beast or fowl to eat ..." (17:11-13).

The first part of the verse is telling us that the blood is the life-force of the body, human or animal. It carries the vital nutrients and oxygen to all the cells. A man, who has defiled his life-force through sin, can offer as atonement the blood of an animal in his stead. The latter part of the verse refers to the flesh of beasts, which are used as food, referring to kosher animals, which cannot be domesticated. Those animals must be hunted down. The verse is pointing out that sacrifices consisted only of domesticated animals – oxen, sheep, and goats; kosher animals, which cannot be domesticated, such as deer, can be used for food only and not for sacrifices. Why is this so?

There are two differences between a domesticated animal and an undomesticated one. Domesticated animals can be trained and tamed. Undomesticated animals cannot. Domesticated animals rely on their owners for food and water. They can not survive in the wild. Undomesticated animals can very easily survive in the wild.

Man is similar to the domesticated animal. Just as the domesticated animal can be trained and tamed so too Man can be taught and civilized. Just as the domesticated animal relies on its owner for food, Man too must realize that he relies on his Creator for sustenance. Since the sacrifice symbolically represents the Man who sinned, it is naturally befitting that an animal be used that best represents man; therefore, a domesticated animal is used.

≈§ THE REFINED AND THE HUNTER

The 187ᵗʰ mitzvah is the mitzvah of covering the blood of a wild animal or fowl that has been ritually slaughtered.

"Any man from the children of Israel, from the convert who lives among you, who hunts meat of a beast or fowl to be eaten, he shall cast the blood (on earth) and cover it with earth" **(17:13).**

When the Torah wanted to describe the evil Eisav, it called him *"a man who knew hunting"* (*Bereishis* 25:27). He hunted just for the sport. The Torah does not endorse nor consider cruelty to animals as a sport. This verse states, *"...who hunts meat of a beast or fowl to be eaten."* Hunting is only permitted for food and not for the amusement value it provides. The Torah values life, all life, human, animal, and even vegetation. The Torah prohibits the wanton destruction of animals. The Torah even prohibits the wasteful destruction of trees (*Devarim* 20:19-20).

The Torah further wanted to teach us to respect animal life. When we must slaughter the animal for food, we should cover the blood as a sign of burial. It shows respect for the life of the animal that was taken for our own benefit (*Ohr HaChaim* 17:13).

By covering the blood before partaking of its flesh, a person displays his refinement above the animal kingdom. Animals kill their prey and eat it right away, in full view of their prey's blood. Furthermore, to emphasize our refinement, our Rabbis teach us that we must cover the blood in a respectful manner, using our hands and not just kicking some dirt over the blood.

✌ KEEPING OUR DISTANCE

"Like the deeds of the land of Egypt wherein you dwelled, you shall not do; like the deeds of the land of Canaan to which I bring you, you shall not do. In their laws you shall not walk" (18:3).

The Torah issues a clear and concise warning against adopting or even imitating the lifestyles and social customs of a non-Jew. Rashi points out that this extends even to attending their theaters and stadiums. What is so terrible about a theater or stadium?

Our Sages (*Avodah Zorah* 18b) give different opinions as to why Jews should not attend theaters or stadiums. Rebbe Meir says it is because the entertainment was given in honor of their idols, much like the Olympic Games in ancient Greece. Rebbe Shimon ben Pazi says that gladiatorial contests were held there. Jews should not even be in the audience who witness such barbarism. The Rabbis say that one is not allowed to be part of a group of those who mock civility and morals.

The Medrash (*Rus Rabbah* 2:23) says that when Naomi wished to dissuade Ruth from converting to Judaism, she said, "We cannot go where the non-Jew goes, such as their theaters and stadiums." The commentaries (*Matnas Kehunah* and *Etz Yosef*) explain that those places were where simple-minded people went to be entertained by frivolous acts.

What sets a Jew apart is that he was commanded to be part of a holy nation, as we shall see in the beginning of the next *parshah, Kedoshim*. What does it mean to be holy? This is a concept that has been understandably misinterpreted. What comes to mind immediately are the reclusive "holy men" such as Monks and Hermits who sequester themselves from all earthly pleasures so as to be pure in spirit. This is clearly not how the Torah expected us to live. Hashem created the world for our benefit. He wants us to experience life's beauty and enjoy it. This notion is better understood when we realize that the pleasures of this world exist for our benefit: a means to aid us in our spiritual growth. For example a person can become closer to G-d through the food that he eats. First he acknowledges that it was G-d who made the food possible. We do so by reciting a blessing before eating the food. We again acknowledge His beneficence by thanking Him again after enjoying the food. Our act of eating has been enwrapped in blessing. The food enables us to become stronger and healthier in order to serve G-d. G-d made the food enjoyable to encourage us to eat and make it into a spiritual experience.

Life's pleasures may be harnessed to become conducive to holiness; however, that is only if the pleasures are not indulged in to an excess. Hashem gave the mitzvah "to be holy" in very vague terms in order to leave the choice of indulgence or abstention to the individual. Each person must seek the path to holiness in a way that enhances his spiritual growth. The Kotsker Rebbe, explained the phrase "*You shall be holy* (19:2)," by stating emphatically, "*Hashem is not short of angels; He has plenty of them up there in heaven. It is holy men down here on earth that He wants.*"

When the Torah instructs us, "*In their laws you shall not walk*" (18:3), it does not mean that we are above the law of the land. Jews are not allowed to ignore stop signs or run red lights. We must pay our taxes and obey the laws of the land. "*The law of the land is the law,*" proclaimed Shmuel (*Nedarim* 58a). The Torah is telling us that when it comes to ethics, morals, and religious values, we must follow the dictates of the Torah and not be swayed by outside influences.

The *parshah* began with holiness in time, *Yom Kippur* and its service. It then told us about holiness concerning place, the *Bais Hamikdash*, that ritual services could not be performed outside its confines. It then spoke about holiness of life, even animal life, the mitzvah of covering the blood. The remaining 24 mitzvos of this *parshah*, with one exception, deal with the holiness of marital relationships.

EGYPT AND CANAAN

"Like the deeds of the land of Egypt wherein you dwelled, you shall not do; like the deeds of the land of Canaan to which I bring you, you shall not do. In their laws you shall not walk" (18:3).

Why were Egypt and Canaan in particular mentioned? Why mention anyone? Also, mitzvah 189, to be explained shortly, mentions the prohibition of a son having an intimate relationship with one's father. What was the origin of that prohibition?

Cham was one of the three sons of Noach. The Torah tells us that while Noach was in a state of unconsciousness due to his excessive indulgence of wine, Cham had a relationship with his father (*Bereishis* 9:2, *Sanhedrin* 70a). Cham's descendants were the founders of two great kingdoms: Mitzrayim (Egypt) and Canaan (Bereishis 10:2). These two nations were notorious for their immorality. When Avraham came to Egypt with Sarah, they had to lie and say that Sarah was Avraham's sister. Otherwise, the Egyptians would have killed him, in order to take Sarah as the king's wife. Avraham, knew in advance the practices of Egypt.

Later we find that Potiphar's wife attempted to seduce Yosef. The Medrash (*Sifrah* 18:3) says that Egypt was known for deviant intimacy.

Canaan produced the degenerate cities of Sodom and Gemorrah. It was in Canaan where the crime against Dinah occurred. Avimelech, king of the Canaanite Philistines, seized Sarah as a wife.

The conclusion one draws is that the vile relationship that Cham had with his father tainted his soul. It caused him to produce genetically deviant offspring. Biologists have yet to discover the genetic makeup of the soul; but there is one. These genes are spiritual in makeup, not physical. If one mistreats these "genes" it can cause a horrible mutation. The Torah is our medical guide as to how we should treat our souls.

THE MITZVOS REGARDING
FORBIDDEN RELATIONSHIPS

The 188th mitzvah in the Torah is the prohibition to even "approach" a relative with whom an intimate relationship is forbidden.
"Any man, to a relative he shall not approach..." (18:6).

The Rambam (*Isurei Biyah* 21:1) interprets "approach" to mean to have physical contact in a manner that expresses physical desire, such as embracing and kissing.

The laws pertaining to sexual morality hold a vital key to Jewish sanctity. Many safeguards regarding sexual relationships were put in place. Animals copulate merely because of instinctive impulses. Many humans also behave according to their unbridled impulses. They are no better than the dog or horse, nor do they care to be better. The Torah tells us that through a pure marital relationship, based on respect, appreciation, and love, we have the capacity to reach great spiritual heights. The Torah gives us direction and safeguards on how to begin to achieve that goal.

There are those who consider the safeguards that protect one from immorality as old fashioned. However, G-d created us with our urges, instincts, and desires. Human nature does not change. The Torah's safeguards are as valid today as they were thousands of years ago. If man harnesses his animalistic urges for godly purposes, then he can cause holiness to dwell in his midst. If however, his urges are not kept under control, he becomes no better than the animal.

This section of the *parshah* is introduced with the verse, *"And you shall keep my statutes (chukim) and my laws (mishpatai) which if a man does them, he shall live. I am Hashem"* (18:5).

Why are these laws called *chukim*, which means "beyond comprehension," and also *mishpatim*, which means logical and comprehendible? How can they be both comprehensible and incomprehensible?

In truth they are comprehensible and logical. Logic says that physical contact with one with whom a relationship is forbidden may very well lead to a violation of that prohibition. However, if a person treats the laws simply as logic, he will think to himself that it does apply to him. He will say to himself that he can better control his urges than the other fellow. In the end, he too will violate the prohibition. Therefore, the Torah instructs him to treat these laws as though they were not comprehensible, as *chukim.*

> **The 189th mitzvah in the Torah is the prohibition for a son to have an intimate relationship with his father.**
> *"The nakedness of your father or your mother you shall not uncover"* (18:7).

As we shall see, an intimate relationship between any two males is forbidden by Torah law; however, such a relationship with a father was doubly repulsive. Therefore, the Torah gave it an additional prohibition. This is the explanation of the beginning of the verse according to the *Sefer HaChinuch* who follows one opinion expressed in the Talmud (*Sanhedrin* 54a). Rashi follows another opinion, also expressed in the Talmud (*ibid*), that the phrase *"nakedness of your father"* refers to a stepmother. Therefore, the 189th mitzvah according to Rashi would be the prohibition to have a sexual relationship with a step-mother.

> **The 190th mitzvah is the prohibition to have an intimate relationship with one's mother.**
> *"The nakedness of your father or your mother you shall not uncover"* (18:7).

As repulsive as this may seem to us, taking one's mother as a wife was an extremely common occurrence in the ancient world. Pharaohs as well as Greek and Roman emperors often married their mothers or daughter: sometimes both.

> **The 191st mitzvah is the prohibition to have an intimate relationship with one's step mother.**
> *"The nakedness of your father's wife you shall not uncover"* (18:8).

According to Rashi, this was already forbidden by mitzvah 189. Rashi interprets this verse to prohibit a relationship with a step-mother even after she is no longer the father's wife.

The 192nd mitzvah is the prohibition to have an intimate relationship with one's sister.

"The nakedness of your sister.... you shall not uncover..." (18:9).

The 193rd mitzvah is the prohibition to have an intimate relationship with one's son's daughter.

"The nakedness of your son's daughter... you shall not uncover... (18:10).

The 194th mitzvah is the prohibition to have an intimate relationship with one's daughter's daughter.

"The nakedness of your daughter's daughter you shall not uncover..." (18:10).

The 195th mitzvah is the prohibition to have an intimate relationship with one's daughter. This mitzvah is unusual in respect that there is no verse that clearly states it; however, it is obviously true. If one may not have a relationship with one's daughter's daughter, then surely he cannot have a relationship with his daughter.

The 196th mitzvah is the prohibition to have an intimate relationship with one's half-sister from the same father.

"The nakedness of the daughter of your father's wife, born of your father, she is (still) your sister, you shall not uncover her nakedness" (18:11).

The 197th mitzvah is the prohibition to have an intimate relationship with one's father's sister.

"The nakedness of your father's sister you shall not uncover." (18:12).

The 198th mitzvah is the prohibition to have an intimate relationship with one's mother's sister.

"The nakedness of your mother's sister you shall not uncover..." (18:13).

The 199th mitzvah is the prohibition to have an intimate relationship with one's father's brother.

"The nakedness of your father's brother you shall not

uncover..." (18:14).

This is the interpretation of the *Sefer HaChinuch*. See next mitzvah.

> **The 200ᵗʰ mitzvah is the prohibition to have an intimate relationship with one's father's brother's wife.**
> " *...to (your father's brother's) wife you shall not approach, she is your aunt*" (18:14).

This interpretation of the *Sefer HaChinuch* renders two mitzvos from the same verse. The verse states, "*The nakedness of your father's brother you shall not uncover, to (your father's brother's) wife you shall not approach, she is your aunt.*" The *Sefer HaChinuch* divides the verse into the aforementioned mitzvos, number 199 and 200. Rashi on the other hand does not divide the verse into two mitzvos. Rashi maintains that the end of the verse explains the beginning. Here is how Rashi interpreted the verse: *The nakedness of your father's brother you shall not uncover.* And what is meant by your father's brother's nakedness? Your father's brother wife. Rashi omits mitzvah 199. In order to achieve a total of 613 mitzvos, Rashi will have to include some mitzvah that the *Sefer HaChinuch* does not count.

> **The 201ˢᵗ mitzvah is the prohibition to have an intimate relationship with one's daughter-in-law.**
> "*The nakedness of your daughter-in-law you shall not uncover*" (18:15).
> **The 202ⁿᵈ mitzvah is the prohibition to have an intimate relationship with one's brother's wife.**
> "*The nakedness of your brother's wife you shall not uncover*" (18:16).
> **The 203ʳᵈ mitzvah is the prohibition to have an intimate relationship with a woman and her daughter.**
> "*The nakedness of a woman and her daughter you shall not uncover nor her son's daughter, nor her daughter's daughter...*" (18:17).

One may not marry a woman and her daughter, even if one is not married to them simultaneously. Therefore, one may not marry his wife's daughter; also he may not marry his wife's mother, who is his mother-in-law, because then he will have married a woman and her daughter.

The 204ᵗʰ mitzvah is the prohibition to have an intimate relationship with one's wife's son's daughter.

"The nakedness of a woman and her daughter you shall not uncover nor her son's daughter, nor her daughter's daughter..." **(18:17).**

The 205ᵗʰ mitzvah is the prohibition to have an intimate relationship with one's wife's daughter's daughter.

"The nakedness of a woman and her daughter you shall not uncover nor her son's daughter, nor her daughter's daughter..." **(18:17).**

The 206ᵗʰ mitzvah is the prohibition to have an intimate relationship with one's wife's sister while the wife is alive.

"A woman and her sister you shall not take as wives to uncover her nakedness while she is alive" **(18:18).**

This prohibition, applies while he is married to his wife and even after a divorce; but it does not apply after the death of his wife. All other prohibited relationships based on a connection to the wife apply at all times: even after the death of the wife. For example, a man is always prohibited from marrying his wife's daughter: while the wife is married to him, even after a divorce, and even after the death of the wife. This mitzvah is the only exception and, thus, a man may marry his wife's sister after the death of his wife.

The 207ᵗʰ mitzvah is the prohibition to have an intimate relationship with one's wife during her menstrual impurity period.

"A woman during her menstrual impurity you shall not approach to reveal her nakedness" **(18:19.**

This begins at the instant menstruation begins and usually ends 12 days later after immersion in a *mikvah.*

The Torah refers to sexual intimacy as "knowing." *"Adam knew Chavah, his wife"* (*Bereishis* 4:1). A husband and wife should know and understand each other emotionally, intellectually and spiritually. Ideally, only after reaching this level of emotional intimacy, should they arrive at the level of physically knowing each other. When intimacy occurs under these circumstances, it can be a medium for expressing a couple's deep emotional feelings and spirituality.

As with all aspects of the physical world, our physical desires contain the potential to reach great moral, spiritual and virtuous heights. However, the more potential something has for holiness, the greater is its potential for un-holiness. Intimacy in its proper time and place can help a couple to achieve a state of marital bliss. It may result in the creation of a new soul, a child.

The Torah and the Sages gave us laws, rules, and regulations to help assure the survival of the marriage. The laws restricting a married couple from physical contact during the state of menstrual impurity renews and revitalizes the relationship each and every month.

The 208ᵗʰ mitzvah is the prohibition to offer one's son as a sacrifice to the fire-god *Molech*.

"From your children you shall not give to pass to Molech, do not defile the name of your G-d, I am Hashem" (18:21).

The *Chasam Sofer* wonders why this prohibition is mentioned in the portion of the Torah that deals exclusively with forbidden relationships. He answers as follows. We see from this portion of the Torah that the institution of marriage is considered holy. The holier something is, the more restrictions apply to it. A child who is born of such a holy union has a special holiness about him. Should a father take his holy son and offer him to the chilling fire-god *Molech*, it is considered a "*chillul Hashem* (blasphemy). Therefore, the verse concludes with "...*do not defile the name of your G-d, I am Hashem.*"

The verse says *"From your children you shall not give to pass to Molech."* The word "from" means "some" You cannot offer some of your children as a sacrifice. If one gives all his children he has not violated this mitzvah (*Sanhedrin* 64b). Many years ago, a Catholic priest asked the *Maharal* of Prague to explain this seemingly illogical law. It would seem to be much worse offering all one's children than only some of them. Why is the father exempt if he offers all of them?

The *Maharal* responded that there is a mitzvah to proclaim part of one's crop to be *trumah* and to give it to the *Kohen*. The law states regarding one who proclaims all of his crops to be *trumah,* that proclamation is totally invalid. What is the logic? The logic is that one who gives everything away is *meshugeh,* crazy. The proclamation of a *meshugineh* is invalid. The same logic applies to one who offers all his children to *Molech.*

The 209th mitzvah is the prohibition against homosexuality.

"With a male you shall not lie as with a woman, it is an abomination" **(18:22).**

The 210th mitzvah is the prohibition for a male to commit bestiality.

The 211th mitzvah is the prohibition for a woman to commit bestiality.

"With any beast he shall not lie to be defiled thereby, and a woman shall not stand before an animal to commit bestiality, it is a perversion" **(18:23).**

The marital act is one of unification. Two distinct individuals become as one. They are united in deed, thought, and emotion. This overwhelming spirit of unity is to give us an idea what it means to be unified with G-d and His creation. It is the highest level of spirituality and holiness. The greater the degree of holiness that can be achieved, the more restrictions and regulations are placed on that act. The most sacred place in this world was the *Kodesh HaKadoshim;* it is the place with the most restrictions regarding who can enter and when. The same principle applies to marital union.

⋚ THE HOLY LAND

"All these abominations were done by the men who preceded you and they defiled the land. (Take heed,) so that the land not spit you out should you defile it as it spit out the nation that preceded you" (18:27-28).

he *parshah* concludes with the warning that if we transgress these mitzvos and contaminate the land of Israel, we will be expelled. This illustrates the greatness and holiness of the land of Israel. Israel is not like any other country in the world. The land of Israel requires a certain standard of behavior, a degree of holiness, and it will expectorate those that contaminate it.

The Ramban explains why only the cities of Sodom and Gomorrah were destroyed because of the inhabitants' immoral behavior, and not those of Egypt and many other countries that were equally as perverse. Sodom and Gomorrah were cities in the land Israel. The Holy Land cannot tolerate being defiled.

The Ramban also explains that Yaakov could marry two sisters (a prohibition in the Torah), because it was before the Torah was given and because he was outside of Israel. He was in Aram. However, these two justifications did not stand up to the standards of holiness in Israel. As soon as he brought his two wives into the Holy Land, his second wife, his beloved Rachel, died.

❧ HAFTORAH ACHAREI MOS

THE *HAFTORAH* IS FOUND IN *YECHEZKIEL* 22:1-16.

This *haftorah* is read only once every several years because *Acharei Mos* and *Kedoshim* are often read together and under those circumstances the *haftorah* of *Kedoshim* is read. In addition, the Shabbos of *Parshas Acharei Mos* can fall out on *Rosh Chodesh* in which case the *haftorah* for *Rosh Chodesh* is read.

The prophet Yechezkiel tells the Children of Israel how dreadfully sinful they are:

"O' city that has shed blood... through your idols that you made you have become defiled" (22:3).

"The princes of Israel within your midst, each for his own power (did he seek)" (22:6).

"A father and a mother did (the people) treat lightly, the convert in your midst you did oppress, the widow and orphan you have wronged" (22:7).

"My holy places you degraded, My Shabbos you desecrated" (22:8).

"Among you were talebearers, in order to shed blood" (22:9).

"They uncovered their own father's nakedness, they forced women during their menstrual period" (22:10).

"A man commits adultery with his neighbor's wife; a man defiles his daughter-in-law, his sister, his father's daughter" (22:11).

"They took bribery and shed blood, you took usury and interest, you enriched your friends with money you obtained through extortion" (22:12).

"I will scatter you among the nations and disperse you among the lands, I will rid you of your impurity" (22:16).

One wonders how the Israelites could have become so depraved and indifferent to their fellow Jews and G-d. What was going through their minds?

The Talmud (*Shabbos* 88a) says that when the Jews stood at Mount Sinai, G-d uprooted the mountain and held it above their heads saying, "If you accept My Torah, all will be well. If not, then here will be your burial place." The Jews had no choice but to accept the Torah.

The Talmud continues to relate that since they had no choice in the matter, then they could not be found guilty if they violated any of the Torah laws: they were forced to accept them. However, during the time of the Babylonian exile, when the miracle of *Purim* occurred, the Jews willingly accepted the laws of the Torah.

It seems, based on that section of the Talmud, before the miracle of *Purim,* the Jews were not really held to be responsible for the laws of the Torah since they were intimidated into accepting them. We can now begin to understand the frame of mind of those rebellious Jews during the time of Yechezkiel. They flagrantly tread upon all the laws and statutes of G-d claiming that it was under duress that they were given and they were not obligated to observe them.

Since they seemed to have had a legitimate argument, why was the prophet Yechezkiel threatening them with exile and the Diaspora? Why, in fact, were they punished with exile?

The answer is found in our *parshah. "All these abominations were done by the men who preceded you and they defiled the land. (Take heed,) so that the land not spit you out should you defile it as it spit out the nation that preceded you"* (18:27-28). The Land of Israel cannot accept being defiled. It will cast out those who defile her. The nations of the Canaanites were destroyed, not because they did not keep the Torah, but because the Holy Land cannot tolerate defilement. Likewise, the Jews were exiled not as a punishment for not keeping the laws of the Torah but because they contaminated the Land of Israel.

This lesson is especially important in our time. In the State of Israel there are political parties that seek to uproot every trace of Judaism that is now present in the land. They demand the right for stores to be open on Shabbos. They demand the right to sell pork and bacon in the markets of Jerusalem. They demand that all forms of conversion be legalized. They demand that civil marriages be instituted, doing away with the sanctity of the Jewish marriage and the Jewish, home. Israel is surrounded by 21 enemy Arab nations. Israel is threatened from within by the anti-religious secularists. Those who seek to defile the land present a far greater threat than those who seek to throw us in the sea. If secularists were to have their way, then the land will spit us out, G-d forbid.

KEDOSHIM

⋛ THE TEN COMMANDMENTS REVISITED

"Be holy" (9:2).

As the Jewish People stood near the foot of Mount Sinai to receive the Torah, G-d told them, *"You shall be unto Me a kingdom of priests and a **holy** nation"* (*Shmos* 19:6).

Hashem was telling the people that the purpose of the Torah is to make every Jew into a holy person. Therefore, the revelation at Sinai and the Ten Commandments were preceded with the declaration *"You shall be unto Me a kingdom of priests and a **holy** nation."* Our *parshah* also begins with the declaration, *"Be holy."* Our *parshah* mirrors and expands upon the Ten Commandments that were given on Mount Sinai. The verses below which are found in Shmos are taken from the Ten Commandments as they were given at Sinai. The verses from *sefer* Vayikra are those same commandments as they are found in our *parshah*. [Please note the chapter and verse of each commandment from our *parshah*: the commandments in our *parshah* are in a different order than those in Shmos. This will have to be examined.]

1) "*I am the L-rd your G-d who brought you out of the land of Egypt*" (*Shmos* 20:2).
   "*I am the L-rd your G-d*" (*Vayikra* 19:3).

2) "*You shall not have other gods before Me*" (*Shmos* 20:3).
   "*Do not turn to idols and molten gods you shall not make...*" (*Vayikra* 19:4).

3) "*You shall not take the name of the L-rd your G-d in vain*" (*Shmos* 20:7).
   "*You shall not swear in My name falsely*" (*Vayikra* 19:12).

4) "*Remember the day of Shabbos to keep it holy*" (*Shmos* 20:8).
   "*My Shabboses you shall keep*" (*Vayikra* 19:3).

5) "*Honor your father and your mother*" (*Shmos* 20:12).
   "*A man shall respect his mother and father*" (*Vayikra* 19:3).

6) "*You shall not murder*" (*Shmos* 20:13).
   "*Do not stand by (while) the blood of your brother (is spilled)*" (*Vayikra* 19:16).

7) "*You shall not commit adultery*" (*Shmos* 20:13).
   "*A man who commits adultery with another man's wife...*" (*Vayikra* 20:10).

8) "*You shall not steal*" (*Shmos* 20:13).
   "*You shall not steal*" (*Vayikra* 19:11).

9) "*You shall not bear false witness against your friend*" (*Shmos* 20:13).
   "*There shall not walk a talebearer among your people*" (*Vayikra* 19:16).

10) "*You shall not desire your friend's house...*" (*Shmos* 20:14).
    "*You shall not seek revenge or bear a grudge against the children of your people*" (*Vayikra* 19:18).

Why is it that the order of the mitzvos in our *parshah* does not follow the same order of the Ten Commandments? The order of the Ten Commandments is as presented above.

The Ten Commandments follow the logical sequence of philosophical and theological importance.

(1) The most fundamental principle in Judaism is to recognize that there is a G-d. (2) Next, it is important to understand that He

alone is G-d and we cannot worship other gods along with Him. (3) Next we must understand that G-d is holy and everything that represents Him is holy. Therefore, His name cannot be uttered in vain. (4) We are obligated to serve G-d because we owe our very existence to Him. He created the universe and everything within it. Therefore, we keep the Shabbos to acknowledge that He is the Supreme Creator.

(5) After we have accepted the authority of Hashem and have realized that He is worthy of our love, respect, and awe we are obligated to show respect to His creations. When a young girl brings home a drawing she made in kindergarten class, the mother hangs it up with pride on the refrigerator door for all to see. Since she loves her daughter, she loves what her daughter has created. How much more so are we obligated to show respect for G-d's creations and creatures? The most important created beings for us to respect is our parents. If one has no sense of appreciation and gratitude towards parents, how can that person expect to have any sense of respect for anyone?

(6) After a person realizes that he owes his existence to G-d and his parents, he understands how precious and wonderful life is. He must then realize that everyone's life is precious and it is a grievous crime to kill another human being. (7) After he has learned to respect other people's lives, he must respect their rights. Adultery is the most egregious form of trampling on another man's rights. (8) Next, he must respect his neighbor's property rights by not stealing. (9) Just as he cannot commit a physical act to harm his neighbor or his property, he cannot even seek to harm him with words, such as false testimony.

(10) Finally, after one realizes that he cannot seek to harm his friend even through words, the Torah tells us that it is not permissible to feel animosity or jealousy towards him.

The Ten Commandments in our *parshah* follow a very different order. We will divide them into 4 groups.

1) "*A man shall respect his mother and father*" (*Vayikra* 19:3).

2) "*My Shabboses you shall keep*" (*Vayikra* 19:3).

3) "*I am the L-rd your G-d*" (*Vayikra* 19:3).

4) "*Do not turn to idols and molten gods you shall not make...*" (*Vayikra* 19:4).

5) *"You shall not steal"* (*Vayikra* 19:11).

6) *"You shall not swear in My name falsely"* (*Vayikra* 19:12).

7) *"There shall not walk a talebearer among your people"* (*Vayikra* 19:16).

8) *"Do not stand by (while) the blood of your brother (is spilled)"* (*Vayikra* 19:16).

9) *"You shall not seek revenge or bear a grudge against the children of your people"* (*Vayikra* 19:18).

10) *"A man who commits adultery with another man's wife..."* (*Vayikra* 20:10).

The mitzvos in our *parshah* are obviously not in the order of philosophical and theological importance. Instead, they follow the order of ethical importance. (1) The rules of ethics tell us that our primary moral obligation is to our parents. (2) The next mitzvah highlights the point that ethical importance, unlike theological importance, has prescribed boundaries. We must keep the Shabbos even if our parents command us otherwise (see *Rashi* 19:3). (3) If the Torah underscores our primary moral obligation as being to honor our parents, why shouldn't their words take priority over Shabbos? Because your parents, as well as you, are required to listen to Hashem. *"I am the L-rd your (plural) G-d."* Therefore, G-d's commandments override any conflict presented by the obligation to honor one's parents. (4) A Jew is strictly forbidden to worship or make idols, regardless of any conflict presented by his or her parents. What did this add to what we have already stated by Shabbos. Maybe we can draw from the case of Avraham. His father, Terach, was in the idol business. Not only did Avraham resist his father's ways, he went so far as to mock his father's business by smashing the smaller idols and placing the weapon in the grasp of the big idol as 'evidence' against it. Thus, the fourth mitzvah perhaps takes our moral obligation in this first group to the limit: a parent with any connection to idols, even just making or selling them for others, forfeits the awesome honor due to them which is incumbent upon their son or daughter. These are the mitzvos of the first group.

The second group is the next stage of ethical importance. (5) One must respect the rights and property of others. (6) One who disregards the rights of others and steals from him, will in the end swear falsely in court denying he did anything wrong (*Rashi* 19:11). This is the second group.

(7) The third stage of ethical conduct is that not only are we prohibited from physically harming our neighbor, we cannot verbally damage him by spoiling his reputation. (8) The next stage of ethical conduct deals with one who thinks that he will not physically harm his neighbor nor will he sully his reputation. Instead, he will stand idly by while someone else is doing him harm. The Torah tells us that one cannot be passive when an injustice is being committed. He is required to act. (9) The next stage of ethical conduct is that not only can we not harm our neighbor, not only can we not stand idly by while harm is being inflicted upon him, we cannot harbor any ill-feelings about our neighbor in our heart. Sometimes we cannot help our feelings; then it is our responsibility to meet with the neighbor and make every attempt to resolve the issue and not allow it to fester.

The final stage of ethical conduct is unique. Those of the first three stages – the parents, the neighbors (property rights), the appropriate interpersonal conduct in speech, deed and thought – all have exceptions. The parents and neighbors can choose to overlook their rights or forgive any misdeeds. A person can talk *lashon ha'ra* about the wicked. We can hate them in our hearts. The fourth stage is an ethical offense that has no exceptions. (10) When it comes to adultery, no one can be *mochel* (forgive) the moral conduct – not the adulterer, not the adulteress, and not her husband.

In summary, at Mount Sinai the Ten Commandments were given in their order of religious importance. That is called *bain adam l'makom*, between man and G-d. Our *parshah* lists the commandments in the order of ethical importance. That is called *bain adam l'chavayro*, between man and his neighbor. Just as we are commanded to be holy in our religious pursuits, we are commanded to be holy in our ethical dealings with others as well.

✑ **UNITY**

When the Jewish People entered the Wilderness of Sinai, the verse states, "*And Israel camped there opposite the mountain (of Sinai) (Shmos* 19:2). Rashi makes note that the verb "*camped*" is used in the singular form rather than the expected plural form. Rashi explains that there was such unity among the Children of Israel when they camped before Mount Sinai, it was as though they were a single entity. Therefore, the verse uses the singular form.

Because there was such unity, brotherhood, and mutual respect among the Israelites, it was not necessary to stress the importance of the mitzvos *bain adom l'chavayro*. G-d gave the commandments in their order of religious significance. Our *parshah* occurred much later on, after the sin of the Golden Calf. By then, the magical spirit of unity and harmony was lost. G-d had to strengthen and invigorate that lost feeling by giving the mitzvos of our *parshah* in a sequence that would show the greatness of those mitzvos which are *bain adom l'chavayro*.

The *Sifsai Chachomim* points out that the other *parshiyos* in the Torah were taught to the Israelites by Moshe in groups. After one group had been taught, they departed and the next group would enter. However, since our *parshah* was taught to stress the importance of unity and mutual respect, it was taught in one gathering to the entire congregation of Israel simultaneously. Therefore, the verse says in the introduction to the *parshah*, "*G-d spoke to Moshe saying: Speak to **all the congregation** of the Children of Israel*" (*Vayikra* 19:1-2).

✑ **BE HOLY**

"Be holy for I, the L-rd your G-d, am holy..." (19:2).

hat does it mean to be holy? What message does the verse mean to convey by ending with "*...for I, the L-rd your G-d, am holy.*" Surely we cannot imitate the holiness of G-d which is above our frail comprehension.

Some people misconstrue the concept of holiness to mean total abstinence. During the time of the Second Temple there was a cult of Jews called Essenes. Here is how the contemporary Jewish historian, Josephus Flavius, describes these Essenes.

These Essenes reject pleasures as an evil. They refuse to marry. They despise wealth. All property is owned communally. One does not own more than another for it is a law among them that those who come to join the sect must give their possessions to the common property of the whole order. They regard fragrant oils as a defilement and if any one of them be anointed without approval, it is wiped off his body. They think to be sweaty is a good thing. They do not put on new shoes until the old ones are torn to pieces.

They neither buy nor sell any thing to one another but every one of them gives away whatever he has to whomever he wishes and anyone may take for himself whatever he needs. All of this is on the condition that the overseer approves. They eat together and are served from the communal kitchen by the baker and the cook. Before they eat, they dress themselves in white robes. The portions are small but adequate. Quiet fills the hall. Only one person is allowed to speak at a time and only if the others grant him permission to speak.

One who steals or tells a lie is punished in a horrible manner. He is cast out of their society and is forbidden to eat food fit for humans. He is reduced to eating grass and eventually dies of starvation. Some are granted forgiveness while in the throes of death and taken back into the fold.

Speaking in an ill-manner of Moses is considered a capital offence. Moving any vessel on the Sabbath is strict-

ly forbidden. Relieving one's self on the Sabbath is frowned upon.

(BASED ON JOSEPHUS FLAVIUS'S WARS OF THE JEWS, BOOK II, CHAPTER 8).

The Essene concept of holiness sounds somewhat like the concept of the Christian monastery and indeed the Essene movement was embraced by the early Christians. However, that is not the Jewish concept or philosophy of holiness. The Talmud (*Yevamos* 20a) tells us that we sanctify ourselves through that which is permitted to us. What does the Talmud mean? The Rambam in the fourth chapter of his introduction to *Pirkei Avos* states the correct manner in which a person should strive to achieve is that of moderation in all his activities. One should eat in moderation. One should dress moderately, meaning not in flamboyant clothing and not in tatters. Just as eating forbidden food is not allowed, overindulgence in permitted food is likewise not allowed. The Ramban in the beginning of our *parshah* says that moderation is the definition of holiness. We are to seek holiness through that which is permitted to us.

The Ramban continues by saying that those things which the Torah prohibited are totally prohibited. But, there are many things which the Torah permitted – eating kosher foods, acquiring wealth, relaxation, etc. One who consumes his time with those activities is not leading a holy lifestyle but rather one of self-indulgence. The Ramban uses an expression to describe the over-indulgent person, *navel birshus haTorah*, a depraved individual who lives within the boundaries that the Torah permitted.

G-d is holy. How does G-d express this holiness? G-d "occupies" himself with the task of benefiting His creatures and sustaining life. He continuously watches over His creation. There is no concept whatsoever of self-indulgence in connection to G-d. The Torah instructs us to be G-d-like. We too are urged to be holy and not to be self-indulgent but rather to seek and improve the welfare of others.

There are two forms of holiness. The first is with respect to man and his Creator. One who *davens* with *kavanah* and is careful with all the laws of Shabbos and kashrus is expressing zeal in the spiritual realm of holiness, the realm of *bain adom l'makom*. We refer to that holy person as a *tzaddik*. However there is another realm for expression of holiness and that is in the physical world. One who keeps the normal standards of dress and cleanliness. One who is considerate of his fellow and shows compassion to the unfortunate is also holy. We refer to that holy person as a *chassid*.

The Talmud (*Berachos* 53b) tells us that one who washes before a meal is making himself holy. One who washes at the conclusion of the meal (*mayim achronim*) is also making himself holy. Washing before the meal is to remove any *tumah*, spiritual uncleanliness; the *kedushah* (holiness) of a *tzaddik*. The washing at the conclusion of the meal is to remove any physical uncleanliness to prepare one's self to *bentch*; the holiness, of a *chassid*.

We are used to thinking that holiness is primarily associated with a *Sefer* Torah or a *shul.* or being constantly in a *Bais Medrash*. The *parshah* is teaching us that holiness is a way of life; that is to be maintained even outside the *shul.* It is a mode of moral, ethical, and social conduct that is to be instilled in our daily activities and throughout our lives.

⋖§ IN AWE OF PARENTS

The 212ᵗʰ mitzvah in the Torah is to fear one's parents.
"A man, his mother and father, should fear..." (19:3).
"Honor your father and your mother" (Shmos 20:12).

Some people are confused by the word "*fear*." What does it mean to fear one's parents? Does it mean that one should treat them nicely out of fear of being punished by them? Of course not. In old English, the term "fear" meant to be in awe or to hold in reverence. The mitzvah is to have reverence for one's parents.

What is the difference between this mitzvah and the mitzvah to honor one's parents mentioned in Shmos (20:12)? Why here does the Torah mention the mother before the father and in Shmos it mentions the father before the mother?

The Talmud (*Kiddushin* 30b-31a) explains that to honor one's parents means to do something for them. If they need a favor, one should do it because of the mitzvah to honor one's parent. A child is usually more anxious to help a mother more than a father, possibly because the mother speaks more kindly to the child and may even reward the child for the good deed. Therefore the Torah mentioned the father before the mother to teach us that we must perform the mitzvah even without being bribed by kind words and a promise of a reward.

The Talmud then explains that to have reverence for a parent means to refrain from something out of respect for a parent, such as not sitting in their seat and not contradicting them. A child usually has a greater reverence for the father for he is commonly the authority figure in the family. The Torah mentions the mother first to teach us that one must have the same reverence for a mother as he or she has for a father.

The Talmud (*Kiddushin* 31a) asks what the extent of this reverence is. The Talmud illustrates with the following story:

A certain gentile, Dama the son of Nesinah, lived in Ashkelon. The Sages sought jewels for the priestly *ephod* and were willing to pay six-hundred-thousand gold *denarim*, but the key to the jewel chest was lying under his father's pillow. Dama refused to awaken his father whose head was gently resting on the pillow. The following year the Holy One, Blessed be He, gave Dama his reward. A red heifer was born to his herd. When the Sages of Israel went to him to purchase it, he said to them, 'I know that even if I asked you for all the money in the world you would pay me. But I ask of you only the money which I lost through honoring my father.' Rebbe Chanina later commented: If a gentile, who is not commanded in the Torah to honor his parents, is rewarded, how much more so we, who are commanded, will be rewarded.

Why did the Talmud feel it necessary to illustrate the extent of honoring one's parent from a gentile? Were their no similar cases of Jews who performed the mitzvah to the same extent?

I believe the answer is as follows. Having respect for one's parents is logical. In fact, even non-Jews respect their parents. The Torah teaches us that having respect for parents extends beyond that which is logical. That is why the father was mentioned before the mother with regards to honor and the mother was mentioned before the father with regards to reverence. The "main" mitzvah begins at a point beyond the logical realm. Anything that we do for our parents out of logic and decency is not included in the essence of the mitzvah. When the Talmud asked "To what extent does reverence go?" it was asking to what extent does this logical realm extend before the main mitzvah begins. The Talmud showed us that Dama the son of Nesinah was willing to forgo a profit of 600,000 gold *denarim* to honor his father. Dama was not motivated by the mitzvah. He was motivated by what he perceived to be logical decency. The Talmud was teaching us that to fulfill the real mitzvah of honoring and respecting one's parents is very challenging indeed. It begins where "the decent thing to do" logically ends.

We can apply this approach to all the mitzvos *bain adom l'chavayro*, between man and his fellow. These mitzvos are quite logical; almost everyone has compassion for the needy or sympathy for those in dire straits. The real challenge is to go beyond your personal feelings of compassion and sympathy. Give a little bit more, do a little bit more. Go beyond the logical realm.

✢ COMPARATIVE RELIGION COURSES

The 213th mitzvah in the Torah is not to turn to idol worship.
"Do not turn to idols" **(19:4).**

hat does it mean to "turn" to idol worship? Why didn't the verse simply say do not worship idols?

The *Sefer HaChinuch* (213) says that the verse means that one is not permitted to study or think about other religions. One is not even permitted to look at idols in a studious or admiring fashion. One who looks at idols or symbols of other religions may come to be curious about their beliefs. He may be tempted to study and evaluate their belief system. This in turn may lead one to think that there is some validity to that religion.

❧ IDOLS 'R' US

The 214ᵗʰ mitzvah in the Torah is the prohibition against making an idol for oneself or someone else. *"Make not for yourselves molten gods"* **(19:4).**

A Jew is not permitted to be involved in the manufacture or sale of any item used exclusively for other religions.

A local rabbi once jokingly commented that a Jew can sell a single fruit and a few branches of common trees for an exorbitant sum. The non-Jew, on the other hand, can sell an entire Christmas tree for a few dollars.

Though the comment was made in jest it does show a basic difference between our approach and others. Every religious item used in the performance of a mitzvah has a multitude of rules and regulations. A *Sefer* Torah, *tefillin, tzitzis,* an *esrog,* a *succah,* matzah, etc have so many laws that, in order to make it suitable for the mitzvah, it adds greatly to the cost. The letters of the *Sefer* Torah must be formed exactly, the leather boxes of the *tefillin* must be made in a certain way, the *esrog* must be totally free of blemishes, the *succah* has many regulations as to what can be used for a covering, and matzah must be baked without the slightest question of it being *chametz*. Just as G-d is perfect, every object used in the service of G-d must be perfect. An object used for a mitzvah has *kedushah,* holiness. It cannot simply be tossed into the trash after it is no longer needed. Some religious objects are required to be disposed of in an honorable fashion; other religious objects require burial. No other belief system has such a comprehensive quest for perfection.

However, even we have one religious item that is often overlooked in our quest for perfection. We do not examine it carefully and sometimes we misuse it in a derogatory fashion. What is that object? It is us. The Jew is the most precious religious object we have. In our search for perfection we may spend hours looking for the perfect *esrog* or spend a small fortune on matzos for Passover. But what about ourselves? The opening verses of our *parshah* tell us to be holy. We too are a holy religious article, the most holy one. We dare not overlook our own physical and spiritual flaws.

◆§ OUTSTAYING ONE'S WELCOME

The 215ᵗʰ mitzvah is the prohibition to eat meat of a sacrifice after the proper time limit has expired.
"On the day you sacrifice, it may be eaten and on the following day (too), but the leftover on the third day you shall burn with fire. If it be eaten on the third day, it is abominable and it is not acceptable" **(19:6-7).**

Sacrifices have a time limit until when it may be eaten; one is not permitted to eat the meat after that time. The Talmud (*Menachos* 6a) tells us that when the priests or Israelites ate from the sacrificial meat, it was considered as though G-d was inviting them to eat at His table. A considerate guest does not overstay his visit. Partaking of the sacrificial meal after a proper time has lapsed is considered a breach of proper etiquette. The Talmud (*Pesachim* 86b) also tells us, *"One must listen to his host in whatever he says except when he says that it's time for the guest to leave."* The Talmud means that the guest should not stay too long so that the host must tell him that it is time for the guest to depart. The guest should leave before he has to be told.

Just as the Torah instructs the Israelites to be a generous host to guests, the Torah also instructs the guests to also be considerate of their hosts and not take advantage of their beneficence.

SHARING YOUR BLESSINGS

The lesson of the following mitzvos is to leave a corner of the not yet harvested field available for the poor to take what they need. We must not feel that we are giving a gift from our own personal property; our harvest is only ours through G-d's kindness. G-d expects us to act as his agent to see that the poor have what they need.

General rules:

The owner of the field may not designate which poor person (s) can take the crops. They must be made available to all the poor.

The non-Jewish poor may also take from the produce.

The corner of a fruit orchard must also be left for the poor.

Though the Torah did not give any precise measure as to the size of the corner that must be left for the poor, the Rabbis instituted that the corner must consist of at least 1/60

of the total yield of the field, vineyard, or orchard.

These mitzvos only apply to produce which is used for human consumption. That would exclude an alfalfa field.

These mitzvos only apply to produce which ripen around the same time of the year, such as wheat. Dates which ripen throughout the summer do not have these mitzvos.

These mitzvos only apply to produce that can be stored for later use. Most vegetables would therefore be excluded from these mitzvos.

If one owned several fields, a corner in each one must be left for the poor. He cannot leave one large section in one field for all the other fields.

The poor are only entitled to the crops they actually pick up. They cannot toss a sheet over part of the corner and claim it is theirs.

If no poor come to claim the produce to which they are entitled, the owner of the field may then retrieve it.

The Rambam (*Matnas Aniyim* 1:14) writes that these mitzvos apply only in Eretz Yisroel, according to Torah Law; however, the rabbis instituted that Jewish farmers throughout the world should adhere to these laws.

The next eight mitzvos in the *parshah* deal with sharing your crops with the poor.

> **The 216th mitzvah in the Torah is to leave a corner of your standing produce in the field for the poor.**
> *"When you cut the harvest of your land... to the poor and the stranger you shall leave them"* **(19:9-10).**
> **The 217th mitzvah in the Torah is the prohibition to harvest the entire field for yourself.**
> *"You shall not cut entirely the corner of your field"* **(19:9).**
> **The 218th mitzvah is to leave those stalks that fall down during the cutting for the poor.**
> *"The gleanings of your harvest... to the poor and the stranger you shall leave them"* **(19:9-10).**

This is called *Leket* (gleaning). This applies to one or two stalks that fell from the hand of the harvester. If more than two stalks fell, the harvester may retrieve it.

> **The 219th mitzvah is the prohibition to pick up fallen stalks to which the poor are entitled.**
> *"The gleanings of your harvest you shall not gather"* **(19:9).**
> **The 220th mitzvah is to leave part of the vineyard for the poor.**
> *"Your vineyard... to the poor and the stranger you shall*

leave them" (**19:10**).

The Rambam and Ramban have differing interpretations as to what part of the vineyard the verse refers. The Rambam (as quoted by *Sefer HaChinuch* 220) interprets the verse to mean that one should leave the corner of the vineyard for the poor. The Ramban (*ibid*) interprets the verse to mean those grapes that do not grow in clusters, but merely a few straggly grapes that are on the vine that do not lean one upon the other, should be left for the poor.

The *Sefer HaChinuch* points out that the Rambam agrees that the straggly grapes should also be left for the poor but derives that from another verse and, likewise, the Ramban agrees that the corner of the vineyard should be left for the poor but derives that from another verse. They only disagree as to the interpretation of this verse.

The 221ˢᵗ mitzvah is the prohibition to harvest the entire vineyard for yourself.

"Your vineyard you shall not gather" (**19:10**).

The 222ⁿᵈ mitzvah is to leave for the poor the grapes that fall from the cluster while it is being harvested.

"The fallen of your vineyard... to the poor and the stranger you shall leave them" (**19:10**).

This applies only to one or two grapes that fell from a cluster as it was being cut from the vine. If more than two grapes fell, they may be retrieved by the harvester.

The 223ʳᵈ mitzvah is the prohibition to retrieve grapes to which the poor are entitled.

"The fallen of your vineyard you shall not gather" (**19:10**).

These mitzvos teach two important lessons. But first we must ask why did the Torah pick the corner of the field and orchard to be left for the poor? Why not some place in the middle? A farmer's work begins at the corner of the field and ends at the corner of the field. When the farmer first sets his flow into the ground, he starts at one of the corners and plows straight to the opposite corner. He then moves the plow to the next row and plows from one end of the field to the other. His work is completed when he reaches the last corner. The planting of the seeds follows the same pattern. It begins at one corner and ends at another corner. The harvesting also begins at one corner and ends with another corner. From beginning to end, from corner to corner, the farmer does what he can to ensure a bountiful crop but he must always rely on the blessings of Hashem that his labors will be fruitful. That is why this series of mitzvos end with the phrase "*I am the L-rd your G-d*" (19:10), to remind us that G-d is the source of all blessings.

To show his feeling of gratitude the farmer is instructed to share his blessings with those who were not as fortunate as he. This theme, of expressing gratitude through sharing, is still with us today. How do we express gratitude to Hashem after the birth of a child? We make a *kiddush* in *shul*. How do we express gratitude and show joy at a bar mitzvah or wedding? We have a beautiful meal in honor of the occasion and invite our relatives, friends, and neighbors. When one recovers from a serious illness, he makes a festive meal and expresses his gratitude to Hashem for his blessings.

The farmer is told not to retrieve the one or two stalks or grapes that have fallen to the ground. The farmer knows that the poor will be attracted to his field to collect from the corners. If he were to pick up those insignificant fallen crops, he is demonstrating that he refuses to give to the poor a single stalk or grape more than is required. He would be displaying miserliness. In all probability he wouldn't stoop to retrieve it except that he wants to prevent the poor from taking it. Miserliness is a debasing trait. The miser has no compassion for anyone and, in the end, no one has compassion for the miser.

The sixteenth century political theorist, Niccolò Machiavelli, in his *The Prince*, claimed that miserliness is a political virtue. "*In our own days we have seen no Princes accomplish great results save those who have been accounted miserly. All others have been ruined.*" No wonder the name Machiavelli has become a synonym for deceit. The Torah's two lessons of these mitzvos are to be magnanimous in sharing and be far removed from miserly behavior. Very un-Machiavellian.

✺ THE OTHER THEFT

The 224ᵗʰ mitzvah in the Torah is the prohibition to steal.
"You shall not steal" (19:11).

The preceding mitzvos dealt with leaving part of your crops for the poor. One who does not conform to those laws is considered to have robbed from the poor. This mitzvah is the general prohibition to steal from anyone, poor or rich.

The concept behind the prohibition to steal needs no elaboration. All ethical systems and cultures understand that such a restriction is necessary in order for a society to function properly. However there is another type of theft which is often overlooked and discounted. Our Sages call it theft of trust.

Theft of trust means to fool or mislead someone. The Talmud (*Chullin* 94a) tells us that this too is strictly forbidden. If another person is placing trust in you, you may not purposely fool him. The *Ritva* (*Chullin ibid*) says that the prohibition to fool another person is included in the Torah's interdiction of *"You shall not steal."* The verse did not say "You shall not steal money" or "You shall not steal property." It simply stated, *"You shall not steal"* to include all forms of theft, even theft of trust. What is meant by theft of trust?

King David had a rebellious son, Avshalom. Avshalom lead a rebellion against his father in order to usurp the throne. During the rebellion, Avshalom came to his father and told him that he wished to repent; however, he was afraid that the supporters of the king would try to kill him. King David gave his son a letter to present to the *Sanhedrin* that they should obey the request of Avshalom and give him an armed guard. Avshalom appeared before the *Sanhedrin*, showed them the letter, and told them that his father agreed to relinquish the throne and to allow Avshalom to reign in his stead. Avshalom told them that the king was instructing the *Sanhedrin* to provide Avshalom with an armed guard so he may safely assume the throne. In the end, Avshalom's rebellion failed and he had to flee for his life. Avshalom's long hair became entangled in the branch of a tree and three of David's men pierced him with darts. The Talmud (*Sotah* 9b) says "*Why was he pierced with three darts? Because he fooled three – the king, the Sanhedrin, and the people?*"

The Talmud does not directly attribute the deserved punishment of Avshalom to his rebellion, to a rebellion against his own father, the righteous king of Israel; but rather, the Talmud attributes his death to the fact that Avshalom fooled everyone. He stole their trust. This gives us an inkling of how great the sin of deceit is.

Our Sages give some examples of theft of trust. When presenting a gift to someone, the presenter cannot misrepresent the gift to be more valuable than it really is (*Chullin* 94a). If an expensive bottle of wine was previously opened, a host cannot tell a guest that it was just opened in honor of his guest (*Rashi, ibid*). It is forbidden for a person to mislead someone so that the other will think favorably of him. If a person is raising money for a certain charity, he cannot say that he is raising money for another charity so that the giver will be more generous. He is fooling the donator (*Rashi, Baba Basra* 11a).

In one respect, stealing trust is worse than stealing property. One who steals property can return it or make restitution. A person who steals someone's trust will find it very difficult to restore that trust.

There is another form of theft that deserves to be mentioned and that is wasting someone else's time. A person enters a store with no intention to buy anything there, but rather to get a product's serial number so he can order it elsewhere. He talks to a salesman to get information about the product, again with no intention of making a purchase there. Not only is he fooling the salesman but he is stealing the salesman's time (See *Baba Metzia* 48b). If restoring stolen trust is difficult, restoring someone else's wasted time is impossible.

When one considers all that is included in the mitzvah of not stealing, it is truly awesome. It requires us to think carefully about many more situations than we previously had considered.

✑ THEFT THROUGH WORDS

The 225ᵗʰ mitzvah is not to deny that something of value that belongs to another is in one's possession.
The 226ᵗʰ mitzvah is not to lie through an oath about owing someone money or property.
"Do not deny, do not tell a lie, a man with another" **(19:11).**

*n*ormally, theft is committed through an action. The thief takes someone else's money or property. Here, the Torah talks about one who has someone else's money or property that was obtained legally. Someone gave him a loan, or he found a lost item and took it with the intention of returning it, or someone deposited an item by him for safekeeping. He later denies having the item or owing the money. He is committing theft through his denial. The Torah is teaching us that this too is considered theft as though he went into another's home and robbed it.

✑ A CITY CALLED TRUTH

*O*ne of the morals we are taught as young children is not to tell a lie. It is taken for granted that the Torah prohibits lying. The verse in our *parshah* says *"Do not tell a lie"* (19:11). The verse in Shmos (23:7) says *"From false words be far."* It seems quite clear that the Torah does in fact prohibit telling a lie. However, upon closer investigation we find that this is not so clear at all. Our verse, according to Rashi, the *Sefer HaChinuch*, the *Rashbam*, the *Sforno*, among others, say that the verse refers specifically to swearing falsely under oath in court regarding monetary matters for personal gain. It does not come to prohibit the telling of a lie not under oath, not in court, not regarding monetary matters. Likewise, the verse in Shmos is interpreted by the commentaries to refer to a lie told in court. What is the law regarding telling a lie?

The Talmud (*Sanhedrin* 97a) records the following:

> One of the Rabbis, Rav Tabus, others say, Rav Tavyomi, who, even if he were given all the money in the world, would not tell a lie. He once came to a town called Truth in which no one ever told a lie and where no man ever died before his time. He married one of their women by whom he had two sons. One day his wife was washing her hair, when a female neighbor came knocking at the door asking for Rab Tabus's wife. Thinking that it would not be etiquette to say that his wife was washing herself, he said that she was not at home. Shortly thereafter, his two sons died. The people of that town came to him and questioned him, "What was the cause of this?" He related to them what had happened. "We pray thee," they answered, "leave this town and do not incite death against us."

Rav Tabus told a very innocent lie. He merely said that his wife was not at home. How many times have we told someone on the phone that the person with whom they wished to speak wasn't at home whereas in truth they were at home? A person could more accurately have said, "I'm sorry, so-and-so is not available." The lie Rav Tabus told was not for monetary gain. It was a misstatement spoken out of modesty; yet, such an inaccuracy could not be tolerated in the town of Truth. How fortunate are we that we do not reside in such a town.

Another story is found in the Talmud (*Yevamos* 63a):

> Rav was constantly tormented by his wife. If he asked her to prepare lentils, she would prepare peas. If he asked for peas, she prepared lentils. When Rav would relay the order through his son, Chiyah, Chiyah would reverse the order. If his father asked for lentils, he would tell his mother that Father wanted peas. In that way, Rav would get what he asked for. Rav remarked to Chiyah that the wife

*has seemed to improve her ways. Chiyah told his father the
secret. Though Rav appreciated his son's intentions, he rep-
rimanded him for not speaking the truth.*

We see from here that Rav himself would not consider utilizing
any strategy to offset his wife's behavior. Harmlessly asking for peas to
ensure that he got lentils was too dishonest for Rav.

We see from these two illustrations that it is strictly forbidden to
tell a lie, no matter how innocent or harmless. However, there is contradictory evidence. The Talmud (*Kesubos* 16b-17a) states:

*Our Rabbis taught: What does one sing at the dance
before the bride? Bais Shammai says that one should utter
words that are appropriate for that bride. Bais Hillel says
that one should sing, "Beautiful and graceful is the bride."
Bais Shammai responded to Bais Hillel, "What if she was
lame or blind, does one say that she is a beautiful and
graceful bride? The Torah said, 'Keep thee far from false
words.'" Replied Bais Hillel to Bais Shammai, "According to
your words, if one has made a poor purchase in the market
and cannot return it, should one praise it to the purchaser
or depreciate it? Surely, he should praise it in his eyes."
Therefore, the Sages have said one should always be pleasant with people. When R. Dimi came to Babylon, he said
that in Israel they sing before the bride "No face powder nor
cosmetics, no setting of the hair, and yet the bride is still as
graceful as a gazelle."*

This excerpt indicates that one is certainly allowed to tell a "white
lie" so as not to hurt someone's feelings. There is another indication
that one is permitted to tell an innocent lie. We are all familiar with
the statement in *Avos D'Rebbe Nasson* that when Aharon, the brother
of Moshe, saw two people who had argued, he would tell each of them
that the other wished to make peace. In that way they would both get
together and make amends. We now have contradictory evidence
whether or not "white lies" are permitted.

The resolution to the contradiction is quite simple. If the motive
of the one telling the "white lie" is for his own benefit, or for the benefit of some other party, then it is strictly forbidden. If the motive for

telling the "white lie" is for the benefit of the one being spoken to, then it is allowed. Rav Tabus, who told the neighbor that his wife was not at home, was not telling the "white lie" for the benefit of the neighbor to whom he was speaking. It was for his wife's benefit. Chiyah told his mother the "white lie" for his father's benefit, not for his mother's benefit. Such lies are not permitted.

Bais Hillel would sing and praise the bride that she was beautiful and graceful because it was for the benefit of the groom before whom they sang. Bais Hillel allowed one to praise a friend's purchase because it was for the friend's benefit. There was no personal gain. Likewise, Aharon was allowed to tell a "white lie" for the sake of the striving parties. There was no personal gain. Lying for personal gain, whether monetary or not is forbidden. Telling a white lie for the benefit of the person to whom you are speaking is permitted.

THE MITZVOS

The 227ᵗʰ mitzvah is the prohibition to break a promise.
"You shall not swear in My name falsely" **(19:12).**
The 228ᵗʰ mitzvah is the prohibition to withhold the property or money to which your neighbor is entitled.
"Do not oppress your neighbor" **(19:13).**

The term "*oppress*" used in this verse refers to withholding money or property. This is derived from the remainder of this verse which states "*...do not rob nor retain the wages of a hired hand with you until the morning.*" Since the end of the verse refers to withholding money or property, so too does the term "*oppress*" refers to withholding.

The 229ᵗʰ mitzvah is the prohibition against robbery.
"Do not rob" **(19:13).**

The difference between this 229th mitzvah, *"Do not rob"* and the 224th mitzvah, *"You shall not steal"* is that a robber is not afraid to show himself to his victim. He usually has a weapon and threatens the victims to part with his money. One who steals is one who sneaks around and stealthily takes property. A burglar is an example of one who steals. A bank robber is an example of a robber. Why the Torah made two separate prohibitions, one for stealing and one for theft will be discussed later.

The 230th mitzvah is not to delay the payment of a hired worker.

"Do not retain the wages of a hired hand with you until the morning" (19:13).

This refers to a person who was hired by the day. He must be paid before the day's end unless other arrangements were made prior to his beginning the work. A person who was hired by the week or the month must be paid before the end of the last day of the contractual period. The law applies regardless whether one hired a person, or rented an animal, or rented an object, payment is due on that last day.

When one hires a baby-sitter, the baby sitter must be paid before the end of the day. If she is baby-sitting at night, she must be paid before the end of the night. According to many authorities, paying by check does not fulfill this obligation. Payment must be made in cash unless prior arrangements were made. The mitzvah applies even to hiring a child, someone under the age of bar or bas mitzvah (*Sefer HaChinuch* 230).

One who withholds wages or rent violates all three mitzvos mentioned in this verse: "(1) *Do not oppress your neighbor* (1), *do not steal* (2), *do not retain the wages of a hired hand with you until the morning* (3)."

The 231st mitzvah is the prohibition to curse another Jew.

"Do not curse the deaf" (19:14).

If it is forbidden to curse a deaf person, one who cannot hear your curse and is therefore not offended, certainly it is forbidden to curse one who can hear it.

This prohibition applies even to someone who curses himself (*Rambam Hilchos Sanhedrin* 26:3).

❧ LEADING THE BLIND ASTRAY

The 232ⁿᵈ mitzvah is not to make a trusting person stumble through misleading advice.
"Before the blind put not a stumbling block" **(19:14).**

The *Sefer HaChinuch* tells us that, in order for a community to function properly, the people have to rely on one another. Each person makes his or her contribution to the welfare of the group. One person may grow vegetables, another may be a shoemaker. One may serve as the rabbi and teacher, another may be a tailor. Each one produces something or provides a service that is needed by others. As a group, they can thrive. A shoemaker living alone in the wilderness could not survive. To whom would he sell his shoes? From where would he get his food? To solve this problem, communities were invented. The community as a whole can take care of the needs of the individual members. But this can only happen if the individuals trust each other. If the shoemaker produces inferior goods but sells them as high quality goods, he will lose the trust of the community. They will stop buying from him. The community will have no shoes and he will have no money for food and clothing. Trust is the pillar upon which a society rests. One who gives misleading advice is breaking that communal trust and chips away at that pillar of society.

This mitzvah includes the prohibition to assist another person who wants to commit a sin. By helping that person sin you are giving him the impression that the sin is not so terrible. Even if the sinner is not aware that he would be committing a sin, one is not allowed to cause another person to sin even inadvertently. An accountant cannot help a client cheat on his taxes.

A Jewish nurse who is required to feed non-kosher food to an irreligious Jewish patient should seek the council of a rabbi. People who work in advertising must be especially careful.

The mitzvah also includes the prohibition to sell something dangerous, whether it is a danger to the buyer or to others. Therefore a Jew cannot sell fireworks or firearms to an irresponsible person.

The Torah painted a very striking picture when describing this mitzvah. Do not put a stumbling block before a blind person. Can you picture someone sticking out his foot to purposely trip a blind person? Who would do such a heartless thing? Giving poor advice or causing one to commit a sin is, in the Torah's eyes, the very same as tripping a blind man.

⇜ JUSTICE MUST PREVAIL

The 233ʳᵈ mitzvah is not to pervert justice in a civil judgment.
"Do no wrong in judgment" (19:15).
The 234ᵗʰ mitzvah is the prohibition for a judge to show favoritism to either litigant.
"You shall not favor the poor nor show honor to the great one" (19:15).
The 235ᵗʰ mitzvah is for a judge to be scrupulously fair to both litigants.
"With righteousness you shall judge your neighbor" (19:15).

*T*he *Sifra* (19:15) tells us that not only a judge but each and every one of us should judge everyone we see and meet fairly and favorably. As the Mishna in *Pirkei Avos* (1:6) says: *Judge every person with the benefit of a doubt.*

The Talmud (*Shabbos* 127b) teaches us two lessons regarding judging people favorably:

He who judges his neighbor and gives him the benefit of the doubt is himself judged favorably. The story is told of a certain man who came from the Upper Galilee and was hired by an individual in the South for three years. On the eve of the Yom Kippur, the hired hand requested his wages.

"Please, give me my wages that I may go and support my wife and children."

"I have no money," answered the other.

"Give me produce," said the hire hand.

"I have none," said the other.

"Give me land."

"I have none."

"Give me cattle."

"I have none."

"Give me pillows and bedding."

"I have none."

The hired hand slung his things behind him and went home with a sorrowful heart. After the Succos festival his employer took his wages in his hand together with three laden donkeys, one bearing food, another drink, and the third various sweets, and went to the hired hand's home. After they had eaten and drunk, the employer gave him his wages. Said the employer to the hired hand, "When you asked me to give you your wages and I answered that I had no money, what did you suspect of me?"

"I thought, perhaps you came across cheap merchandise and had purchased it with all your money."

"And when you requested of me to give you cattle and I answered that I have no cattle, what did you suspect of me?"

"I thought that they may be hired to others."

"When you asked me to give you land and I told you that I have no land, what did you suspect of me?"

"I thought perhaps it was leased to others."

"And when I told you that I have no produce, what did you suspect of me?"

"I thought, perhaps they were not tithed."

"And when I told you that I have no pillows or bedding, what did you suspect of me?"

"I thought perhaps you designated all your property for charity."

"I swear by the Temple's service that everything you have said was so. As for you, just as you judged me favorably, so may G-d judge you favorably."

Though the Talmud does not identify the name of the admirable hired hand, Rashi tells us that he was one of the great Sages of Israel. Possibly, because of his humility, the Sage requested that his name not be mentioned in the story. That is the second lesson the story teaches us. Humility and judging others favorably go hand-in-hand.

❧ PRESERVING THE LIFE AND REPUTATION OF OTHERS

The 236th mitzvah is not to speak slanderously of others.

"Do not go as a talebearer among your people" (**19:16**).

The 237th mitzvah is not to stand idly by when someone's life is in danger.

"Do not stand by the blood of your neighbor" (**19:16**).

The Talmud (*Baba Basra* 11a) says that a person who saves one Jew is considered as if he saved the whole world.

The *Sifra* (19:16) extends this mitzvah to include one who refuses to testify on another's behalf and, as a result, the other will lose a court case involving monetary matters. Not only is one forbidden to stand idle when his friend's life is in danger, one is not allowed to stand idly by when his neighbor's property is in danger.

In our times the moral issue of assisted suicide has arisen. If a terminally ill person wishes to commit suicide but needs the assistance of someone else, is one allowed to assist in the suicide? The *Maharam MiRuttenburg* (*Shailos and Tshuvos* 39) says that this mitzvah, "*Do not stand by the blood of your neighbor,*" also means that if you see someone trying to commit suicide, you are obligated to save him from himself. That being the case, certainly you are not allowed to help him kill himself. The *Chidah* (*Birkei Yosef* 301:6) says that one is even allowed to transgress the sanctity of Shabbos to save a potential suicide victim.

☙ BROTHERLY LOVE, BROTHERLY HATE

The 238ᵗʰ mitzvah is the prohibition to hate another Jew.
"You shall not hate your brother in your heart" **(19:17).**

R ather than harbor hate in your heart, it is better to confront the other person and try to resolve the issues with him. Make your feelings known to your friend and allow him to defend himself or perhaps apologize. Harboring hate eats away at the heart. It is a parasite that eats off its host. It does no one any good, least of all you (Ramban and *Ibn Ezra 19:17*).

The Jew and his Torah are the foundation stone of the universal concept of brotherly love and compassion, yet, they have become the objects of scorn and irrational hatred. Today's world explodes with hatred all over the map. A small sampling of those engaged in destroying each other are as follows: in India, Sikhs and Hindis, in the Balkans, Serbs and Croatians, in Northern Ireland, Catholics and Protestants, in Iraq, Sunnis and Shiites.

We hear of Russian children massacred by Chechnians, mass murders in Africa and gruesome stories of mayhem from all regions based on religious or tribal or ethnic conflict. Yet there seems to be one issue that all the world's bitter adversaries can agree on: that the

Jew is the **real** despised enemy of mankind. All terrorists, regardless of their 'cause', seem to unite in mutual hatred of the Jews. The Medrash in *Shmos* (*Shmos Rabbah* 2:4) tells us that the name Sinai is derived from the word *sinah*, meaning hatred. The other nations resent the fact that the great moral and ethical code is our treasured possession. And even though they developed a corrupted version of our Torah and called it their own New Testament and their own Koran, nevertheless, they still hate us.

This hatred from external forces, however, pales next to the insidious affect on the Jewish People from internal hatred. The sad fact is that today, as throughout our history, we are confronted with our misguided fellow brethren who actually despise the Torah way of life and actively seek to undermine those who are loyal to our religious practices. What can we do? Certainly we do not want to return hate with hate.

The next four mitzvos address this issue. They are contained within the following two consecutive verses: *"You shall surely rebuke your neighbor and do not bear sin because of his account. Do not avenge, do not bear a grudge against the sons of your people"* (19:17-18).

The 239th mitzvah is the duty to rebuke a fellow Jew for improper behavior.
"You shall surely rebuke your neighbor" (19:17).

The word "rebuke" conjures up the image of harsh condemnation, biting criticism, and an elevated voice level. However, the object of this mitzvah is to get the sinner to change his ways. If one rebukes the sinner by shouting at him in public and deriding him, it is unlikely that he will alter his misbehavior. It is more likely that the sinner will become more aggressive in his misbehavior. However, if one speaks softly to the sinner in private, it is more probable that the sinner will amend his ways (*Sefer HaChinuch* 239).

King Solomon said: *Rebuke not a scorner, lest he hate you; rebuke a wise man, and he will love you* (*Mishlei* 9:8). When rebuking someone, we should not just point out his or her faults, thereby making the person feel like a scorner. Scorners do not accept criticism. That will just make them become defensive. Instead, we should point out their positive qualities, making the person feel like a wise and noble person. He will be more receptive and more easily accept the critical rebuke just as the wise person accepts reproach.

The Talmud (*Yevamos* 65b) says that if you know that the sinner is so entrenched in his ways that any manner of rebuke will be futile, then it is better to remain silent. If one cannot douse a raging fire, do not stoke it. Let it burn out on its own.

No one lives in a vacuum. Everyone's life is intertwined with the lives of those around him. As the Torah sees it, every Jew is responsible for the welfare of one's fellow Jew. This concern for our fellow Jew is vital for our own moral and spiritual growth.

The *Dubner Maggid* once settled in a town. The rabbi of the town paid him a visit and complained, "Oh, great *maggid*, the people in this town can hardly support me. How will they be able to support the two of us?" The *maggid* replied, "I will tell you a parable."

There was a farmer who bought a chicken. The farmer was negligent with regards to feeding his chicken. Not long after, the farmer bought a rooster. The chicken complained to the rooster, "The farmer hardly gives me enough to eat. How can two of us survive?" The rooster replied, "Every morning I will crow loudly until the farmer comes and feeds us. Through my cook-a-doodle-doos we will both thrive."

The *maggid* turned to the rabbi and said, "Through my words of rebuke, spoken in love, I will melt the stone hearts of the town's people. They will open their purses widely and we both will thrive."

The 240th mitzvah is the prohibition against embarrassing another Jew.

"Do not bear sin because of his account" (19:17).

In your zeal to correct another's behavior, do not resort to publicly embarrassing him. If you do, your sin will be greater than his.

Our Sages (*Baba Metzia* 59a) say that one who shames his neighbor has no portion in the World to Come. Better to throw yourself into a furnace than shame your neighbor. They also maintained (*ibid* 58b) that shaming a neighbor is tantamount to murder. Tamar, the daughter-in-law of Yaakov's son Yehudah, was willing to have herself executed rather than shame her father-in-law (See volume on *Bereishis*, page 312).

Almost 2,000 years ago, our Temple was destroyed, the holy city of Jerusalem was burned to the ground, and its inhabitants were sold into slavery. The Rabbis traced that terrible episode to a sequence of events that began a few years earlier. At a party, the host embarrassed one of the attendees, Bar Kamtza. Bar Kamtza sought revenge which culminated in the destruction of the *Bais HaMikdash*, Jerusalem, and our people (See *Gittin* 55b-56a.). This connection between being embarrassed and seeking revenge is the connection between this mitzvah and the next one.

The 241ˢᵗ mitzvah is the prohibition against taking revenge.

"Do not avenge" (19:18).

The *Sefer HaChinuch* explains that one should have the true understanding that whatever happens to him, good or bad, is caused by a Divine decree. If one seeks revenge because a neighbor committed some injustice against him, he must realize that the neighbor did not cause the injustice, but rather it was his own shortcomings that allowed such a thing to occur.

The 242ⁿᵈ mitzvah is the prohibition against bearing a grudge.

"Do not bear a grudge against the sons of your people" (19:18).

The previous mitzvah, not to take revenge, means not to take a vengeful action. This mitzvah, not to bear a grudge, refers to words that are spoken in a vengeful manner. The classic example is that one man asked his friend if he could borrow a certain object. The friend refused to lend it. The following day, the friend came to borrow an object from the very same person to whom he had declined to lend. The person said, "Yes, you may borrow the object from me. See, I am better person than you are." Those words were spoken in a vengeful manner.

One of the themes of these mitzvos is that one cannot harbor ill-feelings towards another person. Keeping ill-feelings within you makes you into an unhappy person. It gnaws away at the soul. You become angry with yourself, your family, your neighbors and your friends. In the end, you become angry with G-d. The most important lesson in life is to work out those feelings that cause you distress. You cannot simply will them into oblivion. You must take positive steps to dispel them. This may mean you should talk to the person that you see as the cause for those feelings. But, you must speak in a calm and rational manner. If you are convinced that this will not be fruitful, then seek guidance from one who is well-versed in maladies of the spirit. He will be able to guide you through the wisdom of the Torah and our Sages. This concept is sound preparation for what is perhaps the keystone mitzvah of the Torah: which is the next mitzvah.

✑ LOVE THY NEIGHBOR

The 243ʳᵈ mitzvah is to love the Jewish People.
"You shall love your neighbor as yourself" (19:18).

Rebbe Akiva (*Sifra* 19:18) said that this is the great rule upon which the Torah is based. This is brought out by the well known story recorded in the Talmud (*Shabbos* 31a):

It happened that a certain gentile came before Shammai and said to him, "Make me a convert on condition that you teach me the whole Torah while I stand on one foot." Thereupon Shammai repulsed him with the builder's cubit which was in his hand. When he went before Hillel, he said to him, "What is hateful to you, do not do to your neighbor." That is the whole Torah, while the rest is the commentary thereof; go and learn it.

The Torah said that we must love every Jew. It is stated in the positive, to love. Why did Hillel state it in the negative, *"What is hateful to you, do not to your neighbor"*?

The Torah is talking to the Jewish people. Every Jew is bound together by a common history and destiny. We are bound together in time, spirit, and soul. We are commanded to love every Jew as we love ourselves because we are all one people. Hillel was addressing a non-

Jew. Non-Jews lack this unity. It is impossible to tell non-Jews to love others as they love themselves. The only thing Hillel could tell him was not to hate others just as one does not hate himself. As Rav Kook put it, everyone understands that baseless hatred is wrong. Not everyone can understand that baseless love is a virtue. This explains why the Rambam (*Da'os* 6:3) says that this mitzvah, to love another as he loves himself, though assumed to be a universal Golden Rule, applies only to the Jewish People.

The mitzvah tells us that we must love others as we love ourselves. Love for others is predicated on the assumption that we love ourselves. A person that has low self-esteem or no self-respect cannot esteem and respect others. One who does not love himself cannot love others.

In the previous mitzvah we discussed the harm that harboring hatred within our hearts causes. If we have feelings of hate within us, we cannot experience love. Without being able to experience love, we cannot spiritually advance. We are imprisoned in the pit of negativity. Sadness and depression take over. We are not motivated to do anything, let alone soar to spiritual heights. The goal of life, as stated at the outset of the *parshah,* is to strive for a state of holiness. This can only be achieved through a feeling of love. Love is the vehicle that can convey us to the heavenly realm.

⊰ MIXING APPLES AND ORANGES

The 244ᵗʰ mitzvah is the prohibition to crossbreed different species of animals.
"My laws you shall keep; your cattle to shall not crossbreed" **(19:19).**

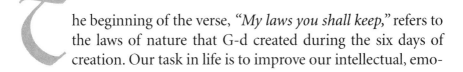

he beginning of the verse, *"My laws you shall keep,"* refers to the laws of nature that G-d created during the six days of creation. Our task in life is to improve our intellectual, emotional, and spiritual selves, not to 'mix' in and try to improve G-d's creation around us. The natural world is already sufficient for our needs. The Torah testifies that *"G-d saw all that He had created and it was exceedingly good"* (*Bereishis* 1:31). One who attempts to "improve" nature by crossbreeding two diverse species is demonstrating that G-d's perception that *"it was exceedingly good"* was not correct. This prohibition would apply to non-Jews as well (See *Sanhedrin* 56b and *Baba Metzia* 90a).

The verse mentions specifically cattle because cattle would be the most likely species people would like to improve upon. However, the prohibition does apply to all animal life (*Baba Kamma* 44b). In our times, this mitzvah would call into question the practice of genetic engineering.

The 245th mitzvah is not to plant two or more species together.
"Your field you shall not plant mixtures" (19:19).

This mitzvah includes two distinct mitzvos. The first is the prohibition to plant two or more edible species together. This applies only in Eretz Yisroel. Because of the sanctity of the land, even planting diverse species next to one another is forbidden

The second part of the mitzvah is the prohibition to crossbreed diverse species of trees through grafting. The concept behind this mitzvah is similar to the prohibition to crossbreed animals.

What is the *halachic* definition of different species? Are oranges and tangerines two different species? Horticulturists say that they are. The answer is that science plays no part in this *halachah*; instead, common sense rules. The average person would agree that oranges and tangerines are related to each other. Therefore, they are not considered two different species. Oranges and apples are. Therefore, as the old expression goes, don't mix apples and oranges.

✦ FORBIDDEN FRUIT

The 246th mitzvah is not to eat the fruit of the tree the first three years.
"Closed off for you is the fruit of the (first) three years, it shall be closed off for you, it shall not be consumed" **(19:23).**
The 247th mitzvah is that the fruit of the fourth year of the tree is considered holy and must only be eaten in Jerusalem in a state of purity (*taharah*).
"And in the forth year shall all the fruit be holy for praise to G-d" **(19:24).**

The first crop of fruit is the most precious one. Anyone who has ever planted a tree knows this to be so. Generally speaking, the fruit of the first three years, while the young sapling is still developing, is of a poor quality in size and taste. Not until the fourth year is the fruit really desirable. The Torah wanted that the first good crop should be taken to the Holy City and eaten there in a state of purity. The one eating the crop would utter words of praise thanking G-d for this wonder blessing and miracle that so often is taken for granted. Before those words of thanks are offered, before that first good crop (the fourth year's) is brought to Jerusalem, no fruit of the tree is to be eaten or any benefit derived thereof.

The next verse says, *"And in the fifth year you will eat its fruit, an increase for you will be its produce."* If one shows his appreciation to G-d in the fourth year, he will be blessed even more the fifth year.

This prohibition applies in our times, even outside the land of Israel. If one purchased a fruit tree from a nursery, he should inquire how old the sapling is to know whether or not the prohibition applies. The three years always end on the 15th day of *Shevat*, *Tu B'Shvat*. One should discuss with his rabbi what to do with the fourth year's crop.

✎﴾ SELF-RESTRAINT

The 248th mitzvah is not to be overindulgent in food and drink.
"Do not eat with the blood" **(19:26).**

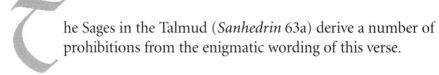

he Sages in the Talmud (*Sanhedrin* 63a) derive a number of prohibitions from the enigmatic wording of this verse.

1) One may not partake of the meat of a slaughtered animal while its blood is still flowing forth.
2) Sacrificial meat cannot be eaten until after the blood has been sprinkled on the altar.
3) After a sinner has been executed, no meal of condolence is eaten at the home of the mourners.
4) The members of the court are not allowed to eat on the day of an execution.
5) Another interpretation is found in the Talmud (*Berachos* 10b). One should not eat breakfast before he prays for himself (his blood).
6) The most commonly understood meaning of the verse is not to indulge in gluttonous behavior (*Sanhedrin* 63a, *Rambam Sefer HaMitzvos Lo sasay* 175).

One may mistakenly think that since there is a mitzvah to love one's neighbor as he loves himself, he is obligated to a self love that includes an indulgence in one's favorite food and drink. The Torah is correcting such a misplaced rationalization. That is not self love; that is self destruction. Habitual self indulgence leads one to an addictive reliance on self-gratification. This habit can conceivably grow out of control; then one who is addicted to self-gratification will be willing to commit criminal behavior to satisfy his lust. The addiction can become so strong, so consuming, that in his immoral stupor he will be willing to commit murder, spilling blood. The Torah is telling us not to eat and drink in a gluttonous manner; a manner that has the potential to lead to the spilling of blood.

⋙ SUPERSTITIONS

The 249ᵗʰ mitzvah is the prohibition to believe in superstitions.
"You shall not practice superstitions" **(19:26).**

There are religions that govern the believer's behavior based on certain trivial occurrences or circumstances. Based on the movement of different creatures, they will alter their behavior. A modern day example would be those who will not cross the path of a black cat because it bodes ill-fortune. The Torah should be our guide in life and not foolish superstitions.

It is interesting to note that during the years that the former Soviet Union prohibited religious practices, the population in general became overly superstitious. Every innocent action took on some ominous meaning. If someone accidentally stepped on your foot, you must immediately step on his foot or you will be trampled upon for the remainder of your days. If someone pats you on the back, have him pull at your clothing seven times or you will never get married. Never shake hands over a threshold: it will lead to a quarrel. Never pour wine with the label facing away from you; it will cause the host to become angry with you. Never leave a place and return immediately without doing something in between. Otherwise calamity will strike. Whistling indoors leads to poverty. So too does wiping crumbs off a table with your hand. The list goes on and on.

All people have an inborn thirst for a belief system. If it cannot be met through normative religious practices, then foolish superstitions are a likely substitute. Therefore, when traditional religions were not available to the Soviet population, superstitions began to guide their lives. This calls to mind to famous quotation of Voltaire, *"If G-d did not exist, man would have to invent Him."*

✍ MAZEL TOV!

The 250ᵗʰ mitzvah is the prohibition against practicing astrology.
"You shall not practice astrology" **(19:26).**

Astrology is the belief that the positions of the stars and planets, the constellations and the zodiac, at any given time indicate what fate has in store. However, we are commanded to place our faith in the Torah and lead our life according to its indications.

The Talmud (*Shabbos* 156a-b) records three interesting events illustrating the Jewish attitude with regards to astrology. The first one regards our forefather Avraham:

> *Avraham pleaded before the Holy One, blessed be He, "Sovereign of the Universe! I have looked at my constellations and find that I am not fated to have a son." G-d responded, "Go away from your planet gazing, for Israel is not subject to planetary influence. What is your calculation? Because Jupiter stands in the West? I will turn it back and place it in the East."*

G-d was telling Avraham that the power of faith and prayer is greater than the signs of the constellations. (Readers familiar with the writings of the controversial Dr. Emmanuel Veliokosky are aware that he describes a major planetary disruption during the Patriarchal Era.)

The next story is about the Talmudic Sage Shmuel.

> *Shmuel and Ablat were sitting when a certain man passed by. Ablat, who was well versed in astrology, said, "That man is passing by but he will not return for a snake will bite him and he will die." Shmuel replied, "If he is an Israelite, he will go and return." While they were still sitting, that man did return. Ablat arose and threw off the man's knapsack and found a snake inside cut into two pieces. Shmuel asked him, "What did you do to merit this miracle?" The man replied, "Every day all us workers pool together our bread. We split it evenly for all to eat. Today one of us had no bread and he was ashamed. I told him that*

I would collect the bread and pretend that I took from him too. That would save him from embarrassment." Shmuel observed, "You have done a good deed. Charity saves from death."

The third story involves Rabbi Akiva.

Rebbe Akiva had a daughter. Astrologers had told him, that on the day she enters the bridal chamber a snake will bite her and she will die. He was very worried about this. On the evening of her marriage, she took off a brooch and stuck it into the wall. By chance, it struck the head of a snake and killed it. "What did you do?" her father asked her. "A poor man came to our door last evening," she replied, "and everybody was busy at the banquet so there was none to attend to him. I took the portion which was given to me at the wedding feast and I gave it to him." "You have done a good deed," said Rebbe Akiva. Thereupon Rebbe Akiva went out and lectured, "Charity saves from death."

The Talmud begins and ends these stories with the phrase "*Israel is not subject to the signs of the constellations.*" The Hebrew word for constellation is *mazel*. When we wish someone a hearty Mazel Tov, in effect we are saying: no matter what the constellations say, I am wishing you the blessing that all should be well. The good wishes of a Jew are more influential than the stars in the heavens.

❧ WHOSE BODY IS IT?

The 251ˢᵗ mitzvah is the prohibition against cutting off the *payos* of the head.
"*Do not round off the corners of your head*" (19:27).

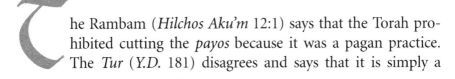

The Rambam (*Hilchos Aku'm* 12:1) says that the Torah prohibited cutting the *payos* because it was a pagan practice. The *Tur* (*Y.D.* 181) disagrees and says that it is simply a decree issued by G-d whose reason we do not fathom.

The 252ⁿᵈ mitzvah is the prohibition against shaving with a razor.

"Do not destroy the corners of your beard" **(19:27).**

There are only three negative commandments in the Torah that do not apply to women: shaving, cutting the *payos*, and the prohibition for a *Kohen* to defile himself (become *tamei*).

The 253ʳᵈ mitzvah is the prohibition against inscribing any permanent tattoo on the skin.

"A tattooed writing you shall not place in your (skin)" **(19:28).**

The battle cry off those who are pro-abortion, euphemistically called pro-choice, is "Whose body is it?" They believe that no one has a right to tell a woman what she can or cannot do with her own body. These last three mitzvos – prohibitions against cutting the *payos*, shaving with a razor, and tattooing, indicate that the Torah can in fact tell us what we can and cannot do with our own body.

✎ NO TALKING DURING DAVENING

The 254ᵗʰ mitzvah is to conduct oneself with the proper decorum in a holy place.

"My sanctuary you shall revere" **(19:30).**

The *Bais HaMikdash* is called the House of G-d and one must conduct himself accordingly. The Rambam (*Bais HaBechirah* 7:5) says that the mitzvah begins even outside the Temple; as one approaches its holy grounds one is not allowed to be light-headed. He must put himself in the proper frame of mind that he is about to enter a holy place.

A person was not permitted to enter the *Bais HaMikdash* just to view its structure – sightseeing. It could only be entered in order to perform a mitzvah. It could not be used as a short-cut. One could not seek shelter from the rain under its roof. One had to remove his shoes and wash the dust off his feet before entering. Sitting down within its sacred courtyard was only permitted for the kings of the Davidic dynasty.

The Rambam (*Bais HaBechirah* 7:7) rules that these laws still apply even after the *Bais HaMikdash* was destroyed. Therefore, besides the laws of purity prohibiting us from walking on the Temple Mount, no sightseeing is allowed either.

Included in this mitzvah is the prohibition to construct a building for personal use that is patterned after the Sanctuary of the Temple. Also, one is not permitted to replicate any of its vessels, such as the seven branch menorah.

The Talmud (*Berachos* 62b) tells us that a synagogue is also a House of G-d and one must display proper reverence for it.

A private house is held together with bricks and mortar, with wood and nails. A *shul* is held together by its *kedushah*. If the members uphold its sanctity, the *shul* will endure. If the proper reverence for such a holy place is not respected, the very glue that holds it together, its *kedushah*, will dissolve. The *Chofetz Chaim* has said that unfortunately many *shuls* were destroyed because the worshippers did not conduct themselves properly. The cement of *kedushah* had dissolved.

✑ GHOST-BUSTERS

The 255ᵗʰ mitzvah is the prohibition to participate in any form of séance.
"Turn not to the ghosts" (19:31).
The 256ᵗʰ mitzvah is to prohibit the ancient practice of using the bones of certain animals through which the spirits would communicate.

"To the spirits do not seek out" (**19:31**).

The council and guidance that we seek is firmly grounded in the Torah and the scholars who study its ways.

◀ **RESPECTING THE WISE**

The 257ᵗʰ mitzvah in the Torah is to honor wise scholars. *"Before the gray-haired you shall arise, you shall show honor before the old"* (**19:32**).

Wisdom is acquired in two ways: through life's experiences and through diligent study. The Talmud (*Kiddushin* 32b) says that the *gray-haired* man before whom you should arise is one who acquired wisdom through life experiences. The "*old*" refers to the one who has acquired our ancient wisdom through diligent study.

The Jewish religion places great emphasis and value on wisdom. Education is a foundation stone of the Jewish People. Parents were commanded to educate their children. Every single Jew was to be educated not just the progeny of the elite. In America, not until the middle of the nineteenth century was education seen to be the right to which every child was entitled. Even in the twenty-first century there are inner-city cultures that downplay the importance of education and wisdom. It is viewed as a mindless folly. The Torah teaches us the great importance of wisdom by commanding us to show respect to those who have acquired it.

The Talmud (*Kiddushin* 32b) tells us that our Sages would show respect to the elderly non-Jew as well. Rebbe Yochanan would rise up before the aged gentile saying, "How many troublesome events passed over those gray hairs."

WEIGHTS AND MEASURES

The 258ᵗʰ mitzvah is the prohibition against cheating with any kind of false measures.
"Do not pervert justice through measure, weights, and volume" (19:35).
The 259ᵗʰ mitzvah is the precept that one's scales, weights and measures should be accurate.
"Just balances, just weight-stones, just volume measures, just liquid measures, you shall have" (19:36).

Cheating a consumer through fraudulent weights and measures is a very subtle type of deception that is difficult to detect. The customer watches as the storekeeper measures the item for sale. The customer assumes that the scales and measures are accurate. He watches everything without suspecting for a moment that he is the victim of fraud. The Torah abhorred fraud to such an extent that it stipulated two mitzvos (258 & 259) forbidding its practice.

Most objects can be used for good or evil. It is up to the one using it to determine in which manner it will be employed. A gun can be used for self defense; it can be used to rob. A fire can be used for heat and light; it can be used to destroy. False weights only have one use – to defraud. Therefore, the Torah prohibited even owning false measures. *"You shall not have in your house different measures, a large and a small"* (*Devarim* 25:13).

The previous mitzvah taught us to honor wise scholars. The advice of a wise man is carefully balanced; he will "weigh" his words carefully. He will speak in "measured" tones. Wisdom is his "merchandise." A fundamental hallmark of this great commodity of true wisdom is integrity. False measures and false weights represent a fundamental absence of integrity. We despise such instruments.

✎ THE MITZVOS

The 260ᵗʰ mitzvah is the prohibition against cursing one's parents.
"Any man who curses his father or mother shall surely be put to death" (20:9).
The 261ˢᵗ mitzvah is for the court to carry out the death penalty of burning on those rare occasions where a guilty verdict is determined.
"With fire shall they be burnt, he and she, there shall be no immorality among you" (20:14).

There are four different death penalties the Jewish court can impose: stoning, burning, beheading, and strangulation.

The checks and balances that were imposed upon the court made a guilty conviction an extremely rare occurrence. Therefore we do not view these penalties to reflect the reality of what the court actually carried out but rather to teach us about the severity of the infractions.

Burning consisted of pouring molten lead down the throat of the guilty party. The following sins can incur this punishment:

Incest with a daughter or granddaughter

Incest with a step-daughter or step-granddaughter

Illicit relations with a mother-in-law

Illicit relations with a mother-in-law's mother

Illicit relations with a father-in-law's mother

A married daughter of a *Kohen* who commits adultery (The male adulterer in this case is punished with strangulation. Only the female, who was the daughter of a *Kohen*, incurs burning.)

JEWISH IDENTITY

The 262ⁿᵈ mitzvah is the prohibition to follow non-Jewish customs and practices.

"Do not go in the way of the nations that I am sending away from before you" **(20:23).**

How does one define Jewish customs? Eating kosher pickles? Buying Israel bonds? Voting Democrat? Buying a condo in Miami? There are ethnic Jewish customs and then there are religious Jewish customs; the latter imbued with Torah values. When we speak of Jewish and non-Jewish customs we refer to those practices which either represent the Torah's ideals or go against the Torah's ideals. Let us give a few examples.

Can one dress like a rapster or hip-hopster? That mode of dress represents the philosophy of those entertainers (I use the term "entertainers" very loosely) who espouse total disrespect for women, the use of gutter language, and anti-social behavior in general. That is undeniably anti-Torah. Therefore, to dress in the rap or hip-hop style would certainly be a violation of this mitzvah. Whether or not one subscribes to their philosophy is not relevant. Simply imitating them is forbidden. Imitation is the highest form of flattery and it is forbidden to flatter a sinner.

On Purim can one dress up like a rapster? Yes. On Purim one who dresses in such attire is in effect mocking them. Mocking anti-Torah ideals is permitted (See *Minchas Chinuch* 662:4).

Can one wear a tie or doctor's uniform? A tie represents neat attire. Neat attire is not anti-Torah. A doctor's uniform represents health and care for the sick. That is not anti-Torah. A tie and doctor's uniform represent concepts that conform to the Torah's ideals. They would be permitted.

"You shall be holy unto Me, for holy am I, G-d, I have set you apart from the nations so that you shall be unto Me" **(20:26).**

HAFTORAH KEDOSHIM

THE *HAFTORAH* IS TAKEN FROM
THE LAST NINE VERSES OF THE BOOK OF *AMOS* 9:7-1.

T owards the end of *Parshas Kedoshim*, the verses (20:22 & 26) read: *And you shall keep all My laws and all My judgments and do them so that the land will not spit you out... Be holy unto Me, for I, G-d, am holy, I have set you apart from the nations to be unto Me.*

Eretz Yisroel is the holy land of G-d. It can only accept a holy nation as its residents. Should the Jewish People not live up to the standards of holiness, the land will spit them out.

In the years prior to the destruction of the First Temple, the prophet Amos rebuked the Jews for not living up to those standards that holiness demands. They had become like the nations of the world. They were no different or better than the Philistines or Cushites. The prophet foretells of the devastation and exile that will soon take place. However, as was the custom of the prophets, he ends with a note of optimism and tells of the future days, after the exile, when the Temple will be rebuilt.

The *haftorah* begins with the phrase, *"Behold, you are like the children of the Cushites to me."* The *Malbim* gives a remarkable insight. Why does the verse compare the wayward Jews to Cushites? The Cushites were a black African tribe. No matter where in the Middle East, Asia, or Europe they moved, they were always readily identifiable by their skin color. No matter how much they tried to assimilate into a foreign culture, they would still stand out. The same is true of the Jewish People. No matter where they moved to, no matter how much they tried to assimilate into a foreign culture, they were always identifiable. There is some unique quality the Jew possesses that no matter how much he tries to disguise himself, the gentile can always see him as a Jew. No matter how hard an unobservant or rebellious Jew tries to extinguish that spark of holiness that glows within his heart, it can never be fully extinguished. He may not be able to see it but the gentile next door can.

EMOR

⮬ **SAY WHAT?**

1n the preceding *parshah*, *Kedoshim*, the general theme was that of sanctity, *kedushah*. The mitzvos of that *parshah* dealt with the commandments that will help the Jewish People to become a holy nation and reach an exalted state. That *parshah* concerned itself with the sanctity of the Jewish People in general. This *parshah* continues the theme of *kedushah*, but narrows the focus on the sanctity of the *Kohanim*, the sanctity of the sacrificial animals, the sanctity of G-d's name, and the sanctity of the Jewish holidays.

This *parshah*, *Emor* contains more mitzvos than any other *parshah*. Sixty-three mitzvos are to be found here.

The laws that apply to the *Kohanim* are considerably more stringent than the laws that apply to the simple Israelite. As we shall see, the *Kohen* is more restricted as to whom he may marry. He is more restricted when it comes to contact with impurities, *tumah*. One must consider the exclusive status of a *Kohen* and the responsibility that goes with it. The Talmud (*Nedarim* 35b) discusses whether the *Kohen* is a messenger of G-d or whether he is the agent of the Jewish People. Of course, both are true. The *Kohen* is the liaison between the Children of Israel and their Heavenly Father. Such an exalted position demands the highest level of purity.

"*And G-d said to Moshe:* **Say** *to the priests, the sons of Aharon, and* **say** *to them...*" (21:1).

Why was the word "**say**" repeated in the verse? The *Ibn Ezra* suggests that the first word "*say*" means that Moshe was to say to the *Kohanim* all the laws in the preceding *parshah* and afterwards he was to say to them the laws of this *parshah* that apply specifically to them.

To expand on the thought of the *Ibn Ezra*, I believe that the double expression teaches us a very valuable lesson. The laws of sanctity in *Parshas Kedoshim* were taught to all the Jewish People, including the *Kohanim*. Why did G-d want Moshe to teach it to them again and then add the special laws of this *parshah* that applied only to them?

The *Kohanim* were an elite and privileged class. They dedicated their lives to the Divine service. They assisted the common folk in their quest for atonement and forgiveness. They were the teachers to the masses. They alone could eat from the most holy sacrificial meat. They alone could eat the sacred *trumah* portion of the crops. The Torah required that the first fruits be presented to them. A portion of every batch of dough and parts of every slaughtered animal were given to them. The priests were regarded as the aristocratic class of the Children of Israel.

As is often the case, members of the upper echelon of society may feel that they are better than everyone else. The can feel that they are entitled to certain liberties that the simple folks are not allowed to take. They can feel that certain laws do not apply to them; after all, they are above everyone else. The laws of sanctity that applied to all the Jewish People were repeated specifically to them to tell them that they are not above the law, especially when it comes to the laws of holiness.

The Talmud (*Yerushalmi Sanhedrin* 6:2) tells a dramatic story that illustrates the point:

> *Shimon ben Shetach was a great and influential rabbi.*

He was the head of the Sanhedrin and the brother-in-law of the king, Alexander Yannai. In his time, a satanic cult of witchcraft thrived in Judea. Shimon led a successful assault against the cult and eliminated it from the land. Shortly thereafter, two witnesses came to the court and testified that Shimon's son had committed murder. A trial was held and Shimon's son was found guilty. As he was being led out for execution, the witnesses bragged to Shimon that they had lied and made up the entire story about his son committing murder. It was their revenge for Shimon's eliminating the cult of witchcraft.

Shimon yelled to the executioner to stop. The witnesses had confessed that their testimony was false. Shimon's son looked at his father and asked, "Is that the law? Surely you know that according to our law, once witnesses give testimony in court, such testimony cannot be recanted. Their confession of guilt is not legally admissible. Let the execution proceed."

Shimon ben Shetach certainly knew the *halachah*. He realized that witnesses on their own cannot retract testimony. They cannot later confess that they had lied. It must be substantiated by outside witnesses, which in this case it was not. Shimon, out of fatherly compassion, felt that just this once, the law could be bent, after all, he was the head of the Supreme Court and his brother-in-law was the king. Shimon's son, the one who was about to be executed, reminded his father that the law can never be bent no matter how great one's status is. And so, the execution went ahead.

Earlier we mentioned a discussion in the Talmud (*Nedarim* 35b) whether the *Kohanim* are considered the messengers of the people or if they are messengers of G-d. The fact may be that they have the great privilege and status of being servants of G-d but they should always view themselves as servants of the people. That view will help them avoid the temptation to bend the rules for themselves.

✒️ SONS OF AHARON

The 263ʳᵈ mitzvah is the prohibition for a *Kohen* to become defiled by coming in contact with a corpse.
"Say to the Kohanim, the sons of Aharon, and say to them: To the dead among his people he shall not defile himself... Holy they shall be to their G-d" (21:1-6).

*T*he usual expression is *"the sons of Aharon, the Kohanim"* (*Vayikra* 1:5, 1:8, 1:11, 2:2, 3:2). *"Sons of Aharon"* is normally mentioned first in a verse in the Torah, followed by *"Kohanim."* This verse is the only time that the order is reversed and reads *"the Kohanim, the sons of Aharon."* Why?

In the previous piece we mentioned the idea, expressed by the *Ibn Ezra,* that the *Kohanim* were specifically told about the standard of sanctity that is expected of all the Jewish People. The *Kohanim* should not feel that they are superior to everyone else and are above the law. Our verse tells the *Kohanim* that there are two things to keep in mind that will help them from feeling superior. First of all, their high degree of sanctity and their social status was not due to any achievement of theirs. Do you know how you got to be a *Kohen*? It was an accident of birth. You are a *Kohen* only because you are a son of Aharon. In addition, you have no choice but to honor the laws of sanctity. The *Bais Din* compels you to keep up those standards. Since your exalted position is merely an accident of birth in which you had no choice and even after birth the *Bais Din* compels you to live up to regulations of a *Kohen,* what is there to feel superior about?

In *Parshas Kedoshim* the phrase is *"Holy **you** shall be"* (19:2). Here, the phrase is *"Holy **they** shall be."* Why here does it say *"they"* instead of "you"? This is especially perplexing, since Moshe was speaking directly to the *Kohanim* he should properly say "Holy you shall be."

Rashi (21:6) supplies the answer to this question. The phrase *"Holy they shall be"* was not said to the *Kohanim;* it was said to the court (*Bais Din*). The *Bais Din* was instructed to see to it that the

Kohanim lived up to the standards that were expected of them. Those standards were to be strictly enforced even against the will of the *Kohanim*.

Rashi (21:1) tells us an interesting fact about the prohibition for a *Kohen* to defile himself. Rashi, quoting the Talmud (*Yevamos* 114a) says that though every parent is obligated to train his youngster in the mitzvos, the child himself is not personally obligated to keep any of the mitzvos until his Bar Mitzvah. The mitzvos of sanctity, regarding a son of a *Kohen* are different. The child is not allowed to defile himself (See *Ramban* (21:1).

Why is the mitzvah of sanctity regarding a *Kohen's* son different than all other mitzvos? All other mitzvos are actions that we are supposed to do or actions we are not supposed to do. A child lacks the understanding why and what he is supposed to do and is therefore exempt from the mitzvos. However, the laws of sanctity are not things the *Kohen* is supposed to do or not supposed to do. The laws of *kedushah* come from what the *Kohen* is. The *Kohen* **is** holy and therefore must protect his holiness. A *Kohen's* young child is also a holy *Kohen.* The father must make certain that the *kedushah* of the child is not defiled.

This lesson can be extended to all Jews. The world holds us to a higher standard. They expect and demand more from us than anyone else. Why? It is because of what we are. We are holy Jews and the world requests that we live up to our holiness.

✑ HITCH YOUR WAGON TO A STAR

*T*he Mishnah (*Kelim* 1:6-9) tells us that there are ten levels of holy places, each more holy than the next. They are:

10 – The lowest level is the land of Israel which is holier

than any other land.

9 – The next level is the walled cities in Israel in which a leper may not reside.

8 – The next level is the area within the walls of Jerusalem where sacrificial meat may be eaten by the one who offered the sacrifice.

7 – The next level is the Temple Mount where a *zav* and *zavah* may not enter.

6 – The next level is the area within the Temple fence where a non-Jew or a Jew who was defiled by a corpse may not go.

5 – The next level is the courtyard of the women where one who has not become totally purified may not enter.

4 – The next level is the courtyard of the Israelites where one who is obligated to offer sacrifices and has not yet done so may not enter.

3 – The next level is the courtyard of the Priests where only those participating in the actual Temple service were allowed.

2 – The next level is the area beyond the Altar where a *Kohen* unfit to perform the Temple service may not enter.

1 – The highest level of sanctity is the Holies in which no one, not even a priest, may enter with unwashed hands and feet.

But the very holiest place of all is the Holy of Holies in which only the High Priest may enter and only on *Yom Kippur*.

What point is the Mishnah trying to tell us? All of these laws can be found scattered throughout the Talmud. What was the purpose of compiling this list? Also, since the Holy of Holies was the very holiest place of all, why wasn't it included in the list of ten holy places?

Perhaps the point of the Mishnah is as follows. Picture someone who is living outside the land of Israel who dreams about being a *Kohen Gadol*; he dreams about entering the Holy of Holies on *Yom Kippur* and experiencing the ultimate state of holiness. Simply dreaming will accomplishes very little. He must take the first step and enter into the land of Israel. After he has accomplished that, he takes the next step of entering the city of Jerusalem. After that, he goes up the Temple Mount. When he gets there, he can pass beyond the fence, then through the women's courtyard, and into the courtyard of the Israelites. He progresses step by step until he finds himself standing in the Holies. By climbing the ladder of *kedushah*, rung by rung, he has arrived at the holiest level attainable by a Jew.

The Mishnah is teaching us, through this list, that goals can only be achieved step by step. What about that person's dream to enter the Holy of Holies? That part of his dream is impossible. It is not obtainable by the average Jew, even if he is a great *tzadik*. Only the High Priest can go there and only on *Yom Kippur*. Though his dream was impossible, but by pursuing it, he attained the highest level possible. He was able to stand in the Holies and bask in the light of the Menorah which burned there.

As American poet, Ralph Waldo Emerson put it, "Hitch your wagon to a star." You may not reach the star, but you'll get a lot further than if you hitched it to a nearby tree.

✍ MAIS MITZVAH: THE MITZVAH TO BURY AN ABANDONED CORPSE

The Hebrew word for a corpse is *mais* (*mem-tof*). When the letters are reversed it spells out *tam* (*tof-mem*), meaning perfect. The *Shem M'Shmuel* says that this indicates that death and perfection are opposites. Rav Shimshon Raphael Hirsch explains that the living human body has the ability to grow both physically and spiritually. Life gives us the ability to serve G-d by providing us the opportunity to perform His mitzvos and emulate Him. Life is our means to achieve purity and instill in ourselves holiness. With the departing of the soul, comes death. Growth ceases. We can no longer grow and emulate G-d. And, with death comes *tumah*, impurity, the antithesis of the sanctity of life.

The Torah describes our father, Yaakov, as, *"Yaakov was a perfect man (tam) who dwelled in tents (of Torah) (Bereishis 25:27)."* Yaakov personified perfection and therefore the Talmud (*Taanis* 5b) says *"Yaakov is not dead."* Perfection is the antitheses of death. Yaakov was perfect and therefore the term "death" cannot be applied to him.

The *Kohanim* had the responsibility of performing the Divine Service in the Temple. Their task was to elevate this lower world to become closer to the world above – from whence all blessings emanate. The *Kohen* represented the pursuit of perfection, both for himself and also for all the Jewish People. Therefore, the *Kohen* was to remove himself from becoming contaminated by "death," the antitheses of perfection.

A *Kohen* may not defile himself by coming in contact with a corpse, attending a funeral service, or entering a cemetery. There are exceptions to this rule. A *Kohen* may defile himself if the deceased was a father, mother, sister, brother, son, daughter, or spouse. Also, if a corpse is found abandoned (*mais mitzvah*) and there is no one to take care of the burial except a *Kohen*, he may defile himself. In fact, he must defile himself. Why are there exceptions to this prohibition? It is very unusual for the Torah to allow for exceptions unless it is under the most dire of circumstances, such as a danger to life. Here, there is no such danger; the deceased has already passed on.

Every Jew is holy. The *Kohen* is the holy of holies. His total focus was expected to be on the spiritual world and to elevating himself. If he would not attend the funeral and burial of his closest relatives, he would be demonstrating insensitivity towards the departed and it would be an affront to the family members. If the *Kohen* would not attend to the burial of the *mais mitzvah*, then this too would be perceived as disrespect for human dignity. Insensitivity and disrespect are not the way to achieve holiness.

Rav Yisroel Salanter once said that someone else's *gashmius* (physical needs) is his *ruchnius* (spiritual needs). This means that when one takes care of someone else's physical needs, he is, in effect, taking care of his own spiritual needs. In the case of the *mais mitzvah,* the *Kohen's* holiness demands that he defile himself. Holiness does not put one above the concerns of others; it puts him directly involved in the concerns of others.

There are those who have the merit to hear the words of Torah from a great Torah scholar. They gather around to soak up the holy words that will elevate their souls. However, among these fortunate ones, there are some that in their zeal to hear the words of Torah and to catch a glimpse of the saintly man, will push and shove those around them. They exhibit a total lack of concern for their fellow Jew. That is not the path to holiness. Holiness is to show respect. If the Torah demanded that the *Kohen* show respect for the dead, how much more so is respect demanded for the living.

⋙ MOURNING

The 264ᵗʰ mitzvah is for a *Kohen* to defile himself by attending the funeral of a close relative and to mourn for that relative.

"Except for his relative that is near to him, to his mother, and to his father, and to his son, and to his daughter, and to his brother, and to his virgin sister who had no husband, to her he should defile himself" **(21:2).**

The Talmud (*Yevamos* 22b) explains the phrase *"Except for his relative that is near to him,"* to refer to a wife, even if she was only *"near to him,"* meaning betrothed but not yet fully married.

Our Rabbis interpret the verse to include all Jews, not only *Kohanim,* in the mitzvah of mourning for the loss of a close relative. If a *Kohen* is obligated to violate his law of sanctity in order to mourn, surely a simple Jew, who would not be violating any law of sanctity, is obligated to mourn.

The Jewish period of mourning is divided into 4 parts.

1 – ANINUS -SUSPENDING DAILY ROUTINE

Death overshadows nearly everything else. The Torah acknowledges the depths of the family's grief and the urgency to attend to needs of the deceased. Therefore, on the day the deceased passed away, the mourners are exempted from prayer. The male mourners are exempted from the mitzvah of *Tefillin*. The *Tefillin* are our sign of glory and this tragic moment is not a time of glory (*Berachos* 11a). After the burial service, prayers once again become obligatory. The mitzvah of *Tefillin* resumes the next day. The mourners may not eat meat or drink wine or partake in an elaborate meal on that day.

When a person hears of the passing of an immediate family member, he or she recites the blessing of *dayon ha'emes*, The Judge of truth. Afterwards, the garments are ripped (*k'riyah*) as a concrete expression of heartbreak. It allows mourners to physically express what words cannot. It shows the depth of their anguish at this time.

No one should perform any mitzvah in front of the deceased. It is considered an affront. It shows that the living can still perform good deeds while the departed cannot.

From the moment of death until the burial, the body is constantly watched and attended. Members of the community take turns sitting with the body, reciting psalms and other prayers to comfort the soul of the deceased. One may not eat in front of a deceased. Even drinking water is forbidden. Our Sages have a delicate sensitivity for the departed.

The human body is considered a holy vessel. It is a great mitzvah to wash the body and purify it before the burial. This mitzvah, called *t'ha'arah* or purification, is performed by the *Chevrah Kadishah*, a voluntary group from the community, rather than by the actual family members. The body is washed limb by limb, starting with the head. Afterwards, a quantity (nine *kav*) of water is poured onto the entire body for purification. The body is then dressed in white linen or cotton. During this solemn procedure, no idle conversation may take place.

The burial should take place on the day of the death. It should not be postponed unless it is for the sake of the honor of the deceased. It cannot be done merely to accommodate family members who have to travel from afar.

Escorting the body to the cemetery is a great mitzvah. If one sees a funeral procession he must escort the body at least a small distance. Not to do so is considered highly contemptuous.

The principle *"from dust you come and to dust you will return"* (*Bereishis* 3:19) dictates many burial customs. Consequently, the body is dressed in a shroud of natural fiber and buried in a coffin of plain wood, which will all decompose at about the same rate; thus the process of returning to the earth is not impeded. In Israel, no coffin whatsoever is used. Bodies are wrapped in a plain sheet and placed directly in the soil. Judaism does not permit embalming or any measures that preserve the body or the coffin.

When the body is lowered into the grave, family members shovel earth onto the coffin. This encourages the mourners to accept the reality of death and allows them to personally assist the body of their loved one into the ground.

2 – THE SHIVA PERIOD

This stage begins upon returning home from the cemetery. Following the funeral, the mourner returns home and eats a "meal of condolence."

The mirrors in a house of mourning are covered. Man was created in the image of G-d. With every death, the very image of God is "diminished" and a reflection of the Divine Image is eclipsed. To symbolize this eclipse, the mirrors in the house of mourning are covered.

Mirrors can only reflect the present. One cannot look into a mirror and see what happened yesterday nor can one see tomorrow. Death takes us away from the present. We reflect on the past life of the deceased. We talk about what he or she did: the acts of kindness, and the consideration and dedication to others. We take a lesson from the departed one's life and allow it to mold our future. Mirrors have no place in a house of mourning.

Mourners sit on low stools or on the floor to indicate the low spirit of the mourner. When a visitor pays a *shiva* call, he or she should enter quietly and sit near the mourner. It is customary to wait for the mourner to speak rather than initiate conversation. Traditionally, conversation should provide an opportunity to celebrate the life of the deceased. It is important to be attuned to the mourner's needs and follow his lead.

During the *shiva* period, work is not done other than necessary domestic requirements. A mourner may not bathe his entire body but hands, feet, and face may be washed with cool water. Mourners are not allowed to learn Torah other than the laws pertaining to mourning.

One does not greet a mourner with the usual *Shalom aleichem*, Peace be unto you, because the mourner is not at peace.

The mourners may not wear freshly laundered garments.

A candle is kept burning during the entire *shiva* period. The flame and the wick represent the body and the soul.

Mourners recite a special prayer, called the Kaddish. Since a *minyan* is required in order to recite the *Kaddish*, a *minyan* will generally convene at the mourner's home to help the mourner fulfill this *mitzvah*.

The text of the *Kaddish* prayer itself has nothing to do with the souls of dead relatives. It is an ecstatic exultation of G-d's glory. The *Kaddish* expresses hope for G-d's rule and for peace to be speedily manifest on earth. It is a reaffirmation of faith of the living during these trying times.

The *Kaddish* also has a sociological impact. Not only is it a way for the mourner to maintain a connection with the deceased in a comforting, structured way, but it also requires the mourning individual to seek out his community. In order to fulfill the obligation of *Kaddish*, the mourner must rouse himself from his pain and become part of an ongoing social group, the *minyan*. Conversely, the *Kaddish* singles out the mourner to the community, reminding them for a full year to embrace one of their members who is in pain.

The practice of reciting the *Kaddish* has taken on a mystique of its own. The words of prayer are offered on behalf of the departed and as such provide a source of comfort to the deceased. It accompanies the soul in its journey to the next world. It entreats the departed soul to pray on behalf of the surviving kin. *Kaddish* is felt to be a great obligation on the part of the mourners: a final act to show their respects. The prayer has such a hold on the imagination that even Jews who had broken all other religious ties were concerned that they be survived by a "*Kaddishel*," a son who would continue to honor them after death with the reciting of the *Kaddish*.

In the event of the death of a spouse, child, or sibling, the *Kaddish* is said for a full thirty days after burial. For a deceased parent, however, the mourner will continue to say *Kaddish* for 11 months. *Kaddish* is also repeated on the *Yarzheit*, the anniversary of the loved one's death.

3 – *SHLOSHIM*: THE FIRST MONTH

Following the *shiva,* there are certain rules of mourning that apply for the remainder of the 30 days after the burial. One should not shave, or have his or her haircut. There are prohibitions against getting married, attending parties, or wearing new clothes. Mourners do not send or receive gifts.

The custom among many is for a mourner to change his seat in the *shul.* This change in place is done with the hope that it should herald a change in his fortune.

4 – THE FIRST YEAR OF MOURNING

The mourner continues to refrain from attending festive gatherings for a term of one year.

After the first year, four times a year, at the *Yizkor* service, we publicly remember those we mourn. *Yizkor* is a memorial service recited on *Yom Kippur* and the last days of Passover, *Shavuos,* and *Succos. Yizkor,* Hebrew for "remember", asks G-d to remember those we mourn and to grant them proper rest.

Many Jews, who do not otherwise enter a synagogue, come for the *Yizkor* service. For many, the prayer represents a kind of pact; by remembering our parents, we ensure that we will be remembered in turn by those who follow us. *Yizkor* can also be a way to help a beloved ancestor: promoting good for that departed soul. We may hope, too, that the loved ones will intercede on our behalf or that the memory of their righteous deeds will bring us favor before God.

The service includes a pledge of charity, given in the memory of a deceased family member. Jewish memory is not a passive affair; we remember loved ones by acts of loving-kindness in this world.

A child is born with a clenched fist. It seems to symbolize his determination to grab it all in. He has already set his sights on seizing all that this world has to offer. When a person dies, he dies with his hands open. It symbolizes that he has seized nothing. Whatever possessions he accrued in this world cannot be taken into the next one. His house, his car, his banks accounts will all be left behind for others to enjoy.

The custom is for someone to close the hands of the deceased. Once again the fists are clenched but this time to show that though there are no material possessions he will carry with him into the next world, the mitzvos and the kind deeds that he performed: securely in his grasp.

THE MITZVOS THAT RELATE TO THE SANCTITY OF THE KOHANIM

The 265ᵗʰ mitzvah is the prohibition for a *t'vul yom* to perform the Temple service.
"They shall not profane the name of their G-d" **(21:6).**

The Sages (*Sanhedrin* 83b) interpret this verse to refer to a *t'vul yom*. A *t'vul yom* is a priest that was unclean and underwent the ritual purification process of immersion in a *mikvah*. Even though he has cleansed himself in the *mikvah*, he still must wait until sunset for the purification to completely take effect. Until sunset he is called a *t'vul yom* (one who immersed that day) and may not yet participate in the Temple service.

Why did the verse use the expression *"They shall not profane the name of their G-d?"* Is not the G-d of the *Kohen* the same as every Jew's G-d?

The unique relationship between G-d and Israel is one of holiness. *"Holy you shall be, for holy am I the G-d your G-d"* (19:2). Because the lives of the *Kohanim* were dedicated to His service, they had a greater degree of *kedushah* than the rest of the people. The *Kohanim* had a closer relationship with G-d. Because of their unique relationship to G-d, He is called "their G-d."

> **The 266ᵗʰ mitzvah is the prohibition for a *Kohen* to marry an "immoral woman."**
>
> *"An immoral woman, a profaned woman, they shall not take (for a wife), a woman divorced from her husband they shall not take, for he is holy to his G-d"* (21:7).

The Rambam (*Isurei Biyah* 18) explains that an *"immoral woman"* includes, among others, the following:

1 – A non-Jewish woman, who would naturally be suspected of committing acts which we consider immoral

Though no Jew is allowed to marry a non-Jew, a special prohibition is given to the *Kohanim*.

2 – A female convert who is suspected of committing immoral acts before her conversion.

3 – A woman who had relations with someone she could not have married: for example a woman who had an incestuous or adulterous relationship.

4 – A woman who was a harlot.

The *Kohen* is held to a higher standard than the rest of the Jewish People. The conduct, purity and holiness of a *Kohen* must always be without blemish. Therefore, the Torah wants him to marry a woman whose background and past are without blemish as well.

> **The 267ᵗʰ mitzvah is the prohibition for a *Kohen* to marry a "profaned woman."**
>
> *"An immoral woman, a profaned woman, they shall not take (for a wife), a woman divorced from her husband they shall not take, for he is holy to his G-d"* (21:7).

If a *Kohen* married a woman to whom he was not allowed, the daughter produced from that marriage is called a "profaned woman" and she is not permitted to marry a *Kohen*.

The 268th mitzvah is the prohibition for a *Kohen* to marry a divorced woman.

"An immoral woman, a profaned woman, they shall not take (for a wife), a woman divorced from her husband they shall not take, for he is holy to his G-d" (21:7).

Marriage is called *kiddushin*, meaning Act of Holiness. Divorce severs that act of holiness. A priest is not permitted to marry a woman who is the product of a broken state of holiness.

The 269th mitzvah is for the Jewish People to treat the *Kohen* with the respect and sanctity his holiness deserves.

"You shall sanctify him (the Kohen)" (21:8).

The *Kohen* is called up to the Torah first as a sign of respect. At a meal, the *Kohen* is to be served first. A *Kohen* is allowed to pass through an open door first. A *Kohen* should not serve or assist another person if it is some sort of subservient act, such as serving food or holding the door for someone else. However, many authorities say that the *Kohen* is permitted to forgo any honor that is shown to him if he feels uncomfortable with it (See *Mishnah Brurah* 128:175).

The *Ramah* (*Orech Chaim* 128:45) says that just as one is forbidden to use sacred objects for his own needs, one may not make use of a *Kohen* because he too is sacred. The *Ramah* is telling us that giving honor and respect to a *Kohen* is not merely because of his position in the community. It is because of his holiness. Holiness demands respect. These lessons are not only important for Israelites to be aware of, the *Kohen* himself must constantly think about the inner sanctity that lies within him. He must be attuned to his own spirituality and live up to that gift which has been passed from father to son, beginning with Aharon, the first priest and the *Kohen Gadol*. Every *Kohen* possesses not only part of the genetic material of Aharon within himself, he also possesses that spark of *kedushah* that has been transmitted through all these generations.

The 270th mitzvah is the prohibition for a *Kohen Gadol*

to defile himself.

"A high priest... unto any of the dead he shall not come, to his father and to his mother he shall not defile himself" **(21:10-11).**

Though no *Kohen* was permitted to defile himself, a special injunction was mentioned to the High Priest because of his special status.

The 271ˢᵗ mitzvah is the prohibition of a *Kohen Gadol* to defile himself even for a close relative.

"A high priest... unto any of the dead he shall not come, to his father and to his mother he shall not defile himself" **(21:10-11).**

Though a regular *Kohen* may defile himself for a close relative, the High Priest was held to a higher standard. The sanctity of his position requires that much more vigilance in his state of purity; thus denying him the same exceptions accorded other *Kohanim* in the attending to the burial of close family members.

The 272ⁿᵈ mitzvah is for a High Priest to marry a virgin.

"And (the High Priest) shall take (as a wife) a virgin" **(21:13).**

The sanctity of the High Priest embodies the ultimate pursuit of perfection. In no way can this be compromised. A woman who had relations previously, cannot offer absolute and perfect love to her new husband. She will unavoidably retain memories of any man with whom she previously had relations. Only a virgin can offer true love and complete loyalty (*Sefer HaChinuch* 272).

The 273ʳᵈ mitzvah is the prohibition for a High Priest to marry a widow.

"A widow, a divorcee, an immoral woman, a profaned woman, these he shall not take" **(21:14).**

See above, mitzvos 266-268.

This mitzvah repeats for the High Priest the prohibitions for marriage that were stated for a regular *Kohen* – a divorcee, an immoral woman, and a profaned woman. In addition to the women that a regular *Kohen* may not marry, the High Priest could not marry a widow.

Even if the widow is still a virgin, the *Kohen Gadol* may not marry her. She too will unavoidably retain memories of her first husband and not be able to offer her true love and loyalty to the *Kohen godol*.

> **The 274ᵗʰ mitzvah is the prohibition for a *Kohen Gadol* to have relations with a widow.**
> *"He shall not profane his seed"* (21:15).
> **The 275ᵗʰ mitzvah is the prohibition for a *Kohen* who has a permanent physical defect to participate in the *Bais Hamikdash* service.**
> *"(A priest) who has in him a (physical) defect shall not come close to offer..."* (21:17).

However, he is assigned other minor tasks in the Temple and is permitted to eat *trumah*.

A *Kohen* represents the pursuit of perfection and holiness. One could mistakenly think that he is to perfect his intellect and may neglect his physical body. The Torah is teaching us that true perfection is not only a spiritual quest, it involves the perfection of the body as well.

The Rambam (*Biyas HaMikdash*, chapters 6-8) details exactly which physical defects disqualify a *Kohen*.

> **The 276ᵗʰ mitzvah is the prohibition for a *Kohen* who has a temporary physical defect to serve in the *Bais Hamikdash*.**
> *"Any man, from the descendants of Aharon the priest, who has in him a defect, shall not come close to offer..."* (21:21).

This verse seems to be a repetition of the previous one; however, Rashi informs us that the word "*any*" comes to include a *Kohen* with a temporary defect. While the defect is with him, he may not serve.

> **The 277ᵗʰ mitzvah is the prohibition for a *Kohen* with any physical blemish to enter the main Sanctuary, the *Ohel Moed* or the *Heichal*.**
> *"But to the curtain (of the main Sanctuary) he may not come..."* (1:23).

The 278ᵗʰ mitzvah is the prohibition for an unclean (*tamei*) *Kohen* to serve.

"They shall separate themselves from the holy things of the Children of Israel" **(22:2).**

The 279ᵗʰ mitzvah is the prohibition for an unclean *Kohen* to eat *trumah*.

"Holy things he may not eat until he is clean (tahor)" **(22:4).**

The Talmud (*Makos* 14a) explains that this verse refers specially to *trumah*

The 280ᵗʰ mitzvah is the prohibition for a non-*Kohen* to eat *trumah*.

"No stranger may eat the holy" **(22:10).**

A "stranger" refers to a non-*Kohen*.

The 281ˢᵗ mitzvah is the prohibition for any Hebrew slave to eat *trumah*.

"The life-long Hebrew slave (nirtzah) of a priest and the six-year Hebrew slave of a priest may not eat holy" **(22:10).**

A *Kohen* may feed *trumah* to his non-Jewish slaves or even to his animals; that is because they are considered his property. Hebrews slaves, however, are looked upon as hired workers and not as the property of the *Kohen*. Therefore, he cannot feed his Hebrew slaves *trumah*.

The 282ⁿᵈ mitzvah is the prohibition for an uncircumcised *Kohen* to eat *trumah*.

"Any man from the descendants of Aharon...shall not eat holy" **(22:4-10).**

The Sages (*Yevamos* 70a & *Sifra* 22:4) derive from this verse the prohibition for an uncircumcised *Kohen* to eat *trumah*. The word "*any*" includes not only an unclean *Kohen,* but one who lacks a *bris*.

The 283ʳᵈ mitzvah is the prohibition for a *Kohen's* daughter who has forfeited her rights to *trumah* to eat *trumah*.

"The daughter of a priest who will be to a strange man, she shall not eat the holy trumah" **(22:12).**

The daughter of a *Kohen* is allowed to eat *trumah*. However if she marries and her husband is not a *Kohen,* she forfeits the right to continue eating *trumah.* Also, the unmarried daughter of a *Kohen* who had relations with a man she was not permitted to marry, she too forfeits the right to eat *trumah.*

The 284th mitzvah is the prohibition for an Israelite to eat from the produce before the *trumah* and other tithes are separated.

"The Children of Israel shall not profane the holy things which they are to set apart for G-d" **(22:15).**

The 285th mitzvah is the prohibition to offer an animal with a physical defect.

"Any (animal) which has in it a defect shall not be offered..." **(22:20).**

The 286th mitzvah is to make certain that the animal that is being offered is a perfect specimen, meaning free from physical defects.

"Perfect it shall be" **(22:21).**

The 287th mitzvah is the prohibition to make a defect in an animal that was set aside to be used for a *korban.*

"No defect shall be in it" **(22:21).**

The 288th mitzvah is prohibition to use any part of the defective animal in the Temple service.

"You shall not offer these to G-d" **(22:22).**

The 289th mitzvah, which is derived from the same verse, is the prohibition to slaughter a defective animal as a sacrifice.

"You shall not offer these to G-d" **(22:22).**

The 290th mitzvah is the prohibition to offer any part of the defective animal on the altar.

"A fire-offering you shall not make of them" **(22:22).**

☙ WHEN THE CAT IS AWAY, THE MICE WILL PLAY

The 291st mitzvah is the prohibition to surgically neuter an animal.

"An (animal which has had its reproductive organs) crushed, torn or severed, you shall not offer it to G-d, in your land you shall not do" **(22:24).**

The end of the verse teaches us that one may not surgically neuter any animal, even one not being used for a sacrifice. Rashi (22:24) tells us that the prohibition applies even to non-kosher animals. Obviously, a human may not be surgically neutered (*Sefer HaChinuch*).

Some authorities (See *Shulchan Orech, Even Ha'ezer* 5:14) extend this prohibition to non-Jews as well. Everyone agrees that a Jew may not give his animal to a non-Jew to be neutered. A Jew who wishes to have a pet that is neutered should acquire one that has already been altered.

G-d created His world in a state of perfection. He left nothing lacking and added nothing excessive. It was His will that creatures should reproduce. He gave us this blessing so that each of the species would continue to endure: every creature serves a purpose. It is not up to man to determine them unworthy or not useful.

A few decades ago, the Malaysian government decided to spray large areas of jungle with DDT in an effort to control the mosquito infestation. The poisoned mosquitoes were devoured by roaches; they in turn fell prey to the lizards. The lizards were slowed down by the DDT in their bodies and they were easy targets of the feral cats. The cats were more vulnerable to the poison and began dying by the thousands. With the cat population safely out of the way, the rats thrived and created a more serious health problem.

The delicate balance of nature is one of G-d's remarkable creations. Man must not play G-d and altar the scheme of creation.

The 292nd mitzvah is the prohibition to accept a defec-

tive animal for a sacrifice from a non-Jew.
*From the hand of a non-Jew you shall not offer...any of
these"* (22:25).

✑ MAKE EVERY DAY COUNT

**The 293ʳᵈ mitzvah is to use an animal for a sacrifice
that is at least eight days old.**
*"An ox, a sheep, or goat, when it is born, for seven days
it shall be with its mother, from the eighth day onward
it will be acceptable as a fire-offering to G-d"* (22:27).

Each of the seven days of creation was instilled with unique spiritual qualities which were reflected by the creations made on that day. Before a *bris* takes place, we wait until seven days have passed so that each day can instill its spiritual quality into the child. The sanctity of the covenant of the *bris* mingles with the spiritual qualities of all seven days.

Likewise, we must wait until seven days have passed before we can use an animal for a sacrifice. Passover is a seven day holiday. The Torah wished that each of the seven days of the week have the added spiritual quality that Passover has to offer, that quality of freedom. *Succos* is also seven days; *Shemini Atzeres* is considered a separate holiday. The Torah also wished for *Succos* to instill its special quality into each of the seven day, the quality of joy.

The *Kli Yakar* asks why the verse refers to a newborn calf as an ox, a newborn lamb as a sheep, and a newborn kid as a goat. Why is the adult animal mentioned when it is referring to the newborn?

The *Kli Yaakar* answers that when these animals are born, they have nearly all the abilities of an adult. Most of their faculties are already developed. One may assume that because of this, the newborn could be offered as a sacrifice since they have almost reached physical perfection. Though the animal may seem to be adult-like, when it comes to being proclaimed holy and being used as a sacrifice, the animal must possess spiritual qualities as well. We must wait until the animal has lived through all the days of the week.

We go through the week thinking that, except for Shabbos, every day is the same as the day before. The week is filled with six days of monotony, drudgery, and hard work. The lesson here is that each day of the week has its special gift to offer us. We must see the blessings of each day so we will be able to take in the wonderful spiritual gift each day has to offer us.

The 294ᵗʰ mitzvah is the prohibition to slaughter a female animal and its offspring on the same day.

"An ox or a sheep, it and its offspring you shall not slaughter in one day" **(22:28).**

This mitzvah applies whether the mother and/or the offspring is for personal use or even if it is for a sacrifice.

We have mentioned numerous times that there is no greater love than that of a mother for her child. It would be inhumane to take a mother and a child's life in the same day. The Ramban explains that the purpose of this mitzvah is directed not toward the animal, but toward man. The observance of these mitzvos, which teach us to have a feeling of compassion towards animals, can help purge man of callousness, cruelty and savagery. Although man is allowed to slaughter animals for food, he should do it with self-discipline and mercy.

SANCTIFYING G-D'S NAME

The 295ᵗʰ mitzvah is the prohibition to do anything that could bring disgrace to G-d's name.
"Do not profane My holy name" **(22:32).**
The 296ᵗʰ mitzvah is to bring honor to G-d's name.

"I shall be sanctified among the Children of Israel" (22:32).

If we love and respect someone, we want others to love and respect him as well. The last thing we wish is to cause others to hate and disrespect the one we love. Our greatest love and respect is for Hashem. It is therefore naturally incumbent on us to have others love and respect Him as well. The most dreadful thing we can do is cause others to resent and disrespect Him.

It is interesting that first the Torah gives us the mitzvah of not causing disrespect for G-d and then it gives us the mitzvah of bringing respect for Him. Shouldn't the Torah first mention the ideal mitzvah of bringing respect? However, the Torah is teaching us the same principle that Hippocrates repeated when he wrote his rules for the physician (*Epidemics, Book I, sect.* 11) almost 2,500 years ago, *"First, do no harm!"* The Torah tells us too, "First, do no harm!" Bring no disgrace to G-d. That is within everyone's grasp. Each one of us has the ability and opportunity to do something terrible that would bring disgrace to G-d: may it never happen. The Torah addresses all of us: do no harm. There are those who have the opportunity and ability to bring honor to G-d's name. The Torah then addresses them and tells them to do so.

People think that to make a *chilul Hashem* (disgracing G-d's name) means to act improperly in front of non-Jews. Such actions may cause the non-Jews to think ill of our people. That is how most of us look at this mitzvah. However, the verse says, *"I shall be sanctified among the Children of Israel."* The primary mitzvah is not to make a *chilul Hashem* **among the Children of Israel**, among our fellow Jews.

There are some misguided Jews who in their zeal of opposing the State of Israel side with Palestinian terrorists. These Jews who curry favor among extreme Anti-Semites dress like ultra-Orthodox Jews and, therefore, to the world they represent Orthodox Jews. When these deranged folks hold a demonstration, how do normal people react? A normal non-Jew will react with bewilderment. Some might make erroneous conclusions about Orthodox Jews and others will assume it is the actions of some demented individuals. How do Jews react? We feel embarrassed that a fellow Jew can publicly behave so poorly. We regretfully feel ashamed to have such dishonorable members among our people. That is a real *chilul Hashem*, when one Jew behaves in a disgraceful manner that makes another Jew feel that he has been publicly shamed by that behavior.

Conversely, a *kiddush Hashem* is to make another Jew feel proud of his fellow Jew. How can one do that? Not long ago, there was a man, not particularly committed to his Jewish faith, who desperately needed a kidney transplant. A donor was found, an Orthodox Jew. After the transplant, the convalescing recipient called the convalescing donor to thank him profusely. The donor said, "Don't thank me. I'm not in the habit of giving away my body parts. However, our Torah teaches us that we must do whatever it takes to save another Jew. I am simply following the words of our Torah."

We can imagine how impressed the recipient must have felt about the donor's commitment to the Torah. We can imagine how proud the recipient must have been of that fellow Jew and how proud he must have felt to be a Jew. That is a *Kiddush Hashem*.

◄§ THE FESTIVALS OF LIFE

The remaining 29 mitzvos of the *parshah* deal with the sanctity of the holy days of the year – Shabbos, Passover, *Shavuos, Rosh Hashanah, Yom Kippur*, and *Succos.*

The three festivals, when pilgrimages were made by all the Jewish People to the *Bais HaMikdash*, are Passover, *Shavuos*, and *Succos*. These three holidays have a dual identity. First, they reflect major occasions in Jewish history. Passover is when the Children of Israel gained their G-d-given freedom from the land of Egypt; *Shavous* is when the Children of Israel received the Torah from G-d. *Succos* commemorates when the Children of Israel were granted G-d-given sustenance and shelter in the desert. They survived and thrived on the *manna* and were protected by the Clouds of Glory.

The second aspect of the three festivals has nothing to do with history; it is the timeless aspect of the three phases of the agricultural season. Passover is the time the harvest first begins to sprout forth from the ground. *Shavuos* is when the grains are harvested. *Succos* celebrates the ingathering of the fruit and grains that were left in the fields to dry.

Why do we have this dual nature of our holidays? Why are two sets of seemingly unrelated reasons given for their celebration?

Quite possibly, the dual nature of our festivals is not unrelated at all and this dual nature reveals a very important lesson regarding the Jewish national holidays. Passover is when the Children of Israel left the land of bondage. The grains sprouting forth and 'exiting' their entombment of the ground symbolize this event. However, the Jewish nation did not as yet have any set of laws or ideals giving them a unique identity. All they had so far was their sad memories of slavery in Egypt. Nostalgically they were still attached to the land of Egypt. On *Shavuos,* when they received the Torah, they attained a new identity. They now were completely severed from the land of bondage. This is symbolized by the harvest of the grains when the stalks are severed from the ground.

The Sages often describe the giving of the Torah at Sinai as a wedding between G-d and Israel. However, the wedding contract is not completed until the groom feeds and shelters his bride. That honoring of the contract is celebrated with the festival of *Succos* when we recall how G-d fed and sheltered the Israelites in the wilderness of Sinai. This is symbolized by the ingathering of the produce when the new crops are brought in the homes.

The overall lesson is an important one. The three festivals do not merely commemorate events from the past but they are timeless, just like the agricultural events. They occur year after year. Every year we must free ourselves from being enslaved by the habits and misdeeds of the past. Every year we must recommit ourselves to receiving the

Torah. And, every year we must renew our realization that it is G-d who nourishes and protects the Jewish People.

Not only do the festivals reflect the present yearly cycle of agriculture and yearly growth of every Jew, they also represent the history and destiny of the Jewish Nation. Passover commemorates the past, when we were born out of the womb of Egypt amidst the labor pains of slavery. *Shavuos* represents the present. Each and every day we are expected to receive the Torah. The blessing we recite each morning and again when we are called to the Torah ends with *"Blessed are You, G-d, Who gives the Torah."* We do not say "Who gave (past tense) the Torah," but rather *"Who gives* (present tense) *the Torah."* *Succos* represents the future of Israel when the *Mashiach* will come and rebuild the Temple. In that time, G-d's providence and His sustaining of the Jewish People will become revealed to all. It will be a time of universal peace when swords will be beaten into plowshares and the lion will lie down with the lamb. It is no wonder that we refer to the next Temple as the *Succah* of Peace in our nightly prayers (*Hashkivaynu*), *"Spread over us the Succah of Your Peace."*

The Torah portion of the festivals begins with *"The seasonal (holidays) which you are to proclaim..."* (23:2). The Talmud (*Rosh HaShanah* 25a) tells us that it is up to the Jewish People (via the *Sanhedrin)* to establish when the New Moon (*Rosh Chodesh*) should be proclaimed each month. Even if they err and proclaim it on a wrong day, that day is still *Rosh Chodesh.* Even if they willingly proclaim it on the wrong day in order to establish a more convenient calendar arrangement, (so *Yom Kippur* will not be on a Friday or Sunday), it is validly proclaimed. When *Rosh Chodesh* will be observed is determined by the Jewish People. Therefore, in effect, the Jewish People have control over the timing of the festivals. That is why the festival blessing concludes with *"Blessed are You, G-d, who sanctifies Israel and the timely festivals."* We mention Israel before the festivals because Israel has control over them.

The festivals represent the destiny of the Jewish People. We should never view ourselves as victims of circumstances. We should never see ourselves as straw blown in the wind or driftwood randomly carried by the ocean's waves. We are active participants in the outcome of our individual and collective destiny.

✌ PASSOVER

The 297ᵗʰ mitzvah is to rest from work on the first day of Passover.
"On the first day (of Passover) shall be to you a holy proclamation, all servile work you shall not do" (23:7).
The 298ᵗʰ mitzvah is derived from the same verse and it is the prohibition to do work on the first day of Passover.
"On the first day (of Passover) shall be to you a holy proclamation, all servile work you shall not do" (23:7).

There are two mitzvos (297 & 298) teaching us not to work on *Yom Tov*. The first is a positive commandment. The second is a negative commandment, called a prohibition.

The reason why we have two commandments here is as follows. We are rewarded for doing positive commandments. We are not punished if we do not do them. For example, we are rewarded for the positive mitzvah of eating matzah on Passover. We are not punished if we do not eat matzah. With regards to negative commandments, prohibitions, the reverse is true. We are punished for violating the commandment; we are not rewarded for not violating them. For example, one is punished if he violates the prohibition against eating non-kosher. He is not rewarded each moment that he refrains from eating non-kosher.

Resting on every *Yom Tov*, as well as on Shabbos, is both a positive and a negative commandment. Therefore, we are rewarded if we keep the positive command and rest from work. We are punished if we violate the negative command and do work.

The 299ᵗʰ mitzvah is to offer the special communal sacrifices (*korbon musaf*) each day of Passover.

"And you shall offer a fire-offering to G-d seven days" **(23:8).**

The 300ᵗʰ mitzvah is to rest from work on the seventh day of Passover.

"On the seventh day, a holy proclamation, all servile work you shall not do" **(23:8).**

On the seventh day of Passover, the Egyptian army drowned in the Red Sea. The redemption from Egypt was then completed.

The 301ˢᵗ mitzvah, derived from the same verse, is the prohibition to do work on the seventh day of Passover.

"On the seventh day, a holy proclamation, all servile work you shall not do" **(23:8).**

The 302ⁿᵈ mitzvah is to offer the barley meal-offering on the second day of Passover: it is called the *korban Omer*.

"And you shall bring the Omer..." **(23:10).**

The next three mitzvos are listed below followed by the verse that all three are derived from.

The 303ʳᵈ mitzvah is the prohibition to eat baked goods made from *chodosh*.

The 304ᵗʰ mitzvah, derived from the same verse, is the prohibition to eat roasted grain that is *chodosh*.

The 305ᵗʰ mitzvah, derived from the same verse, is not to eat soft grains that are *chodosh*.

"Bread, roasted grain, soft grain you shall not eat until that very day, until you have brought the (Omer) offering of your G-d. It is an everlasting statue for all your generations and throughout all your dwelling places" **(23:14).**

Any grains that sprouted from the ground after the second day of Passover were not allowed for consumption until the next year's second day of Passover: after the *Omer*-sacrifice was brought. If no *Omer* was offered, then it was permitted at the end of the day. This grain that sprouted after the second day of Passover is called *chodosh* and can not be eaten until the next year. Since the verse says that it is *"an everlasting statue for all your generations,"* that implies the mitzvah still applies today in Israel. The verse also states that the mitzvah applies *"throughout all your dwelling places."* Whether this refers only to dwelling places in Israel or if it refers to all your dwelling places even outside the land of Israel is a lengthy discussion amongst the rabbinical authorities.

⋙ COUNTING THE OMER AND SHAVUOS

The 306ᵗʰ mitzvah is to count the 49 days, seven weeks, between the first day of Passover and *Shavuos*.
"And you shall count from the morrow of the day of rest, from the day you brought the Omer for waving, seven weeks, complete they shall be" **(23:15).**

Shavuos is unlike all the other holidays. All the other holidays are assigned a calendar date by the Torah. Passover is the 15ᵗʰ of *Nissan* (23:6), *Rosh HaShanah* is the 1ˢᵗ of *Tishrei* (23:24), *Yom Kippur* is the 10ᵗʰ of *Tishrei* (23:27), and *Succos* is the 15ᵗʰ day of *Tishrei* (23:34). *Shavuos* is not assigned a calendar date. Instead, it is assigned to the 50ᵗʰ day after the first day of Passover. *Shavuos* is, in effect, an extension of the holiday of Passover. When Moshe told Pharaoh, *"We will go with our young and with our old, with our sons and with our daughters, with our flocks and with our herds will we go; for we must celebrate a festival to G-d (Shmos 10:9),"* he was referring to *Shavuos*. The ultimate purpose of the Exodus was to receive the Torah at Sinai. *Shavuos* is a climax of the Passover holiday.

The 307ᵗʰ mitzvah was to offer a special communal meal-offering on *Shavuos*, called "the two loaves", *shtai ha'lechem*.

"And you shall offer a new meal offering to G-d" (23:16).

This meal-offering was made from the finest wheat flour that had just come into season. The two loaves represent the two tablets of the Ten Commandments. This symbolizes that it is only through the merit of our Torah mitzvos that we are able to enjoy the fine produce of the land of Israel.

The next two mitzvos are derived from the same verse.

The 308ᵗʰ mitzvah is to rest from work on *Shavuos.*

The 309ᵗʰ mitzvah is the prohibition to work on *Shavuos.*

"And you shall proclaim that very day a holy proclamation for yourselves, all servile work you shall not do" (23:21).

◄ ROSH HASHANAH

he next two mitzvos are derived from the same verse.

The 310ᵗʰ mitzvah is to rest from work on *Rosh HaShanah.*

The 311ᵗʰ mitzvah is the prohibition to do work on *Rosh HaShanah.*

"On the first day of the seventh month, it shall be to you a day of rest, memorialized (by the) blasting (of the shofar), a holy proclamation" (23:24).

It is interesting to note that the word "*shofar*" is not mentioned in the verse. This hints at the fact that we do not blow the *shofar* on Shabbos *Rosh HaShanah*. We merely recall the mitzvah of blowing the *shofar* in our prayer service.

The 312ᵗʰ mitzvah is to offer the special communal

sacrifices (*musaf*) on *Rosh HaShanah.*
"And you shall bring a fire-offering to G-d" (23:25).

✺ YOM KIPPUR

**The 313ᵗʰ mitzvah is to fulfill the mitzvos of absten-
tion on *Yom Kippur*.**
**The 314ᵗʰ mitzvah, derived from the same verse, is to
offer the special communal sacrifices (*musaf*) on *Yom
Kippur*.**
*"However, on the tenth day of this seventh month is a
Day of Atonement, a holy proclamation it shall be to
you, and you shall humble yourselves and offer a fire-
offering to G-d"(23:27).*

On the first *Yom Kippur* after the Exodus, Moshe came
down from Sinai with the second set of tablets. This signi-
fied that the Israelites had atoned for the sin of the Golden
Calf and that they were forgiven.

Our Sages interpret the phrase "*to humble yourselves*" to mean
that we are required to fast, refrain from washing, refrain from using
perfumes, refrain from wearing leather shoes and abstain from marital relations on *Yom Kippur*.

Most translations say that on *Yom Kippur* we are "*to afflict ourselves.*" Perhaps a more accurate translation is "*to humble ourselves.*"
Affliction and suffering do not guarantee that we will be forgiven. If
we would have someone twist our arm until we screamed "Uncle!"
would that assure us of a portion in the World to Come? Certainly
not. The goal on *Yom Kippur* is to make oneself humble before G-d,
to apologize, and say that he will never do such and such sin(s) again.
Wearing sneakers on *Yom Kippur* is not an affliction but it is a sign of
a humble status. Could you imagine Queen Elizabeth wearing sneak-

ers! The Hebrew word used in the verse is *anisem* (*ani* without the suffix). It is related to the word *anav*, a humble person.

The 315ᵗʰ mitzvah is the prohibition not to work on ***Yom Kippur.***

"All work you may not do on that same day for it is a day for atonement to you before the L-rd your G-d" **(23:28).**

The 316ᵗʰ mitzvah is the prohibition to violate the laws of humility (eating, etc) as they apply to ***Yom Kippur.***

"For any soul who does not humble himself on that same day shall be cut off from his people" **(23:29).**

The 317ᵗʰ mitzvah is to rest from work on ***Yom Kippur.***
"A solemn day of rest it shall be to you" **(23:32).**

⋞ SUCCOS

The 318th mitzvah is to rest from work on the first day of *Succos.*

The 319ᵗʰ mitzvah, derived from the same verse, is the prohibition to work on the first day of *Succos.*

"On the fifteen day of this month is the festival of Succos, seven day to G-d. On the first day (it) shall be a holy proclamation, all servile work you shall not do" **(23:34-35).**

The 320ᵗʰ mitzvah is to offer the special communal sacrifices (*musaf*) on each day of the festival.

"Seven days you shall offer a fire-offering to G-d" **(23:36).**

he next three mitzvos are listed below followed by the verse that all three are derived from.

The 321ˢᵗ mitzvah is to rest from work on the 8th day of *Succos, Shemini Atzeres.*

The 322ⁿᵈ mitzvah, derived from the same verse, is to offer the special communal sacrifices (*musaf*) on the eight day of *Succos.*

The 323ʳᵈ mitzvah is, derived from the same verse, is the prohibition to work on the eighth day of *Succos.*

"On the eight day shall be a holy proclamation it shall be to you, and you shall bring a fire-offering to G-d, a day of refraining, all servile work you shall not do" **(23:36).**

The 324ᵗʰ mitzvah is to take the four species (*esrog, lulav, hadassim,* **and** *aravos***) on** *Succos.*

"And you shall take for yourselves on the first day (of Succos) the fruit of the goodly tree, a palm of a date tree, branches whose wood is thickly (covered with leaves), and willow of the brook, and you shall rejoice before the L-rd your G-d seven days." **(23:40)**

The beginning of the verse tells us that we must take the four species on the first day. At the end of the verse it tells us to take it for seven days. Which is correct, the first day or all seven days?

The end of the verse refers to the *Bais HaMikdash.* In the *Bais HaMikdash* the four species were taken every day of *Succos.* That is the meaning of the phrase "*and you shall rejoice before the L-rd your G-d seven days.*" "*Before the L-rd your G-d*" means in the *Bais HaMikdash.*

Outside the Temple, the four species were taken only on the first day of *Succos.*

Today, Jews everywhere take the four species on all seven days of *Succos,* except Shabbos. This is to remind us of the *Bais HaMikdash* which no longer stands, yet we anticipate that it will be speedily rebuilt in our times.

The 325ᵗʰ mitzvah is to dwell in the *Succah* **for seven days.**

"In booths you shall dwell for seven days ...so that your generations shall know that in booths I made dwell the

Children of Israel when I brought them out of the land of Egypt" (23:42-43).

❧ THE FOUR SPECIES AND THE FORGOTTEN JEW

Each of the four species is unique and each one represents a unique category of Jews. The *esrog* has two qualities – it has a fragrant smell and its fruit is edible. The fragrance that it gives out to whoever is near represents kind deeds that a Jew performs and gives out to his fellow man. The *esrog* also has a taste which one can take in and enjoy. That represents Torah knowledge which one can take in and savior its wisdom. The *esrog*, which has both fragrance and taste, represents the Jew who not only has Torah knowledge, but he shares it with others and performs kind deeds for his fellow man.

The *lulav* (date) tree has no fragrance but its fruit has taste. This represents the Jew who has Torah scholarship but does not share his knowledge. He does not concern himself with others and therefore does not perform kind deeds.

The *hadassim* have a pleasant fragrance but no taste. They represent those who have little Torah scholarship but do perform many kind deeds. They concern themselves with the plight of their fellow Jews.

The *aravos* have neither fragrance nor taste. They represent the Jews that have lost their way: who have no Torah scholarship and perform no kind deeds.

On *Succos* we hold all four species tightly together and wave them about. That demonstrates that as long as there is unity among the Jewish People we can survive no matter what comes our way. Whether the ill-winds of misfortune come from the north, south, east, west, up or down, unity and brotherhood is our key to survival.

If one of the four species is missing, the mitzvah has not been performed at all. Even if it is the lowly *aravos* that are missing, there is a lack of unity and the mitzvah has not been fulfilled.

These correspond to the Four Sons of the Passover Seder. The **esrog** is the Wise Son who possesses Torah knowledge and shares it. The *lulav* represents the Wicked Son who has knowledge but refuses to share it. He keeps it within himself. The *hadassim* represent the Simple Son. He has no Torah knowledge yet he still concerns himself with others. The *aravos* represent the Son Who Does Not Ask. He is not concerned with Torah and therefore asks no questions. He is not concerned about others and does not ask if they need anything. He simply doesn't ask about anyone or anything; he is unfortunately lost in his own misguided world.

The *aravos* seem to be the least significant of all four species yet it is the *aravos* that seem to require from us the most effort and attention. As a rule, the *esrog, lulav,* and *hadassim* hold up fairly well over the seven days of *Succos.* The *aravos* on the other hand begin to wither almost immediately. We try placing them in a glass of water or placing them wrapped in the refrigerator. Often, it is all for naught. They wither away and we must go out on *Chol HaMoed* (the intermediate days of the Festival) and purchase new ones because without them there is no mitzvah.

The same is true of what we consider to be the least significant Jew: the one who has no Torah learning and does not concern himself with the Jewish community. We try to bring him into the fold of Jewish brotherhood. The task is daunting and takes our greatest efforts and much of our communal time. Sometimes, in spite of all our efforts, we do not succeed. But still we must try because without him there can be no unity among the Jewish People. Without him there is no mitzvah.

~§ THE BLASPHEMER
AND THE SHOWBREAD

"And he went out, the son of an Israelite woman and the son of an Egyptian man..." (24:10).

here is very little in the way of narrative in *Sefer* Vayikra; it is mostly a book of mitzvos. Our *parshah* does conclude with a brief story. It is the story of the infamous blasphemer (See the volume on Shmos, *Parshas Shmos, The Story Behind the Story,* page 13).

The story is as follows. An unidentified man, known only as the son of Shlomis bas Divri, ridiculed the mitzvah of the Twelve Showbread (*Lechem Ha'panim*). The *Lechem Hapanim* were typically placed on the Table in the *Mishkan* every Shabbos and were not to be removed until the next Shabbos when new loaves replaced the old ones. At that point the *Kohanim* ate the *Lechem Hapanim* of the previous week. The blasphemer argued that a King should be served with warm, fresh bread and not weekold, stale bread (*Vayikra Rabbah* 32:3).

The blasphemer was not given a suitable reply by his Jewish neighbors and this encouraged him to become more contentious and argumentative. In the end, he cursed G-d and was stoned to death. Had the blasphemer been a bit patient he would have seen the answer to his question. Each week a miracle occurred in the *Mishkan* and later in the *Bais HaMikdash*. The *Twelve Showbread* remained warm and fresh throughout the week. When the *Kohanim* ate from the *Showbread*, they ate warm fresh bread. Had the blasphemer had the patience to wait one week he would have known that G-d does not need fresh bread every day. He would have learned to curb his contentious behavior and he would have lived.

There are many situations that occur in life when we are apt to question G-d's actions. However, we are not privy to G-d's thought process so the question goes unanswered, just as the blasphemer's question went unanswered. Sometimes, with the passage of time, things begin to make more sense and we can see the righteousness of G-d's actions. The blasphemer had little faith and trust in G-d. He was not willing to wait even one week to see the miracle of the *Showbread*. Patience is indeed a virtue.

The story begins with the phrase *"And he went out, the son of an Israelite woman and the son of an Egyptian man...."* It says that he went out, but where was he headed? The Torah does not say. Possibly it could be suggested that the blasphemer himself did not know where he was going. He was a lost soul. He had a troubled childhood, coming from a mixed union of a Jewish mother and Egyptian father. He was looking for something. What that might be, no one knows. But usually when one wanders around aimlessly with nowhere to go, he will usually end up in trouble. Unfortunately, today, many youths who come from dysfunctional homes often times wander the streets of the city, and the streets of life, aimlessly, without a goal. They have no purpose or sense of direction; they have no place to go. They do not realize the dreadful direction in which they are headed. The neighbors of the blasphemer may not have been able to help him or save him from himself, but we cannot stand idly by with so many of our young boys and girls "going out." They need our concern, our compassion, our friendship, and our patience. We must provide for them a safe and friendly place to go. They need our help and direction. These lost souls should be one of our primary challenges and concerns.

The *parshah* concludes with the death of the blasphemer. It is a sad ending to a *parshah* so full of the hope of sanctity and spiritual potential. Each and every Jewish child and adult is a holy soul and has a potential for greatness. It is a tragedy to lose even one, even a blasphemer. We cannot afford any more tragedies, especially in our turbulent times. It will be up to the *haftorah* to lift our spirits.

◆⁊ HAFTORAH EMOR

THE *HAFTORAH* IS FOUND IN *YECHEZKIEL* 44:15-31.

In the last nine chapters of *Sefer Yechezkiel*, the prophet describes in graphic detail the *Bais HaMikdash* that is to be built by *Mashiach*. In the portion from which the *haftorah* is taken, Yechezkiel describes the laws that pertain to the *Kohanim* who will serve in the future Temple. The prophet reviews and repeats many of the laws regarding the *kedushah* of the *Kohanim* that are found in our *parshah*. However upon closer scrutiny, we are in for an unexpected surprise.

The prophet proclaims *"They shall wear linen clothes, wool shall not be upon them (44:17)."* Linen clothes were not worn by the Temple *Kohanim*; only the *Kohen Gadol* wore linen and only on *Yom Kippur*. How odd.

The prophet continues, *"They shall remove the (sacred) clothes in which they had ministered and leave them in the holy chamber, they shall don other garments so that they not mingle with the people while wearing their (holy) clothes* (44:19)." This law too only applied to the High Priest on *Yom Kippur*. He was not allowed to wear the special garments for the *Yom Kippur* service when he mingled with the people. The other priests were allowed to keep their garments in place even while mingling with the Israelites. How odd.

Yechezkiel goes further, *"They shall keep their heads trimmed* (44:20)." This law also only applied to a *Kohen Gadol*. His hair had to be trimmed very close to the scalp.

"No Kohen may drink wine when he enters the inner courtyard (44:21)." No *Kohen*? According to Torah law, only those *Kohanim* that were engaging in the service could not drink wine. Those *Kohanim* who had a physical defect and were performing minor tasks, such as sorting and cutting wood for the altar, were permitted to drink wine. Yet, the prophet says *"No Kohen!"*

"They shall not take a widow or divorcee for wives but only virgins from the House of Israel (44:22)." Only a *Kohen Gadol* was not

permitted to marry a widow; a regular *Kohen* was permitted. Only a *Kohen Gadol* had to marry a virgin.

The *Malbim* explains that in the time of *Mashiach* there will be a great spiritual elevation. The regular priests will become like the High Priest. The priest with a defect will become like a blemish free priest. The nation as a whole will be spiritually elevated. But there is one law, Yechezkiel tells us, that pertains to a regular priest now that will still be enforced in the future. Regarding that law, the regular *Kohanim* will not be regarded as High Priests. Which law is that?

"Unto a human corpse you may not become unclean, however, each may become unclean to (the corpse) of his father, mother, son, daughter, brother, or sister who has not been married to a man (44:25)." During the eras of the *Mishkan*, First Temple, Second Temple, and even today, the regular *Kohen* was permitted to defile himself to the corpse of a close relative. Only a *Kohen Gadol* was not permitted to do so. Why will that law still remain in effect even when the regular *Kohen* attains the status of a High Priest? Shouldn't that law also be abolished? The reason is because that law is based on respect for the deceased As well as compassion for a *Kohen*'s bereaving family members. When spirituality is heightened, respect and compassion is heightened, not abolished.

May we merit seeing this heightened spiritual compassion and respect speedily in our days.

BEHAR

"And G-d spoke to Moshe on Mount Sinai saying..." (25:1).

The *parshah* begins with G-d telling Moshe the mitzvos of *shmitah* and *yovel*. Shmitah refers to the seventh year of a seven year cycle. All work in the field is forbidden in the *shmitah* year. *Yovel* is the fiftieth year in a cycle of fifty years. During the *yovel* year work in the field is also forbidden, Hebrew slaves are freed, and all land in Israel is returned to their original owners. The Medrash (*Sifra* 25:1) asks why the opening verse mentioned Mount Sinai. After the giving of the Torah at Mount Sinai in the book of Shmos, the name Mount Sinai is mentioned very rarely. In fact, it is mentioned only five times in Vayikra, only twice in Bamidbar and not at all in Devarim. Why was it mentioned here regarding the laws of *shmitah* and *yovel*? The Medrash answers that Mount Sinai is mentioned to teach us that just as all the laws of this *parshah*, which details the mitzvos of *shmitah* and *yovel*, were given on Mount Sinai, so too all the details of every mitzvah were given to Moshe on Mount Sinai. One should not think that on Mount Sinai G-d told Moshe only the general terms of the mitzvos. The fact is that every mitzvah was elaborated upon and taught in detail to Moshe during the forty days and nights he was on the mountain.

The question is posed by the commentaries why the Torah chose *shmitah* and *yovel* as the examples of mitzvos that were taught in detail on Sinai? Any other mitzvah could have been chosen as well.

The *Chasam Sofer* explains as follows. Almost any mitzvah could have been invented by a person. A person could convince others into thinking that they should not work on Saturday because everyone needs a day off. They could convince others to abstain from non-kosher food because its not healthy to eat; they could convince others to eat matzos to commemorate Passover. However, can you imagine a person telling others not to work in their fields for a full year and G-d will take care of them. After not working in the field for three months, and nearing starvation, that mitzvah would certainly be abandoned. The incredible demand requested by these two mitzvos and the fact that the Israelites were able to successfully fulfill the mitzvah, *shmitah* after *shmitah*, proves that the Divine origin of the Torah and its mitzvos are from Sinai.

✎§ 7+50 = GREAT INSIGHTS AND MYSTERIES

Fifty days after the Exodus, the Children of Israel received the Torah at Mount Sinai. Later, the Torah commemorated these fifty days with the mitzvah of counting the *omer*. The mitzvah is to count seven weeks, totaling 49 days, and then the following day, the fiftieth day, is the holiday of *Shavuos*. We count, for example, on day 25, "Today is the 25th day which is 3 weeks and 4 days in the *omer*."

During the era of the *Bais HaMikdash*, the *Sanhedrin* would count the years of the *yovel* cycle. The *shmitah* was every seven years. After seven *shmitohs*, the following year, the fiftieth year, was proclaimed to be the *yovel* year. For example, on the 25ᵗʰ year the Sanhedrin would proclaim, "This year is the 25ᵗʰ year which is 3 *shmitah* cycles and 4 years in the *yovel* cycle." We see there is some unique relationship between the seven weeks spanning Passover and *Shavuos* and the seven *shmitah* cycles between the first *shmitah* year and *yovel*. In both cases there is a mitzvah to count and just as the fiftieth day is *Shavuos*, the fiftieth year is *Yovel*. Obviously, the numbers seven and fifty have some mysterious, Kabbalistic meaning.

The Ramban in *Bereishis* (2:3) says that the six days of creation and the day of Shabbos that followed, the first week ever, represented the future history of the universe. The seven days represented the future 7000 years of mankind. On day one, **light** was created. This represented the first 1000 years of mankind. Man was created. He had the intelligence, the **enlightenment**, to recognize G-d as his Creator. Adam, the first man, the first to have such intelligence, lived just 70 years short of 1000 years (Actually he was destined to live 1000 years, but he gave 70 of his years to King David).

On the second day, the waters parted in order to **divide** between the realm above and the realm below. During the second thousand years of mankind, the great floodwaters of Noach came and made a **division** between the spiritually worthy and the rebelliously wicked.

On the third day dry land appeared and the trees gave forth their **fruit**. That represented the third thousand years, which began with Avraham extending his kindness to others. He taught the ways of righteousness and justice to his generation and to his children who passed it along from father to son until the day the Israelites stood at Mount Sinai. Kindness, righteousness, and justice are the true **fruits** of our labors.

On the fourth day the stars and the great luminaries, the sun and the moon, were created. The sun represented the great light emanating from the first *Bais HaMikdash*. And, after the sun had set below the horizon, when the Babylonians destroyed the Temple, the moon rose. The moon represented the glow of the second *Bais HaMikdash*. Though the miracles of G-d's presence were not manifest during that time, still, the dim glow of His aura could be felt in the Second

Temple. And then, the moon at the end of its lunar orbit disappeared. The Second Temple was destroyed.

On the fifth day, creeping and swarming creatures were created. These nightmarish entities represented the nations of the world who tormented the Jewish people during the millennium after the destruction of the Temple.

Early on the sixth day, the higher forms of animals and wild beasts were created. That day's creation concluded with that of Man, created in the "image of G-d." This represents the sixth millennium, our millennium. It contains higher forms of animal life, representing the nations who began a quest for cultural advancement, which produced the renaissance and the age of enlightenment. At the same time, however, this "advanced" culture also produced savagery, inflicting greater cruelties upon our people than any nations before them. This millennium will conclude with the climax of creation, the coming of *Mashiach*, which will restore the "image of G-d" contained within mankind to its rightful place.

The next millennium will be the day of Shabbos, the realm of the World to Come.

The Ramban (*Vayikra* 25:1) says that just as the seven days of *Bereishis* contain great insights and mysteries, likewise the seven years of the *shmitah* cycle and the seven *shmitah* cycles of the *yovel* contain great secrets. The fifty years in a *yovel*, represent the fifty Gateways of Understanding. Now we know the Mishnah in *Avos* refers to the *mem tes sharei binah* – the forty-nine Gateways of Understanding. The Ramban, however, states that there is a fiftieth gateway; one that was not revealed even to Moshe. It is well beyond human comprehension. The fiftieth year – the *yovel* – which follows the seven cycles of seven years, also contains mysteries beyond our comprehension. It represents the era of the World to Come when true freedom will be proclaimed and each soul will be reunited with its source.

✑ TIME IS THE CURRENCY OF LIFE

Perhaps you have never noticed, but there is no Hebrew name for the days of the week. Instead, Sunday is called "first day", Monday is called "second day", etc. At the conclusion of our morning prayers, we recite the chapter in *Tehillim* that was recited that day by the *Leviim* in the *Bais HaMikdash*. We preface each day's chapter with, "Today, is the first (or the second or the third, etc.) day of the week upon which the *Leviim* recited in the *Bais HaMikdash...*" Since we recite this every day, in effect, each and every day we are counting the days of the week.

What is the significance of counting? We count things that are important. People count their money. Governments take a census and count their citizens. By counting days, weeks, and years, we are showing the great importance of time. If each day of creation contained the potential history of a millennium, who can even imagine the tremendous potential contained in a whole week or a whole year? But one thing we can be sure of: time is important. Time is the currency of life; we must spend it wisely.

✑ FAITH IN THE FUTURE; FAITH IN TODAY

"Six years you shall sow your fields, six years you shall prune your vines, and gather your crops. On the seventh year, a (year of) rest it shall be to the land, a rest to G-d" (25:3-4).

In most lands of the world, farmers plants crops for one or two years and let the field lie fallow (inactive) the following year. Allowing the earth to remain fallow gives the field time to rejuvenate and replenish itself with the nutrients needed to produce a crop. A farmer would divide his property into several fields. While one is lying fallow, the others were being worked. Thus he had crops each and every year. The *Kli Yakar* (25:2) points out that the Torah tells us not to follow that practice in Eretz Yisroel. The verse says *"Six years you shall sow your fields..."* We are told to work all the fields each and every year for six years. It needs to lie fallow on the seventh year. G-d's Holy Land is different.

Lest you think that the land of Israel needs a rest on the seventh year, the verses teaches us that we allow the field to lie fallow on *shmitah* so that it should be a *"rest to G-d."* The land does not need any rest at all. We, the people need a rest, a rest that will allow us to restore our faith in G-d. It is a year that will allow us to rededicate ourselves to Torah and the spiritual goals of life.

The Land of Israel is truly a miraculous land. Even its deserts can blossom forth with orchards. We have witnessed that the barren Negev has become the breadbasket for the country. When Palestine was under the control of the Ottoman Empire, most of the country was a wasteland. The Jews brought the earth back to life. We made the brown and yellow sand produce greenery and fruits. We changed deserts into gardens. Did I say "We"?

Humans tend to take credit for things to which they are not entitled. We did not bring the land to life. It is the *kedushah* of Eretz Yisroel, the merits of our mitzvos, and ultimately the blessing of Hashem that brings the land to life.

We tend to think of faith as something that will give us the strength to face the future. That may be so, but there is also a faith that addresses the present. Today's crops grow not because of our special talents, but because of Hashem's blessing. If we understand and have faith in today's blessing, that can give us the strength to have faith in the future.

The mitzvah of *shmitah* teaches us to work the fields all six years. We must have faith that Hashem will give His blessing each and every year. We must refrain from agricultural labors during the seventh year to restore our faith that Hashem will take care of us in the future.

The Children of Israel wandered in the desert for forty years.

During that time there was no such thing as private real estate. No one owned any land. They were not farmers or businessmen. They lived off the heavenly blessings of G-d in the form of manna and miraculous wells. G-d fed, clothed, and sheltered His holy nation. The hand of G-d was evident. This freedom from labor allowed the Jewish nation to totally dedicate themselves to the Torah. After the Jews had conquered the land of Canaan, they became farmers, herdsmen, and businessmen. The hand of G-d was not so readily evident. However, during the *shmitah* year, all land and produce was proclaimed to be ownerless. No one owned land. The people had to rely on the hand of G-d and His heavenly blessings. All the people now had the freedom to dedicate themselves to Torah. Now, once again, during the *shmitah* the Children of Israel spiritually returned to the wilderness of Sinai.

◄§ A LIVELIHOOD

A livelihood is supposed to be an occupation that enables one to earn enough money that (with the help of G-d) can satisfy life's needs. However, all too often the livelihood becomes the center of one's life. There is no time for family, no time to relax, no time to learn, no time for others, and no time for G-d. The lesson of *shmitah* is that it is not the farmer's occupation that sustains him; it is G-d's blessings that sustain him. Even when the farmer abstains from working in his field during *shmitah,* he and his family can survive. The lesson of *shmitah* can be applied to every kind of occupation, not only agricultural endeavors. It is not the job that sustains us, it is G-d.

This lesson is wonderfully expressed in the last Mishnah in *Kiddushin*:

> *Rebbe Meir said: One should always teach his son a*
> *clean and easy craft and pray to Him to Whom all wealth*

and property belong. Every craft contains the potential to enrich and the potential to impoverish for neither poverty nor wealth comes from the craft. It all depends on one's merits.

⋐ THE ULTIMATE CHARITY

The thing that stands in the way of man achieving his spiritual potential is his attachment to materialism. People feel attached to things they own, especially to their land and the crops they grow. A productive yield and harvest requires hard work and much time. During *shmitah*, when one proclaims his crops to be public property, he severs that possessive bind he has to his materialism.

With his newly found freedom he can soar to spiritual heights. The root of the Hebrew word *shmitah* means to withdraw. He withdraws from work in the fields and he withdraws from his attachment to materialism.

The *Sefer HaChinuch* (*Mitzvah* 84) points out that when one declares all his crops to be public property it is the greatest act of charity. It benefits the receiver, the poor, and it benefits the giver. The poor benefit because they are not embarrassed to partake of the crops that are left for them. The giver benefits because it is a true act of charity. He yields his land and his crops without consideration for any return benefit; there is no thought as to what's in it for him.

✍ **FAITH OR GREED**

"And if you shall say: 'What shall we eat the seventh year? Behold, we shall not sow, nor gather in our produce.' I will command my blessing upon you in the sixth year, and it shall bring forth fruit for three years. You shall sow the eighth year, and eat still of old fruit until the ninth year; until its fruits come in you shall eat of the old store" (25:20-22).

ashem is pledging His blessing on the sixth year's crop that it will be able to sustain for the sixth year, the seventh year, until the end of the eighth year when the new crop planted after *shmitah* will be ready for harvest.

It would seem that when one sees the abundance of the sixth year's crop he will realize that he can easily refrain from work during the *shmitah* year. If so, why is *shmitah* considered a test of faith?

A non-observant storekeeper told a rabbi that he would like to become a Shabbos observer but he desperately needed the income he earned on Shabbos. The rabbi told him that if he would close his store on Shabbos, then Hashem would give him a blessing that he would earn twice as much on Friday to make up for the loss. Sure enough, after a few weeks of closing shop on Shabbos, the storekeeper noticed that his Friday revenues increased two-fold. He then thought to himself, that if business is picking up so much on Friday, he would make a fortune if he kept open on Saturday too. His greedy temptation got the better of him and he opened his store on Shabbos. Surprisingly to him, he did not make his fortune. The business floundered and he was forced to close down.

Human greed tempts us to ignore the divine source of our blessings. Once we make that leap to trust our own resourcefulness and forget about Hashem, our blessings quickly dissipate.

✍ KEEPING THE LINES OF COMMUNICATION OPEN

"And if you shall say: 'What shall we eat the seventh year? Behold, we shall not sow, nor gather in our produce.' I will command my blessing upon you in the sixth year..." (25:20-21).

The verse seems to be referring to Israelites, who lacked faith in G-d. They questioned the reward promised if they keep the mitzvah of *shmitah*. It appears that in return for their lack of faith, G-d promises them that they will have a three-fold increase during the sixth year. One who questions the mitzvah of *shmitah* is rewarded with a promise of abundance. Why is G-d rewarding what seems to be less than desirable behavior?

It may be true that they are questioning the mitzvah of *shmitah*, but to whom are they complaining? To G-d. Anyone who talks to G-d, even a complainant, is not overlooked. As long as the lines of communication between a person and his Creator are open, there is hope. Not only is there hope, there is even a reward.

This lesson can be applied to everyday life. In families and among friends there are times of argument and strife. But as long as the warring parties still keep the lines of communication open, there is not only hope, but the issue will eventually be resolved.

A man once asked Reb Moshe Feinstein the following question. "My son has married outside the faith. Do I have to sit *shiva*?" Reb Moshe asnswered, "*Shiva*? No! Call him every week to ask him how he is doing. If your son feels that he can still talk with you there is hope he may come back. If you sit *shiva*, dead people cannot come back."

·ᢒ THE MITZVOS OF SHMITAH

The 326ᵗʰ mitzvah is the prohibition to work the land during the *shmitah* **year.**
"And the seventh year shall be a rest to the land" **(25:4).**
The 327ᵗʰ mitzvah is the prohibition to work during *shmitah* **on vines and trees to enable them to produce better crops.**
"Your vineyards you shall not prune" **(25:4).**
The 328ᵗʰ mitzvah is the prohibition to harvest all for yourself the crops that grew by themselves during *shmitah.*
"That which grows wild of during the harvest (season) you may not harvest" **(25:5).**
It too must be declared public property.
The 329ᵗʰ mitzvah is the prohibition to harvest all for yourself the grapes or fruit that grew during *shmitah.*
"The grapes of your vine you shall not gather" **(25:5).**
The 330ᵗʰ mitzvah is the precept to count seven cycles of the *shmitah* **years.**
"And you shall count for yourself seven shmitah cycles, each seven years, seven times..." **(25:8).**

·ᢒ THE MITZVOS OF THE JUBILEE YEAR (YOVEL)

After counting seven Sabbatical cycles of *shmitah*, the following year (number 50) is proclaimed a *yovel* or jubilee. On *Yom Kippur* the *yovel* was proclaimed by blowing the *shofar.* The *yovel* heralded three things

1 – Abstention from any farming or working of the land as in a *shmitah* year.

2 – Freedom was granted for all Jewish slaves. Even those slaves who had bored their ears and proclaimed everlasting service to their master are set free.

3 – All purchased property in the land of Israel reverted back to their original owner.

> **The 331ˢᵗ mitzvah is to blow the *shofar* on the *Yom Kippur* of *yovel* in the same manner we blow the *shofar* each and every *Rosh HaShanah*.**
>
> *"And you shall blow the shofar a blasting sound in the seventh month (Tishrei) and the tenth of the month, on Yom HaKippurim"* (25:9).

The significance of the *shofar* was to proclaim the liberation of the servants. Sounding the *shofar* typically arouses the heart of human beings to either peace or war. Liberating a servant, who has served his master for a lengthy amount of time, is very difficult for the master. Therefore, to inspire the heart of the master and to encourage his good spirit, the *shofar* is sounded.

> **The 332ⁿᵈ mitzvah is for the *Sanhedrin* to officially proclaim the fiftieth year as the *yovel* year.**
>
> *"And you shall make holy the fiftieth year and proclaim freedom in the land, a jubilee it shall be to you"* (25:10).
>
> **The 333ʳᵈ mitzvah is the prohibition to work the land during the *yovel* year just as it is forbidden during the *shmitah* year.**
>
> *"Yovel it shall be the fiftieth year to you, you shall not sow..."* (25:11).
>
> **The 334ᵗʰ mitzvah is the prohibition to harvest all for yourself the crops that grew by themselves on *yovel*.**
>
> *"Do not harvest that which grows wild..."* (25:11).

It too must be declared public property.

> **The 335ᵗʰ mitzvah is the prohibition to harvest all for yourself the grapes or fruit that grew during *yovel*.**
>
> *"Do not harvest the vines"* (25:11).

❧ LAWS OF WRONGING ANOTHER JEW

One of the laws of *yovel* is that all Hebrew slaves are to be freed. Since the Torah mentioned Hebrews that were sold as slaves, it will mention a few laws regarding the treatment of Hebrew slave and the proper conduct of the sale itself. Since it will mention the sale of Hebrew slaves, this section of the Torah begins with a general introduction that all sales are to be conducted according to *halachah*.

The 336th is the mitzvah is the precept of effecting justice between buyer and seller.

"When you sell a sale to your neighbor..." (25:14).

This is derived from the seeming redundancy of the words "sell a sale." It means that when you sell, it should be in accordance with the laws of sales.

Why does the verse say *"When you sell a sale to your neighbor...,"* since one must follow the proper laws of sale even with regards to a non-Jew? Rashi explains that if the item that you wish to purchase is available from both a Jew and a non-Jew at the same price and all other circumstances are equal, it is preferable to give the business to a fellow Jew and assist him in earning his livelihood.

The 337th mitzvah is the prohibition against wronging anyone in buying or selling.

"A man with his brother he shall not do an injustice." (25:14).

This mitzvah includes the law against defrauding anyone in business. This applies to both the seller and buyer alike. A seller cannot overcharge, or mislead a person regarding a product. A buyer is equally warned not to mislead the seller and buy something of great value at below market prices. The Sages say that an unreasonable overcharge means that the seller has made a profit of more than 1/6 after taking into consideration his costs and overhead.

Some misguided individuals think that we must only be scrupulous with Jewish customers and that we are permitted to take advantage of non-Jews. The *Tosefta* (*Baba Kamma* 10:8) says that it is worse to cheat a non-Jew than to cheat a Jew. If one Jew cheats another Jew, the victim will call the seller a cheat. If a Jew cheats a non-Jew, the non-Jew will call all Jews cheats. That is a *chillul Hashem*, a desecration of G-d's name.

The 338ᵗʰ mitzvah is the prohibition to mistreat any Jew under any circumstances.

"A man shall not do an injustice with his neighbor" **(25:17).**

One cannot offend another Jew verbally, nor can he provoke him or give him bad advice. The precept of this mitzvah is to be careful of how we speak to our fellow Jew and not to cause him any pain or distress; i.e. bringing up past events that may make a person uncomfortable.

The mistreatment to which the verse refers is verbal abuse (*Baba Metzia* 58b). The Medrash (*Vayikra Rabbah* 33:1) comments:

> *"Death and life are in the power of the tongue" (Mishlei 18:21). Ben Sira says: If a man has a glowing coal before him, then if he blows on it gently, he makes it flare up. If he spits on it, he extinguishes it. Rabban Shimon ben Gamaliel said to Tabbai his servant: 'Go and buy me good food in the market.' He went and bought him tongue. He then said to him: 'Go and buy me bad food in the market.' He went and bought him tongue. Said he to him: 'What is this? When I told you to get good food you bought me tongue and when I told you to get bad food you also bought me tongue! ' He replied: 'Good comes from it and bad comes from it. When the tongue is good there is nothing better, and when it is bad there is nothing worse.' Rebbe made a feast for his disciples and placed before them tender tongues and hard tongues. They began selecting the tender ones, leaving the hard ones alone. Said he to them: 'Note what you are doing! As you select the tender and leave the hard, so let your tongues be tender to one another.'*

≈§ LAWS OF SELLING LAND IN ISRAEL

The 339ᵗʰ mitzvah is that it is forbidden to sell your land permanently in the land of Israel.
"And the land (of Israel) you may not sell forever for to Me is the land, for strangers and dwellers you are with Me" (25:23).

The land of Israel belongs to G-d. We can exercise ownership rights only within the strict

rules defined in the Torah. Thus all sales of land in Israel are subject to divinely ordained contingent clauses.

"If your brother becomes impoverished, and sells parts of his ancestral heritage (land), his redeemer who is his closest relative, shall come and redeem his brothers sale" (25:25).

Land is a person's most treasured possession. Unlike moveable items, land cannot be stolen nor ruined beyond repair. This was especially true of land in Israel that was allotted to each family of every tribe according to the Divine will as expressed through the lottery conducted by Yehoshua. A person would not sell land unless he was in desperate straits. Therefore the Torah made several rules regulating the sale of land.

The first rule is that land could not be sold in perpetuity. It could only be leased until *yovel*. When *yovel* arrived, the lease automatically expired and the land was returned to its owner. Another rule was that the original owner had the right to break the lease and could "buy" back his land on a pro-rated basis. For example, if the land was "sold" for $10,000 on the 40ᵗʰ year of the *yovel* cycle, since there are 10 years until *yovel*, that means the rent is $1,000 per year. If the original owner wanted to buy back his land after 6 years have gone by, since there are 4 years left until *yovel*, he must pay the tenant $4,000 to get his land back. If he does not redeem his land until *yovel*, the property is returned with no charge to the seller.

In order to be fair to the renter, the land could not be redeemed by the owner during the first two years of the sale. This gives the buyer the opportunity to recoup his purchase by being able to reap several harvests.

STRANGERS AND DWELLERS

"If your brother becomes impoverished, and sells parts of his ancestral heritage (land), his redeemer who is his closest relative, shall come and redeem his brothers sale" (25:25).

The *Dubner Maggid* asked what this verse meant by *"strangers and dwellers."* The Hebrew word for stranger is *ger* which means a temporary resident. The Hebrew word for dweller is *toshav* which means a permanent resident. Which are we, a temporary resident or permanent resident?

He answers that if the Children of Israel regard themselves as temporary residents of the land and willingly relinquish their rights on *yovel*, G-d will consider the Jews to be permanent dwellers in Israel and they will retain the right to live in the Holy Land. However, if the Children of Israel consider themselves to be permanent residents on their land and refuse to give it up on *yovel*, G-d will consider them to be temporary residents in His holy land and they will be driven into *galus*.

340ᵗʰ mitzvah is to release all land holdings in Israel and return it to its original owner on *yovel*.
"All the land of your possession, you shall grant a redemption to the land" (25:24).
The 341ˢᵗ mitzvah is the precept of redeeming land in

a city that is surrounded by walls.

"If a man sells a dwelling house within a walled city, it may be redeemed until a whole year from its sale, during those days shall be its redemption" **(25:29).**

A walled city was a city that was walled during the conquest and division of Yehoshua. Unlike the mitzvah of an unwalled city (See mitzvah 339), a walled city's property could only be redeemed during the first year of the sale. After that time expired, it remains in the possession of the buyer forever. This dwelling, which has its roots back to the time of Yehoshua, was considered the most precious land holding of all. The Torah wanted to encourage the seller to get it back as soon as possible, and therefore only allowed him to buy it back during the first year of the sale.

The exception to that rule is a dwelling that was in one of the Levite cities. Those could be redeemed at any time; and if the owner did not redeem it, then it is returned to him on *yovel* (See the next mitzvah and *haftorah*).

The 342ⁿᵈ mitzvah is to adhere to the laws regarding Levite cities (See the preceding mitzvah).

"The cities of the Levi, the houses in the cities of their possession may be redeemed in perpetuity... The open fields of their cities may not be sold..." **(25:32-34).**

Unlike the other tribes that were allotted definite geographical areas, the Leviim were given 48 cities scattered throughout the land. In addition, they were the landholders of the 6 cities of refuge. Those are the cities to which one who accidentally committed a homicide could seek refuge and protection. In total, the Leviim had 54 cities.

The Levite cities were centers for Torah studies – dedicated to the service of G-d. These cities were beautifully constructed and maintained. The 1,000 cubit area all around the outside of the cities were to be left open with no construction or planting there. This would prevent a sneak attack from an enemy since their movements could be seen by the Levite guards stationed on the city walls.

The 2,000 cubits all around and beyond the 1,000 cubit open area was designated for the Levite fields and vineyards. Since this pattern for the Levite cities was outlined in the Torah, no changes could be made. The open area had to remain open and the land for the fields and vineyards had to remain only for that purpose.

❧ STRENGTHEN YOUR BROTHER – THE GREATEST FORM OF CHARITY

The 343rd mitzvah is the prohibition of lending money to a Jew with interest.
"If your brother becomes poor and his hand is failing with you, you shall make him strong... do not take from him interest or increase... your money you shall not give to him as interest or increase..." **(25:35-37).**

A lender is prohibited from accepting goods or services from a loan he made to another Jew. Everything a man possesses is a gift from G-d. Therefore, one who charges interest denies this as a gift, and uses it to exploit the poor. A man is prohibited to put himself in a position whereby he has control over his fellow man.

This prohibition was mentioned in mitzvah 68. It is repeated here to teach us the severity of the prohibition (See volume on Shmos, page 189).

What does the verse mean if *"his hand is failing with you, you shall make him strong?"* Rashi explains that if you see that someone is falling, do not wait until he is on the ground and cries for help. As soon as you see that he is starting to fall, strengthen him. Help him before the situation becomes desperate. The Rambam (*Matonos Aniyim* 10:7) says that to intervene and help a person from becoming poverty stricken is the greatest form of charity. Help him by offering a loan or investing in his business or offering him a job. In this way he will still be able to maintain his dignity.

Rashi gives a very appropriate parable. If a burden on a donkey's back is shifting, one man can straighten it out. But if you wait until the donkey collapses from its awkward burden, even five men cannot get the donkey to rise again.

The verse *"If your brother becomes poor and his hand is failing with you, you shall make him strong"* literally says "If you brother is low and his hand is failing, you should make him strong." This also includes a friend whose spirits are low. Saying some encouraging words to lift his spirits and giving him *chizuk*, strength, is also a great form of charity.

≈§ YOUR BROTHER SHALL LIVE WITH YOU

"And you shall fear your G-d and your brother shall live with you" (25:35).

Reb Shlomo Kluger commented on this verse. There are Jews who are very scrupulous with mitzvos that are between man and his Creator. They buy the best *tefillin*, the nicest *esrog*, they *daven* a very long *shmoneh esrai*, but they are not very considerate when it comes to their fellow Jews. They are abrupt and sometimes discourteous. They distance themselves from others because they feel it would interfere with their relationship to G-d. This verse tells us that their attitude is completely misplaced. *"And you shall fear your G-d and your brother shall live with you."* If your brother is not included in your life, then you do not fear G-d.

EMPATHY

"If your brother becomes poor and his hand is failing with you, you shall make him strong... your brother shall live with you" (25:35).

The Torah is telling us not to simply have pity, compassion, or sympathy for the poor. Your sense of pity or sympathy can be allayed with a few dollars. Giving the poor man five dollars will make you feel better. The Torah is telling us to empathize with the poor. You must regard the poor man's misfortune as though he was your own brother who lives with you.

Today, it is the fashion that the poor come knocking at our door with ever increasing regularity. Unfortunately it has also come into fashion that we either have become so insensitive as to ignore the knock, or to answer with an abrupt and disparaging tone. Keeping in mind everything this *parshah* has taught us, we must remember that there is only a small difference between the person who collects money and the person who gives it. The difference is to whom G-d has chosen to give the money to first. Our hard work or intelligence was not the deciding factor in our wealth. It is for this reason that we must show so much respect to those who come and ask for money. We must have empathy for them. After all, he's our brother.

The *Toldos Yaakov Yosef* says that when a poor person prays to G-d asking for money, G-d answers every poor man's prayer. But, G-d does not give the money to the poor man directly. He gives it to the wealthier people. In this way, the wealthy can benefit by getting the mitzvah of *tzedakah* and the poor can benefit by getting the money G-d wanted them to receive.

So, the next time your brother comes knocking at the door, remember, you are just giving him his own money that he prayed for. It was his prayer that landed it in your hands.

≈§ LAWS REGARDING JEWISH SLAVES

his *parshah* only discusses the laws of a Jew who sold himself into slavery because of extreme poverty (See *Parshas Mishpatim* for the laws of one who was sold into slavery because of theft). The rules regarding the ownership of a Jewish slave are very demanding. So much so that as our Sages (*Kiddushin* 22a) say, "*Whoever purchases a Hebrew slave has purchased a master over himself.*" A Jewish master is obligated to sustain not only the slaves but also the wife and children. We are as responsible to a Jewish slave as he is to us. We must treat the slave with the utmost respect and dignity and take into account his feelings. We must bear the responsibility of his welfare: provisions, working conditions, plus a lot more.

The whole idea of a Jew owning a Jewish slave is to help put him back on his feet. It should be viewed as an act of compassion. Ultimately, the owner could have been the slave, while conversely the slave could have been the owner. We must also keep in mind that we are all G-d's slaves. Thus, the way you treat a slave, should be the way you want G-d to treat you.

The precept of the next few mitzvos lies in that man should consider that just as a Jewish slave was sold to him because of his unfortunate circumstances, so to it could happen that his good fortune changes due to sin and he or his children get sold into slavery. Someone who possesses the character trait of loving-kindness and compassion toward his fellow Jew will undoubtedly stay away from sinning.

Perhaps it could be said that the same kindness that we were taught must be extended to slaves, is one that, in our days, should be shown to people that come to our house and ask for financial charity. If we keep in mind the lessons, stated above, that there is a slim difference between the person who collects money and the person who gives it and that our hard work or intelligence was not the deciding factor in our wealth, then we will hopefully realize how much respect is due to those who come and ask for money. It is those who ask for money that are bestowing a great opportunity upon the potential giver. It is the opportunity to demonstrate to G-d, by properly performing this mitzvah, that he is worthy of the financial success that He has given to him.

> **The 344ᵗʰ mitzvah is the prohibition to treat a Hebrew slave in an undignified manner.**
> *"If your brother becomes poor and sells himself to you, you shall not make him serve the service of a slave"* **(25:39).**
>
> **The 345ᵗʰ mitzvah is the prohibition to sell a Hebrew slave in the manner that a regular slave is sold**
> *"For they are My servants whom I brought forth from the land of Egypt, they shall not be sold as one sells a slave"* **(25:42).**

Hebrew slaves were not to be placed on an auction block, a stage for all to see, and sold to the highest bidder. The sale of a Hebrew slave is to be conducted in a professional businesslike manner that allows the slave to maintain his dignity.

> **The 346ᵗʰ mitzvah is the prohibition to give a Hebrew slave work that is deemed oppressive.**
> *"You shall not rule over him oppressively"* **(25:43).**

Our Sages define oppressive work as something the master does not really need done, but it is assigned to the Hebrew slave merely to prevent him from being idle. The *Sefer Hachinuch* describes hard work as something that has no time limits or work that has no need. For example one must not say, "keep digging around this tree until I come back" for there is no time limit. Rather he should request the digging around the tree be done until a specific hour or accomplishment. Likewise one should not say "heat this cup for me" when there is no need for it.

> **The 347ᵗʰ mitzvah is the precept of keeping non-Jewish slaves permanently.**
> *"And (non-Hebrew slaves) shall be an inheritance for your children after you to inherit as a possession, forever they shall work for you"* **(25:46).**

Non-Jewish slaves are kept permanently in the family, even

through inheritance. They should not be liberated except in the case of a loss of a limb, organ or eye that was deliberately caused by his master. One was expected to treat his slave humanely and with compassion.

The 348ᵗʰ mitzvah is to not allow a non-Jew to work a Hebrew slave oppressively.

"(The Hebrew slave) like a hired hand for the year he shall be with you, he shall not rule over him oppressively in your sight" **(25:53).**

When the verse says *"he shall be with you,"* it means that a Hebrew slave should not sell himself to a non-Jew who will not permit him to keep the mitzvos. He should sell himself to **you**, another Jew. When the verse says *"he shall not rule over him oppressively in your sight,"* the word "he" refers to a non-Jew. If the Hebrew sold himself to a non-Jew, which was not permitted, and you see that the non-Jew is treating the Hebrew oppressively, then you must do everything in your power to see to it that the non-Jew ceases from such behavior.

✑ REDEMPTION OF ISRAEL

The beginning of the verse above says that a Hebrew slave is like a hired hand for the year. A Hebrew slave goes free after six years, or *yovel*, whichever comes first. The Hebrew slave has the right to buy himself back, redeem himself, any time during his indentured service on a pro-rated basis. If he was bought for $6,000 for 6 years and after 4 years he wants to redeem himself, he pays the master $2,000 and goes free.

Our Sages tell us that if Israel's merits are worthy, then *Mashiach* will arrive sooner. Someone asked the *Chofetz Chaim* that if the earlier generations who had great *tzaddikim* were not worthy of hastening the arrival of *Mashiach*, how can we expect our merits to hasten his arrival?

The *Chofetz Chaim* answered that each year a Hebrew slave can redeem himself and acquire his freedom. This is done on a pro-rated basis. If he redeems himself on the first year it will cost him a lot more than if he redeems himself on the last year. The same applies to the redemption of Israel from the *galus*. During those earlier years the "price" for redemption was very high. Even the merits of those great *tzaddikim* could not meet the "price." However, in our times, we are holding near the end of the *galus*. The price is much cheaper. Perhaps, now we can try and meet the asking price.

≈ᶾ GREED AND POVERTY

The Talmud (*Kiddushin* 20a) says:

> *Immediately after the portion of shmitah and yovel it is written "If you sell to your neighbor or buy from the neighbor's hand... (25:14)." This teaches that one who does not observe the laws of shmitah and yovel will suffer financial difficulties and have to sell his possessions. If he has learned his lesson, all will be well. If not, then the verse says, "If your brother becomes poor and sells his estate... (25:25)." He will have to resort to selling his fields. If he then learns his lesson, all will be well. If not, then the verse says, "If a man sells his dwelling... (25:29)." He will have to resort to selling his house. If he then learns his lesson, all will be well. If not, then the verse says, "Do not take interest or increase... (25:36)." He will have to borrow money; yet, he will find no one to lend him unless it is with interest. In the end, he will be unable to repay the debt on*

account of the mounting interest. The verse then says, "Your brother will grow poor and sell himself... (25:39)." He will have to sell himself into slavery.

This fellow who did not keep the laws of *shmitah* and had to sell his possessions, his land, his home, and in the end had to sell himself, the Torah calls him your brother. "*Your brother will grow poor and sell himself...*" You are not to regard this suffering Jew as a sinner. He is being made to pay for his indiscretions. Do not say to him, "You've made your bed, now lie in it." You are to treat him with compassion because he is your brother. As our Sages (*Sanhedrin* 44a) say, "*A Jew who sins is still a Jew!*"

The Medrash (*Yalkut Shemoni* 658) says:

Why do the laws of poverty-stricken Jews follow the laws of shmitah and yovel? To teach us that one who is greedy and refuses to allow his land to be fallow during shmitah and yovel, will in the end be driven from his possessions. During the era of the First Temple, many Jews refused to adhere to the laws of shmitah and yovel. As a result, the Jewish Nation was driven from their land into galus. They lost everything. Even their Temple was destroyed. When the Jews bemoaned their fate, G-d told them, "Because of your sins I have sold My house (the Bais HaMikdash) to strangers. But fear not, when the jubilee of redemption arrives, you and I will be restored to what is ours.

The 349ᵗʰ mitzvah is the prohibition to bow down and prostrate oneself on stone flooring.

"A stone floor you shall not place in your land to bow down upon" (26:1).

The *Sefer HaChinuch* (349) quotes the Rambam who says that bowing on a stone floor was a pagan practice. For a Jew to imitate the pagans, even if the Jew's intention is that he is bowing before G-d, is prohibited.

The prohibition is to prostrate oneself directly on a stone floor. Some authorities say that even if the floor has permanent carpeting, the prohibition still applies. Therefore, on *Rosh HaShanah* and *Yom*

Kippur when we prostrate ourselves on the floor many synagogues have the practice to see that each congregant has a sheet of paper to place between himself and the floor.

Why does the *parshah,* which dealt primary about the laws of *shmitah* and *yovel* and the punishments for those who do not adhere to those laws, conclude with a law pertaining to idolatry? To teach us that one who still has not learned his lesson, after having to sell himself as a slave, will eventually be sold into a temple of idolatry (*Kiddushin* 20a).

HAFTORAH BEHAR

I n the *parshah* we learned that one who sold his field has the right to buy it back (redeem it) from the buyer. If the seller is unable to redeem his property, there is a mitzvah for a relative of the seller to redeem it. It then becomes the possession of the relative until *yovel.*

The *haftorah* begins with the prophet Yirmiyahu confined to a courtyard in the royal palace by order of the king, Tzidkiyahu. The king was displeased with the prophet's forecast of a Babylonian conquest of the Holy Land and therefore restricted Yirmiyahu's movements among the people. The Babylonians had already begun their siege of the city. The remaining days of Israel's freedom were numbered. The exile was imminent.

Yirmiyahu's cousin, Chanamel, tells the prophet that he had no choice but to sell a field in the Levite city of Anathoth. Chanamel was not able to redeem the land and pleads to his cousin to redeem the field and buy it for himself. Though under confinement, Yirmiyahu was able to redeem the field. It was now his. He had the deed of sale placed in an earthen container. The container was sealed and buried in a safe place. All of this was done according to the instructions of G-d.

Yirmiyahu wonders why G-d would instruct him to buy land in Israel when the country is about to be overtaken by the Babylonians. Within a year, the Jews would be exiled. What good would the land do him in exile?

The *haftorah* does not supply the answer to the prophet's question. Instead, it ends with G-d posing a question of His own, "*Can anything be hidden from Me?*" The explanation of G-d's reply is found in the book of *Yirmiyahu* shortly after the *haftorah* ends. G-d tells the prophet that the exile will not be long. Israel will return to their land. The act of sealing the deed to the land in an earthen container and burying it in a secure place symbolizes the covenant between G-d and

Israel and their eventual return to their land.

The lesson of the *haftorah* is especially meaningful in our times. Yirmiyahu could have just as easily allowed the Babylonians to take possession of the land; later on, when the Jews returned from exile, they would once again take possession of their land. The prophet is told to buy and treasure the fields of Israel even during the time of *galus*. If one treasures the possession of the holy land even during the exile, then that expression of devotion will secure the land's eventual return to the Jews. It demonstrates their faith in G-d's promise to redeem His nation. Today, are we allowed to turn over Jewish land to the Palestinians in return for a promise of peace (somehow assuming that promise is not completely hollow)? Should we lay back and just wait for the arrival of *Mashiach* when the land will be restored to us? Or, must we treasure every inch of Jewish soil and do whatever it takes to retain possession? These are serious questions for the great rabbis of our generation to consider.

BECHUKOSAI

≈§ BECHUKOSAI

"If you walk in My statutes and keep My commandments and do them, I will give the rains in their season and the land shall yield her produce and the trees of the field shall give forth their fruit..." (26:3:4).

Parshas *Bechukosai* brings to a close the book of Vayikra. The theme of Vayikra was sanctity – the sanctity of the *Mishkan*, the sanctity of the land of Israel, the sanctity of the festivals, the sanctity of the Jewish nation, and the sanctity of the individual.

Bechukosai begins with a series of blessings and curses. Those who instill sanctity bring with it blessings and those who defile sanctity bring curses. The *parshah* begins with the word "*if*" to teach us that blessings and curses are all up to us.

Rashi explains the phrase "*If you walk in My statutes*" to mean the diligent study of the Torah. The Hebrew word for statute is "*chok*," which means a law that is beyond human comprehension and logical explanation, such as the laws of kashrus. The question arises: although laws, such as kashrus, may be beyond logic and comprehension, certainly studying those laws in order to observe them correctly is not beyond logic and comprehension. Why then does the Torah refer to study as a *chok*?

Perhaps two answers can be suggested. The first answer is that the great reward that awaits those who immerse themselves in the study of Torah is beyond our comprehension. We cannot fathom the magnitude of the blessings that lie in store for us.

A second answer may be the fact that we are rewarded for studying Torah. The mere fact that we are learning the words and will of the Creator of the universe should be a reward in itself. King David (*Tehillim* 19:9) said "*The laws of Torah are just, they make glad the heart.*" Studying Torah should be its own reward, why are we given additional rewards and blessings? That is what is beyond logic and comprehension. A rabbi of mine once said that he had the greatest job in the world. He has the opportunity to learn and teach Torah and to interact with curious young minds. And, not only that, he gets paid for it! That is the *chok* of learning Torah; we are getting paid for it.

◆§ SPIRITUAL REWARDS VS. MATERIAL REWARDS

"If you walk in My statutes and keep My commandments and do them, I will give the rains in their season and the land shall yield her produce and the trees of the field shall give forth their fruit..." (26:3:4).

All the blessings and curses are phrased in the plural, "*Im bechukosai taylaychu, if you (plural) walk in My statutes... V'im lo sish'mehoo li, if you (plural) do not listen to Me...*"

Why are they phrased in the plural? Doesn't an individual merit blessings if he keeps the mitzvos? Doesn't an individual deserve curses if he does not keep the mitzvos?

An even more basic question is based on the Talmud (*Kiddushin* 29b) that states, "*There is no reward for mitzvos in this world.*" The Talmud is stating that the reward for mitzvos is given in the World to Come and not in this world. The reward is spiritual and not material. Yet, the blessings that are mentioned in this *parshah* – rains in their season, abundant crops, peace in the land, etc., are all material rewards. How do the words of the Talmud reconcile with the words of our *parshah*?

The *Maharsha* (*Kiddushin* 29b) explains that every individual is rewarded or punished according to his or her deeds. That reward or punishment is spiritual in nature and given in the World to Come. That is what the Talmud was referring to when it said that there is no reward in this world. However, not only are we judged as individuals, the Jewish People are judged as a whole. If, as a whole, they are worthy, they will be given material blessings in this world. That will not take away from the individual's reward in the World to Come. If, as a whole, the Jewish People, do not merit blessings in this world, then they will suffer the consequences of the curses in this world. The *parshah* is phrased in the plural because it refers to the Jewish People as a nation and not individuals. Only the nation as a whole is rewarded in this world.

Perhaps another answer can be suggested to the question arising from *Kiddushin*. The *parshah* is talking about blessings. The Talmud is talking about reward. Reward is "payment" for the mitzvos we have done. This payment is given in the next world. Blessings are extras or bonuses. When a *tzadik* gives a person a *brocha*, a blessing, the *tzadik* is not rewarding the person for the mitzvos he or she has done. The *tzadik* is praying that Hashem will give the person a bonus, something extra. Blessings are bonuses that are given in this world. The *parshah* is outlining the circumstances for which we will merit the bonus of blessings.

According to this explanation, rewards are given in the next world for the mitzvos we have done. Punishment is also given in the next world for sins we have committed. That explains rewards and punishments. What about blessings and curses? Blessings are bonuses that are given in this world. But, what are curses? We would expect that they are the frustrations in life. If blessings are extras, then maybe curses are those things that diminish from our basic expectations. However, as the *parshah* unfolds, we seem to discover that every curse is really a blessing in disguise. There are two types of blessings: one that is obviously good and the other that is hidden by disguise. The harshness and severity of the curse serves as an exceptional disguise; but, underneath it all, as we shall see, it is nonetheless a hidden blessing.

STUDY IN ORDER TO DO

"If you walk in My statutes and keep My commandments and do them..." (26:3).

Rashi comments that the verse is telling us that we must learn Torah not merely for its own sake but in order to observe and fulfill the mitzvos. Learning is not to be regarded as some academic exercise. We learn in order to do.

Rav Eliezer Zusia Portugal (the previous Skulener Rebbe) commented: One who studies Torah is compared to one who plants seeds. One who applies what he has studied and observes the commandments is compared to one who harvests what he has planted. One who studies Torah but does not live a Torah way of life, is likened to a foolish farmer who plants but never bothers to harvest the crop. He will not survive the harsh winter. One who studies and does the mitzvos is likened to the farmer who planted and harvested. He will survive the harsh winter.

The *Chedushi Harim*, (the first Gerer Rebbi) saw two of his

Chasidim dancing on *Simchas Torah*. As he observed, he pointed out one of them and quietly predicted that he would stop dancing first. The Chasidim around him watched, anxiously waiting to see the outcome. Soon, just as the Gerer Rebbi predicted, that Chasid stopped dancing first. They asked the Rebbi how he was able to tell who would be the first to stop. He responded as follows. The one who stopped dancing first was motivated by all the Torah he had learned from the previous year. He had learned for the sake of learning, not doing. Such learning was limited and, therefore, his strength to dance was limited. He would tire first. However, the other fellow, who kept dancing, was motivated by all the Torah he had learned as well as the mitzvos he was going to do as a result. Those mitzvos will be done over and over again; therefore it is unlimited. Therefore his dancing was fueled by an unlimited source of fervor.

❧ EVERYTHING IN ITS SEASON, EVEN BLESSINGS

"I will give your rains in their season..." (26:4).

Recently there was a tripling in price of tomatoes. It seems that the heavy rains fell on the Florida crop while the plants were in blossom. The deluge destroyed the flowers causing a dearth of tomatoes. Rain in its season is a blessing but when it falls out of season either it is not productive or it can be a curse.

This is true of all blessings: in the appropriate time it is welcome, in an inappropriate time it can be destructive. Blessings that come at the wrong time or to the wrong people can be a curse.

A Texan who worked in the stock room of a Home Depot thought his life had turned around: he hit the Texas Lottery jackpot and was $31,000,000 richer. But, as we have all heard but don't really believe, money can't buy happiness. His wife became more demanding; his relatives and friends expected to share in the bounty. In order to buy happiness, the confused lottery winner gave into all their demands. Within twenty-four months, he told his financial adviser, "Winning the lottery was the worse thing that ever happened to me." Later than night, he went upstairs to his bedroom and shot himself.

A New Jersey woman won that state's lottery not once but twice. Who could be 'luckier?' But, she had always had a problem with money: she was an addicted gambler. She now lives in a trailer park. Her $5,4000,000 is gone. She relies on handouts from sympathetic friends.

Such stories are startling and require due reflection. There is even an organization to help people cope with their burden of blessings. Everything has its time and place, even blessings.

✍ ABUNDANCE AND SECURITY

> *"And your threshing (will be so abundant that it) will reach the time for harvesting grapes, and the harvest of grapes will (be so abundant that it) will reach the time for sowing. You will eat your bread with satiety and will dwell in your land in safety. I will give peace in the land and you shall lie down (at night) unafraid..."* (26:5-6).

These blessings need further analysis for they appear to follow an unusual pattern. The Jews will achieve great prosperity, so much so, that all will be satiated. Then the Torah states that there will be peace in the land. Satiety and peace usually do not go hand in hand. This is what makes these blessings so unique. Jewish history has shown that when the Jews are in a period of satiety and contentment, their social structure begins to crumble and conflicts arise. This is human nature. We learned from the time of the Great Flood, life was so good that people no longer felt the need for G-d. Our Sages blamed the decay of that civilization on the people's lack of need for a higher being. The more enriched their lives became, the more detached they grew from the source of their fortune; they abandoned G-d.

Much of our misfortune is derived from complacency and comfort. Just sixty years ago we endured a horrible holocaust The Jewish population of Eastern Europe had achieved great prosperity. They integrated themselves far too deeply in the German social structure. They considered themselves to be prosperous Germans rather than successful Jews. The affluent German-Jews fled the Jewish neighborhoods, moved to the big cities, and mired themselves in German culture. They adopted a secular way of thinking. Too many abandoned their heritage; intermarriage was on the rise. They lost their spiritual connection to their past, present and future. They were no longer aware of their source of blessings.

While we must look upon the horrors wrought upon our people as a punishment, we must also come to understand how this moment in our history signaled Jews from all over the world to take stock in their Judaism. The horrors of the death camps saved our nation from the total annihilation of assimilation. As we have seen throughout history, assimilation and abandonment of our Torah placed us into these compromising positions where exile, misfortune and the threat of annihilation were close at hand. G-d, in His mercy, reminded us that we are still in Exile, preventing us from becoming totally assimilated which would mark the end of our nation as a spiritual entity.

What G-d is saying in no uncertain terms is that when times are good if you stand I will reward you, however, if you falter, my reminders will be severe.

✐ UNITED WE STAND

"And you shall chase your enemies and they will fall by the sword. Five of you will chase a hundred and a hundred of you shall chase ten thousand..." (26:7-8).

R ashi points out the inconsistency of the mathematics in the verse. If 5 can chase 100, then that is a ratio of 1 to 20. Thus, 100 should only be able to chase 2,000. Yet, the verse says that 100 will be able to chase 10,000. Rashi provides clarity to this apparent inconsistency by stating that one cannot compare the unity of 5 people to the unity of 100 people. The Jewish people have always maintained their strength through unity. Greatness in our unity leads to greatness in our strength. "United we stand; divided we fall." As long as we stand together, we will ward off our enemies. The greater the unity the less we have to struggle to do it.

✐ PRIDE AND HUMILITY

"I am the L-rd your G-d who brought you out of the land of Egypt from being slaves unto them. I have broken the bars of your yoke, I made you walk upright" (26:13).

R ashi comments that the word upright means with an upright posture. This is a bit astounding since the Talmud (*Berachos* 43b) prohibits even taking four steps with an upright posture. Such a stance is a sign of haughtiness. Why then does the verse say that G-d will make us walk with an upright posture?

We need to distinguish between a self-serving pride and a pride in serving Hashem. If one takes pride in his accomplishments as if to pat himself on the back and to show his superiority, such arrogance is contrary to the Torah. Whatever achievement a person accomplishes, whether it is a spiritual, financial or academic achievement, it is attributed to G-d's beneficence and blessing. We are to express our humble thanks and gratitude. An upright posture is out of place and out of line. Such pride can lead to the withholding of G-d's blessings and the onset of curses.

G-d redeemed the Children of Israel from the slavery of the cruel Egyptians taskmasters. He took us to be His servants: to serve Him and mankind. To take pride in the fact that we are the servants of the Holy One, Blessed is He, is not only permissible but it is laudable. One should take pride in the fact that he is a Jew. If one is embarrassed that he is a Jew, he will not be a reliable servant of G-d. The first thing he will do is remove his yarmulke. Since he has no head-covering, he will not recite a brocha and in the end he will come to eat non-kosher food. One who keeps his yarmulke on takes pride in the fact that he is a Jew. He will be mindful that others see him as a Jew. He will do his utmost to make a *Kiddush Hashem* by being true to others, himself, and G-d. In such cases, pride leads to blessing.

⋙ THE CURSES

"If you do not hearken to Me, and you will not do all these commandments... I will appoint over you a sense of terror, consuming disease, great fevers, the eyes will fail, and the soul will languish, you will plant in vain for your enemies shall eat of it" (26:14-16).

hy does G-d have to punish the Jewish People if they sin? Why not simply stop the blessings?

When a parent sees his or her child doing

something praiseworthy, the child is rewarded. When the parent sees his or her child doing something wrong, the child is punished. Why punish the child? Simply do not reward bad behavior. Obviously, if the parent would not punish the child, the child would not realize that it is doing wrong. He would continue his misbehavior. Likewise, curses and punishments that befall the Jewish People are G-d's ways of letting us know that we are doing something wrong. He is getting our attention. We must then analyze what it is that we are doing wrong and correct our behavior.

If the child corrects his behavior after the punishment, all will be well. If he does not correct his behavior but commits the infraction again, the next punishment will be more severe. The same is true with our relationship with G-d. We must strive to learn our lesson from any punishment so that the cause of this "sense of terror" is removed. If we don't, then the sense of terror will become very real. The enemy shall eat our grain.

⇜ THE ENEMY FROM WITHIN

> *"And if you despise My statutes... I will appoint over you a sense of terror, consuming disease, great fevers...and you will be smitten by your enemies and those who hate you shall rule over you"* (26:15-17).

Rashi explains that the terror and disease will strike inside the city while the enemy will strike from outside the city. These verses allude to the two types of enemies of the Jewish People: the enemy from outside our ranks and the enemy from within. It is the enemy within, the disease, which weakens us so that we fall prey to the enemy outside our walls.

Those who are familiar with the story of Tisha B'Av know that the war-mongering Jewish zealots within the city walls killed more

Jews than the Roman enemy outside the city. The Romans had more compassion than the anti-religious zealot generals. The baseless hatred that the zealots had towards their pacifist brethren is what destroyed the Holy Temple. (See *A Time to Weep* by Rabbi Leibel Reznick for a dramatic and graphic description of that heart-rending era.)

In America, Jews are rarely exposed to overt anti-Semitism. When an occasional act of vandalism surfaces, such as a menorah desecration or anti-Semitic graffiti sprawled on the outside wall of a synagogue, the press and the politicians condemn those acts in no uncertain terms. In Israel, however, Orthodox Jews are often depicted in the newspapers, magazines, and on TV shows as vampires, leeches and apes, sometimes with hooked noses, warts and stooped backs. The Charedim (Orthodox Jews) are accused of controlling the government like a puppeteer. They are presented as lecherous, money-grubbing parasites. Such ugly imagery is chillingly reminiscent of Nazi-era depictions of Jews.

Do the Israeli politicians come to our defense? To the contrary, segments of the political arena are devoted to maintaining, if not promoting, these anti-religious sentiments. These

'leaders' have made significant inroads into the mindset of our misguided secular Israeli brethren.

Author, Joe Lockard, a self-proclaimed Jewish atheist, said of one such 'leader,' "*Discrimination against and demonization of orthodox and ultra-orthodox believers has become the anti-Semitism of some secular Jews, a development equally as unacceptable as religious coercion. Such thoughtless secular reactions scorn the rich ethical and intellectual potential of religious faith, abandon the bonds of community, and forget that secular and religious Jews share a common history and future.*" And that comes from an atheist.

As the great twentieth-century American philosopher, Pogo, said, "*I have seen the enemy and they are us.*"

✑ SEVENFOLD

"If you still do not listen to Me, I will increase your afflictions sevenfold on account of your sins" (26:18).

hy sevenfold and not some other number? Rashi (26:14-15, 18) explains that sin follows in seven steps.

1. Sin begins with neglecting the study of Torah.
2. That leads to neglect of the mitzvos.
3. That leads to the resentment of those who are more religious and do the mitzvos.
4. That leads to the hatred of the Sages who instruct others in doing mitzvos.
5. He will try to spread his personal resentment by trying to stop others from doing mitzvos.
6. He will believe and get others to believe that the Torah is not G-d's word.
7. In the end, he will deny G-d's existence.

Ben Azai said, (Avos 4:2): *One sin leads to another sin; the reward for sin is the opportunity to sin again."*

Regrettably we have witnessed this procession of self-destruction in our recent history.

The so-called Age of Enlightenment, some 200 years ago, attracted hundreds of thousands of Jews to falter in steps 1 and 2, listed above. Although these Jews did not see their behavior as even the least bit anti-religious in ideal, the ensuing generations proved Rashi's steps to be prophetic. With steps 1 and 2 secure, large segments of our people passionately pursued steps 3, 4 and 5 from the mid 19th century into the mid 20th century.

The recent decades have seen a frightening percentage of our fellow Jews wallowing in the ways of steps 6 and 7. Whether it is the complacent atheism of America, and other parts of the world, or the openly hostile secularism of Israel, the results of these seven steps have been devastating to our people. But the real lesson, here, for the religious Jew is the awesome responsibility incumbent on us never to neglect our Torah study; never to tread upon step one. Devoted Torah study is essential for our survival; neglect of this pursuit, no matter how innocuous the intention, will certainly lead to spiritual destruction.

∝§ THE BLESSING OF THE CURSE

"And I will make desolate the land and the enemy who dwells in it will be astonished" (26:32).

Though this verse is one of the curses, it is a blessing in disguise. After the Romans conquered the land and the Jews were driven out, the land was no longer productive. For 2,000 years it was a vast wasteland, unable to support the subsequent invaders. The Romans, the Byzantines, the various warring Arab factions, the Crusaders, the Mongols, the Turks, and the British were all unable to make the Holy Land into a viable country. Had Palestine been a productive land during the years of *galus*, it is unlikely that the United Nations would have voted in 1948 to grant the land as a Jewish homeland. Granting this arid wasteland to the remnants of the holocaust was the least they could do. It was also the most that they were willing to do.

At the height of the 1936-39 Arab riots against the Jewish population in Palestine, a royal commission came from London to investigate the roots of the Arab-Jewish conflict and to propose solutions. The commission, headed by Lord Robert Peel, heard a great deal of testimony in Palestine, and in July 1937 issued its report. Part II, chapter IX, of the Peel Commission Report contains an astute observation. "The Arabs claimed that the Jews bought up all the best farming land in the country. Yet, when this same land was under Arab control, it was nothing more than sand dunes and swamps. "

In other words, it was apparent to an independent source, whose objective was to simply document the situation, that the Arab claim that the Jews had taken the better land for themselves was simply unjustified. What was duly noted was that the land that the Jews cultivated was, at one point, no more conducive for cultivation than the Arab land.

The amount of cultivatable land in Palestine was negligible. It was a cursed land. Most of it was heavily swamped and throughout history many people died of malaria trying to work on it. The commission knew that agriculturally there was not enough cultivatable land to fit all the Jews on this land. There were millions in Europe plus upward of a half a million possible refuges of Jews in Arab countries, plus those that were currently on the land. The commission felt it was unrealistic for the land to hold all these Jews.

The Commission proceeded to document a plan whereby the governing British body would partition the land of Israel and regulate immigration. In its wildest calculations it never estimated a greater number of Jews than Arabs living in Palestine; considering how unmanageable the land was it sought to divide up the land in equitable ways.

It was concluded that the land could hold 2,000,000 people (Jews and Arabs). Today we have two and half times that amount – a total of over five and a half million Jews in the Land of Israel. Today, the land is vibrantly productive and exceptionally workable; the same land that was formerly evaluated in the world's eyes to be unmanageable and inhospitable.

The Peel Commission was witness to the blessing of the curse.

✑ SCATTERING THE TRADITION AMONG THE NATIONS

"I will scatter you among the nations..." (26:33).

Rashi explains how painful this curse is. When the inhabitants of one country are exiled to a common place, they can seek comfort from one another. With this curse, the curse of scattering, they will be unable to do so.

Like all of G-d's curses, this one has a hidden blessing. If G-d forbid, all the Jews had been exiled to one place, we would have ceased to exist a long time ago. If Jews in one part of the world are being persecuted, those in other parts of the world can continue to survive.

In addition, the Rabbis tell us that the *galus* not only serves as punishment for the Jewish Nation, it benefits the other nations of the world. When the various civilizations are exposed to the Jews, they also become exposed to the Jewish faith and its ideals. People speak of the Judeo-Christian values of western civilization. Actually, there are no Christian values per se. Christian values are all derived from the Torah. As the Christian peoples abroad came in contact with the Jews, they absorbed Jewish values. Judeo-Christian values simply means Jewish values that were adopted by the Christians.

If all the Jews had been exiled to a single country, only that country would be exposed to Torah ethics. It would take forever for Torah ethics to spread throughout the world. The scattering of the Jews allowed the Torah's idealism to spread more rapidly.

Of course, once other nations adopted the Jewish value system, they condemned the Jews for not always living up to the high moral and ethical standards of the Torah. The Christians and Moslems claimed to be the true inheritors of the Sinai tradition and the Jews were trying to steal it from them.

✑ THE SUPREME TEST

"Your land will be desolate and your cities a waste, then the land will be appeased on account of the Sabbaths..." (26:33-34).

I n *Parshas Behar* we learned that the punishment for not keeping the laws of *shmitah* and *yovel* is *galus*. If the Jewish People will not honor the sanctity of the land, then the land will reject them and they will be cast into exile. Rashi (26:35) tells us that during the era of the First Temple, many Jews did not keep the laws of *shmitah* and *yovel*. There were seventy *shmitos* and *yovelos* that were not kept. And so, the exile by the Babylonians lasted seventy years.

Why is the curse of *galus* attributed to the disregard of *shmitah* and *yovel* and not some other mitzvah or prohibition? All the other mitzvos and prohibitions do not require a great leap of faith. Had the Torah not given us civil law, we would have invented such laws ourselves. Had the Torah not given us holy days, we would have invented holidays. Every nation has holidays. Had the Torah not given us laws of restricted foods, we would have invented them. Most major religions have restrictions on certain things they can or can not eat. The most unique mitzvah in the Torah is not to work the fields during *shmitah* and *yovel* years. As we saw from the words of the *Chasam Sofer* in the previous *parshah*, *shmitah* and *yovel* could never have been invented by man. Those mitzvos are the supreme test of faith in G-d. If we fail that test, then we forfeit our right to live in His holy land.

EVERLASTING BOND: FOR BETTER OR WORSE

> *"And yet in spite of this, when they are in the land of their enemies I will not despise them nor abhor them so as to destroy them, to break My treaty with them, for I am the L-rd their G-d"* (26:44).

G-d assures the Israelites that no matter what happens, the unique bond between G-d and Israel can never be severed. This unique relationship does not exist between G-d and the other nations. They have been utterly destroyed. The ancient Egyptians, Babylonians, Philistines, Persians, Romans, Greeks, have all disappeared but the Children of Israel continue to exist and thrive.

As the prophet Yeshayah (50:1) quotes G-d saying, "*Is there a document of divorce?*" Thus, the bond between G-d and his bride, Israel, still persists, even during the years of *galus*.

The Jewish People have a remarkable, G-d-inspired ability to bounce back. During the stressful years of exile and persecution, the Jews were able to adapt themselves and set up academies for learning. There were yeshivos in Babylon, in Rome, in Spain, in Germany, and in America. They managed to retain their traditions and maintain their identity. However, every new generation seeks to carve out its own identity and, thus, exposes itself to the pit of assimilation. Therefore, there are always those who reject the ways of their elders and rebel against the constraints of tradition. They strive to absorb the culture of their new homeland and to share in the wealth it has to offer. They shed their ancient mode of dress and foreign sounding names. Torah and its mitzvos fall by the wayside. "Berlin is the new Jerusalem!"

Rav Meir Simcha of D'vinsk, the *Meshech Chachmah,* tells us that at such times these Jews need a reminder that they are G-d's people. They are not Greeks or Romans or Germans. They are Jews. Berlin is not the new Jerusalem. It is the new *gehennom.* The renewed persecution drives home the message and reminds them of their G-d and their heritage. The curse of exile and persecution is the cursed blessing that keeps the Jewish People alive. It stops assimilation and intermarriage when the Jews are not willing to stop it themselves.

It is so very sad that we have to be taught this lesson through great pain and suffering. How unfortunate it is that it takes tragedy to keep us together as a nation. Not only were our Sages aware of this phenomenon, our enemies were also aware of it. In *Mein Kampf,* Hitler writes: *The Jew is only united when a common danger forces him to be.*

✢ THE MITZVOS

The *parshah* concludes with the laws of "*Erechin*" values, regarding donations to the *Mishkan*. This is a case if a person takes a vow to donate himself, his home, possessions or animals to G-d. The value of each must be calculated according to its worth. An entire tractate in the Talmud (*Erechin*) is dedicated to these laws.

The 350ᵗʰ mitzvah is if a person vows to give a gift to the *Mishkan* of a certain value, he must give that exact value.

"A man who utters a vow (to give) according to the evaluation of persons to G-d..." (27:2).

The Torah ascribes a monetary value for men and women in different age brackets. If one pledges to give to the *Mishkan* a donation based on the Torah evaluation of a certain individual, he must honor his pledge. These pledges are called *erechin*.

MALES:
1 month – 5 years = 5 shekels
5-20 years of age = 20 silver shekels
20-60 years of age = 50 silver shekels
60 years of age and upward = 15 shekels

FEMALES:
1 month-5 years = 3 shekels
5-20 years of age = 10 silver shekels
20-60 years of age = 30 silver shekels
60 years of age and upward = 10 shekels.

The list reflects the value of people sold in a slave market where males generally fetched a higher sum than females.

The *Sefer HaChinuch* (350) says that the primary aspect of this mitzvah is to keep one's word and honor his pledge. Words are our ability to communicate ideas and emotions to one another. When G-d created man, the verse says *"And the L-rd G-d formed man of the dust of the ground and breathed into his nostrils the breath of life; and man became a living soul*" (*Bereishis* 2:7). The *Targum* explains that a "*living soul*" means one that is able to communicate, to talk. Our ability to talk comes from the breath of G-d that was instilled in us. We must treat this G-dly ability with the greatest respect. A person must honor his words and commitments. To do otherwise is to denigrate that breath of G-d that is within us.

The monetary value for each individual is based solely on his or her age, not on intellect, strength or beauty. This means that a 20-year-old simpleton is valued at more than a 65-year-old scholar. This is because we believe that although one person may be smarter then another, or stronger then another, it is their potential that has to be taken into consideration. The realization of potential takes time. Take for example the 20-year-old simpleton. Though he seems to be a simpleton now, his potential to grow is great. He still has a great deal of time to absorb knowledge and possibly become greater then the 65-year-old Torah scholar. As time goes on his true value will depend on how he uses this time.

Possibly this is the reason that the laws of *erechin* come after the curses given to the children of Israel. Individuals should never become so depressed that they believe that they cannot rise above their own personal curses and *galus*. Everyone has problems and difficulties, be it problems at home, at school or at work. G-d is telling us that every Jew has a value. Never become so disheartened that you feel you can't rise above it. As long as there is time, we can achieve anything.

The 351ˢᵗ mitzvah is the prohibition to exchange an animal that was pledged to the *Mishkan*.

"*If an animal that can be offered as a sacrifice to G-d (is his pledge)... He may not alter it or exchange it, whether for better or worse*" (27:9-10).

An entire tractate in the Talmud (*Temurah*) is dedicated to these laws. If one pledged an animal to the *Mishkan* or *Bais HaMikdash*, he is not allowed to change it for another one even if the second animal is a better specimen.

The 352ⁿᵈ mitzvah is to treat both the original animal and the one it was exchanged for (if he violates the

prohibition of exchanging) as sacred.

"And if he does change it, one animal for another, both it and the exchange shall be holy" (27:10).

The 353rd mitzvah is to honor one's pledge concerning the value of any animal that cannot be used as a sacrifice.

"If an unclean animal (or) one that is not fit for a sacrifice... The Kohen shall evaluate it..." (27:11-12).

Since the animal itself cannot be used in the Temple service, only its value was considered sacred. The owner was expected to give the value of the animal to the sanctuary.

The 354th mitzvah is to honor one's pledge concerning a house that was proclaimed to be holy.

"A man who sanctified his house to be holy to G-d, the Kohen shall evaluate it" (27:14).

It is the value of the house that is holy and not the actual structure.

The 355th mitzvah is to honor one's pledge concerning his field.

"If from the field of his possession he shall proclaim holy to G-d, its evaluation is (to be made) according to its area, a kor-area is fifty holy silver shekels" (27:16).

The evaluation of land in Eretz Yisroel was not made according to its real-estate value; therefore, whether it be an acre of prime real estate in central Jerusalem or an acre of land in the desert, the evaluation was consistent. All land in Israel is holy and therefore, from a spiritual point of view, all land is equal in spiritual value. Evaluations were made according to the size of pledged property. Each *kor*-area (approx. 3.9 acres) was "valued" at 50 silver shekels (approx. 50 ounces of silver).

The evaluation also took into consideration how many years were left until *yovel*. The 50 shekels assumed that there were a full 50 years until the next *yovel*. If one pledged his property when there were only 25 years left until *yovel*, then the value would be 25 shekels per *kor*-area.

The 356th mitzvah is the prohibition to change an animal that was designated for one type of sacrifice to be used as another type of sacrifice.

"*However, the first born (animal) which is (to be proclaimed as) a first-born sacrifice to G-d among the animals, no man shall proclaim it as (to be another) holy (sacrifice)*" (27:26).

The 357th mitzvah is to honor one's pledge of a gift to the Temple priests.

The 358th mitzvah is the prohibition to sell items which were designated to be a gift to the *Kohanim*, even if his intention is to give the money to the priests.

"*Any devoted property to G-d's (Temple priests), from all that he has, whether man (servant) or animal or field of his possession, it shall not be sold nor redeemed (by the one donating it) all devotions are (to be given to the Temple priests) for it is the holiest to G-d*" (27:28).

Once the item is given to the *Kohen*, the *Kohen* may do with it as he sees fit. There are no longer any restrictions on that property.

The 359th mitzvah is the prohibition to sell or redeem land that was designated for the *Kohanim*.

"*Any devoted property to G-d's (Temple priests), from all that he has, whether man (servant) or animal or field of his possession, it shall not be sold nor redeemed (by the one donating it) all devotions are (to be given to the Temple priests) for it is the holiest to G-d*" (27:28).

Generally, the seller can redeem land in Eretz Yisroel that has been sold; in the event that it is not redeemed, it is returned to the owner on *yovel*. The owner cannot forcibly redeem land donated to the *Kohanim*, nor is it returned to him on *yovel*. It becomes the property of the *Kohen* in perpetuity.

The 360th mitzvah is to designate 1/10th of the animals that are born that year as a sacrifice.

"*Every tenth (animal) of the herd or flock (that is born that year) shall pass under the rod, (every) tenth one shall be (proclaimed) holy to G-d*" (27:32).

The 361st mitzvah is the prohibition to sell or redeem

any tenth animal.
"It shall not be redeemed" **(27:34).**

Even if his intention is to give the money to the *Bais HaMikdash*, it is forbidden. The actual animal must be presented and used for the sacrifice.

Three times each year – before Pesach, *Shavuos,* and *Succos* – the flock herders and cattlemen would place their newborn animals in a pen. The pen door was opened narrowly so only one animal could pass at a time. The herder or cattleman would stand near the opening holding a stick dipped in red paint. He would count the animals as they passed under the stick. Every tenth one was touched with the stick to mark it as a *ma'aser* (tenth) sacrifice.

Unlike other sacrifices, in which case it was considered praiseworthy to present a choice animal as a sacrifice, here, it was left solely to chance; the one to pass under the rod was the *ma'aser.* How poetic it is that on the High Holy Days we recite the awe-inspiring prayer, *U'Nesaneh Tokef,* which compares the Jewish People on the days of judgment to those sheep in the pen.

> *"Let us tell of the great sanctity of the day for it is awesome and fearful. On this day Your Kingship is elevated yet higher; Your throne is set with kindness... The mighty shofar blasts, a weak voice is heard, angels hurry about, there is a gripping fear and trembling, behold it is the judgment day... All the creatures of the world pass before You, like young sheep. Just as the shepherd examines his flock and passes his sheep under his rod, so too, You let pass and You count and examine the soul of every living being. You declare the number (of days) for every creature and write the final judgment decree."*

We are like the sheep that everything seems to be left to chance. We lead our lives as though there will be no reckoning. But, there is a day of counting, a day when our deeds are counted and marked: Judgment Day. Each one of us passes by in a single file. We cannot hide in the crowd. And, as we pass by, we are numbered, one, two, three, etc. Maybe we can be that number ten, the tenth one designated for Hashem. But that is left to chance. Or is it?

❧ THE LESSON OF SEFER VAYIKRA

A few weeks after the herder and cattleman separated their *ma'aser* animals they would bring it with them as they were making their thrice-yearly pilgrimage to the *Bais HaMikdash*. The *ma'aser* animals were sacrificed and the meat was given to the owner to eat in Jerusalem. He was allowed to share it with anyone he saw fit, as long as the person was a Jew and was not unclean, *tamei*. Obviously, he could not eat all the sacrificial meat by himself. He would share his blessings with some of the hundreds of thousands of other festival pilgrims.

Sheepherders and cattlemen lived out in the plains, away from the cities, away from centers of Torah and mitzvos. The opportunities to study were greatly restricted by lack of free time and dearth of Torah scholars. His opportunities to perform acts of kindness were restricted by the fact that he resided in a sparsely populated area. The mitzvah of *oleh regel*, to make three pilgrimages a year, gave him the opportunity to be exposed to great Sages in Jerusalem and to hear their teachings. The mitzvah of sharing his *ma'aser* meat with his fellow pilgrims gave him the opportunity to do acts of kindness in a manner that he was unable to do the rest of the year.

The book of Vayikra began with the mitzvos of the *korbanos*, the sacrifices: laws concerning the spiritual relationship between Man and his Creator. The book of Vayikra concludes with sacrifices, sacrifices that offer the opportunity to do kindness unto others: laws between Man and his Fellow. The ultimate goal of spiritual values is to make this progression of recognizing our obligation to serve our Creator and expressing that obligation fundamentally through having concern and compassion for others; that is the ultimate lesson of *Sefer Vayikra*.

✑ HAFTORAH BECHUKOSAI

THE *HAFTORAH* IS FOUND IN *YIRMIYAHU* 16: 19 – 17:14.

T he *parshah* told of the blessings intended for the Jewish Nation when they follow in the ways of G-d and the curses for them when they abandon their Father in Heaven. Since *Behar* and *Bechukosai* are often read together in *shul* on the same Shabbos, the *haftorah* also refers to the theme of *Parshas Behar*, namely *shmitah*.

At a very young age, Yirmiyahu was assigned the task of being the prophet of doom. The people had abandoned G-d and His Torah. Idolatry was prevalent and *shmitah* was not observed. A treaty was established with Egypt that called for Egypt to come to the defense of Israel in the event of an attack from the Babylonians.

At times, Yirmiyahu felt that his prophecies were an exercise in futility. He bemoans the fate of the Jewish People and bemoans the horrible spectacle to which he will bear witness, the destruction of Jerusalem and her Temple.

"*Hashem, my strength! My stronghold! My refuge in the time of distress*" (16:19). In this opening line of the *haftorah*, Yirmiyahu braces himself for the destruction that will surely come. He reaffirms his faith in G-d and makes a final plea that G-d should revoke His decree against Israel. "*(In the end) all the nations will come from the ends of the earth and say: It was all falsehood (the belief in idolatry) that our ancestors inherited, emptiness that could accomplish nothing. Can man make gods? They are not gods*" (16:17). The prophet is asking that G-d spare His nation; in the end they and all the nations will eventually realize the foolishness of their ways. Spare them the pangs of exile; let them come to the realization on their own.

G-d responds: "*The sin of Judah is inscribed with an iron pen, with a hard nail, etched into the tablet of their heart and onto the corners of your altars*" (17:1). Their sins are so ingrained that they will never come to the true realization on their own.

G-d continues: "*You will (be forced to) **withdraw** from the inher-*

itance which I have given to you..." (17:4). The Hebrew word for "*withdraw*" is *shamat*, from which the word *shmitah* is derived. G-d is alluding to the imminent future when Israel will be forced to withdraw from their land because they had no faith in Him and did not keep the laws of *shmitah* and *yovel*.

G-d then addresses the treaty the Jews had made with Egypt. "*Cursed is the man who trusts in people and makes flesh his strength and turns his heart away from G-d*" (17:5).

The verse gives a wonderful parable regarding a man who places his faith in a foreign nation. "*(Like) a partridge calling (the chicks) it did not bear...*" (17:11). Some birds lay their eggs in the nest of the partridge so they won't have to sit on them to incubate the eggs. They let the partridge do all the work. But, as soon as the eggs hatch, the fledglings fly away, feeling no attachment to the partridge that sat on the eggs. The Jews are like the partridge that cultivated a warm relationship with the Egyptian eggs. But as soon as the eggs hatch and are exposed to the reality of the world, the fledglings fly away. The partridge is left with nothing.

This is true not only of misplaced trust but also of ill gotten gains. "*So is one who amasses wealth unjustly, in the middle of his days it will leave him, and in the end he will be considered a repulsive person*" (17:11). In the time of Yirmiyahu the people felt a false sense of security. They seemed to have it good even though they did not follow in the ways of the Torah. But, this feeling of good was an ill-gotten gain. It would soon leave them. The Jews would be exiled and considered to be a repulsive nation in their new-found home, Babylon.

Yirmiyahu and his prophecies were subjected to ridicule by the royalty and by the people. The prophet became emotionally ill from the entire matter. However, it was not the ridicule that made him sick; it was the knowledge that Israel's Temple would soon be destroyed and the people exiled that distressed him. In the closing line of the *haftorah*, Yirmiyahu begs of G-d, "*Heal me, O' G-d, save me, and I shall be saved.*" The *Malbim* explains that because of the futility of trying to save the Jewish People from themselves, Yirmiyahu wishes to be released from his task as prophet. In that way, he will no longer have to bear the terrible vision of the dreadful events that lay ahead.

We now know what lied ahead. Yimiyahu's visions of doom are our reality. We are in exile, yet we seem to have it good. Is the freedom of religion we have, the freedom to pursue our educational and vocational dreams deserved? Or, are these ill-gotten gains that will leave us soon? We must constantly ask ourselves these questions because the answer is of dire importance. Our physical and spiritual lives are at stake.

ABOUT THE AUTHOR

Yochanan "Jeff" Kirshblum is a graduate of Shaarei Torah of Rockland County and received his B.A. in economics from Queens College, New York.

Though pursuing a career in business, his passion has been for the Jewish People. He has served as the New York Director of the 5% Mandate, an organization whose goal is to enable yeshivas to become tuition free. He is the founder of the a recreational center for Teens at Risk program in Monsey, New York, venturing to bring back into the fold Jewish teens who have lost their way.

Jeff is the innovator of the "I Can't Take It Anymore"-Insurance for Rebbayim Program. The program has seen nation-wide success in having yeshivos insure their mechanchim the financial protection for their families.

Mr. Kirshblum has been a guest speaker at the conventions of Torah Umesorah and Agudath Israel.

This is his third of a five-volume series on the Torah. He has successfully molded the age-old writings of our Sages into our modern lifestyle. A Jew must not only think like a Jew but must also have the heart of a Jew. These volumes, written from the heart, speak to the heart of every Jew.